Mindfulness-based Emotion Focused Counselling

Padmasiri de Silva

Mindfulness-based Emotion Focused Counselling

Foreword by Mahinda Deegalle

palgrave
macmillan

Padmasiri de Silva
Philosophical, Historical & International Studies
Monash University
Melbourne, VIC, Australia

ISBN 978-3-030-64387-4 ISBN 978-3-030-64388-1 (eBook)
https://doi.org/10.1007/978-3-030-64388-1

This Palgrave Macmillan imprint is published by the registered company Springer Nature Switzerland AG
The registered company address is: Gewerbestrasse 11, 6330 Cham, Switzerland

Dedicated
to the Ma Ma Charitable Foundation & Lectureship,
the University of Hong Kong Program in Buddhist Counselling,
and to the memory of Professor Robert C. Solomon,
the acclaimed pioneer of emotion studies,
portraying the rhythms of the emotions in our life.

Heartfelt gratitude to
the nurses at Regis where I live
heroes & heroines of our times,
born to blush unseen!

To Rick Hanson—wonderful insights for developing self-compassion

Foreword

Professor Padmasiri de Silva (b. 1933) is an eminent, veteran scholar of international recognition in the field of the psychology of Buddhism. He is a philosopher with sophisticated comparative training in both Asian and Western philosophy. As Professor of Philosophy, for nearly a decade (1980–1989) he headed the Department of Philosophy and Psychology at the University of Peradeniya, Sri Lanka. He has held many distinguished teaching and research posts at the National University of Singapore, and Monash University, Melbourne, Australia, among others.

After he departed from Sri Lanka in 1989, Professor de Silva's research trajectory has expanded to new areas of applied interdisciplinary study. In particular, in the last decade, Professor de Silva has become very interested in Buddhist therapy and continues to publish in this novel field.

Professor de Silva has engaged in emotion studies for an extended period, making it at times a 'virtual hobby'. His professional training in the 'philosophy of mind' is extensive: he studied for two years at the East–West Centre, Hawaii, and conducted doctoral research on the philosophy of emotions at the University of Hawaii by completing a dissertation on 'Buddhist and Freudian Psychology' (1967).

Professor de Silva has published numerous monographs. One of his most influential and pioneering studies is *Buddhist and Freudian Psychology* (1973 and 2010) on a theory of the psychology of motivation. Professor de Silva's *Introduction to Buddhist Psychology and Counselling: Pathways of Mindfulness-Based Therapies* (2014), completed before the word-processing age during the JVP (Janatha Vimukthi Peramuna, 'People's Liberation Front') brutalities in Sri Lanka (1987–1989), became a best-seller with a long history of many editions (third, fourth and fifth editions in 2000, 2005 and 2014). With sales of over 800 copies in the first year and glowing reviews, it became his most popular publication due to its lucid clarity, formidable inspiration and depth. Even today it offers a comprehensive introduction to Buddhism and is used widely for courses both in Sri Lanka and abroad. His most recent Palgrave Macmillan publication is *The Buddhist Psychology of Emotions and Humour in Buddhism* (2018).

For Professor de Silva, the study of emotions has been 'not merely' as something academic, 'but a lifetime adventure'. As a therapist, his training and practice in counselling for six years led to developing a 'mindfulness-based, emotion-focused therapy' (EFT) delineating cross-cultural work on emotions. His first publication on emotions was *Twin Peaks: Compassion and Insight—Emotions and the 'Self' in Buddhist and Western Thought* (1991).

This book recognizes and highlights a key Buddhist principle of 'uncertainty', often philosophically identified as 'impermanence' (P. *anicca*) and expressed eloquently as 'one never knows what is around the corner'.

In this newest contribution to the study of emotions, Professor de Silva draws on extensive personal and professional experience. The book makes an important contribution by capturing Professor de Silva's lifelong immersion in Buddhism and the practice of meditation that nourished his work as a counsellor. Insight to emotions is combined with long-time meditation practice with the Venerable U. Dhammajīva of Mītirigala.

Concerning the Western and Buddhist analysis of the concept of 'interoception,' Professor de Silva maintains clearly that such comparative analysis in neuroscience is valuable and insightful, but there is an absolute necessity today to go to deeper insights into Buddhist meditation as 'found in the authentic tradition and Buddhist *suttas*'. With tradition-specific claims, Professor de Silva argues that meditation practitioners are expected to work 'within certain boundaries of humility and equanimity', cardinal principles of Buddhist training, which are required codes of practice for making deeper claims on meditation and its attainments.

This book contains clear guidance for methods to achieve the calm, harmonious, compassionate and uplifting emotions that the entire world needs today.

In addition to regular meditation practice, Professor de Silva gained further inspiration for working on emotions through living at Regis in East Malvern, Victoria, Australia. He witnessed at first-hand the expressions of compassion that enveloped the nursing profession. The relaxed and peaceful atmosphere there enabled Professor de Silva to go deeper into reflections on emotions.

Professor de Silva's participation in the Poetry Club at Regis provided further resources for the lively line of communication that he followed through in producing an innovative path (see his poetry compositions included in Chapters 29–31). This enabled him to go beyond getting entangled in a philosopher's muddle of logical puzzles. When moral psychology is becoming a widening tool for doing ethics today, Professor de Silva is committed to working on a forthcoming publication on *Buddhist Moral Psychology*.

Back in the 1980s I was one of Professor Padmasiri de Silva's postgraduate students at the University of Peradeniya (1985–1987) in the newly established MA Programme in Comparative Religion. Since then, I have been greatly inspired by his exemplary example of effectively communicating essential guidance to any young scholar who wanted to become established as an academic.

With gratitude and conviction, I recommend this book very highly for any reader who is interested in understanding mindfulness in emotion-focused therapy in depth. Lucid writing with richness in clarity is a blessing for any reader. It combines many years of personal experience and insight, combined with scholarship and practice. It is a lucid treatment for the understanding of emotions. The poetry section displays a closer link between meditation and the creativity that flows from it.

Mahinda Deegalle
Bath Spa University
Bath, UK

Preface

The African version of the Buddhist concept of *dukkha* is 'Famine sleeps under the basket used for grain.' Although the grain basket is full today, one never knows when it may be empty. The proverb refers to the fact that one never knows what is around the corner (Stewart 2019).

In writing this book, I wish to bring before the reader the memory of Robert C. Solomon (1942–2007), the foremost pioneer of emotion studies. The book dedicated to his memory, *Passion, Death and Spirituality* (Higgins and Sherman 2012) enumerates in detail the monumental contributions to emotion studies Solomon made over the years. I am indebted to him for his guidance and inspiration which led to my own long-held interest in the study of emotions my virtual hobby. My chapter in this memorial volume, 'The Lost Art of Sadness', integrates the deep feelings of sadness at his untimely death with an examination of his own reflections of grief in his book *True to Our Feelings: What Our Emotions are Really Telling Us* (2007).

The early roots of my interest in the study of emotions lie in my participation in a cross-cultural emotions study group at the Culture Learning Institute of the East–West Centre in Hawaii several decades ago, as a professional associate undergoing training for two years. My first entry to the subject was through my studies in the philosophy of mind. This included a doctoral dissertation at the University of Hawaii on the psychology of motivation in Freud and Buddhism (de Silva 2010).

The philosophy of mind lectures with their focus on motivation and emotions at the University of Hawaii, conducted by Professor Abelson in his house with its open windows was a highly memorable experience. It led me to become immersed in the study of emotions not merely as an academic pursuit but as a lifetime adventure, and in another phase of my life as a therapist, it influenced what I describe as mindfulness-based, emotion focused therapy (EFT).

My debt to Robert Solomon dates back to an unforgettable meeting. My first attempt to write on emotions was the book *Twin Peaks: Compassion and Insight* (1991), published while I was at the University of Singapore where I taught for three years. It was when I participated in a philosophy conference in Queensland that I met Soloman and was delighted to give him a copy of my book. To my amazement, he and Professor Roger Ames selected two of the chapters for two forthcoming anthologies: one titled the *Buddhist Theory of Emotion*, the other titled *Pride and Self in Buddhist and Western Thought*. This was the beginning of my longstanding academic interest in emotion studies.

Basic Orientation of the Present Study

My early training until I earned my Ph.D. at the University of Hawaii was in the was in the philosophy of mind and the research area that I selected was the philosophy of emotions. I realized that it required an energizing breeze from the interdisciplinary field of emotion studies.

My lifelong immersion in Buddhism, and especially the practice of meditation, nourished my work as a counsellor. Today, a new series on the *Moral Psychology of the Emotions* (Rowman & Littlefield) with a number of volumes on sadness, anger, compassion, forgiveness, and disguist, etc., illustrates the richness of the field. The series is in search of a new interdisciplinary model of moral philosophy which has practical relevance for mental health, issues of violence and forgiveness, compassionate healthcare, etc. I sincerely congratulate all the scholars participating in this project, for very special reasons. The problems in the world today have relevance to the broad field of ethics or applied ethics, and the different varieties of applied ethics, emerging from time to time, though they need to go beyond offering a plaster for limited contextual breakdowns in ethics.

The development of the *Moral Psychology* series with a strong interdisciplinary flavour running through emotion studies, psychology, philosophy, neuroscience, education, anthropology, counselling and different traditions of therapy provides an energizing framework for research that is relevant to a wide variety of issues: crime and punishment, forgiveness, healthcare, economic crises, the tragic collapse of the environment and endangered animal lives—all of which generate issues where emotion studies provide a nourishing base for new thinking. I particularly found the book *Compassion* very relevant to the tensions that dominate the world today. It focuses on both physical and mental health, with an excellent chapter on Buddhist perspectives on compassion. But I discovered that after reading through five volumes in the series, except for the excellent article on compassion in Buddhism, analysis of the Buddhist contribution to emotion studies has been neglected in other volumes. Even the excellent article by celebrated philosopher Owen Flanagan, with its interdisciplinary flavour, regrettably does not present the exact Buddhist position. Apart from that, his focus on the emotions and empirical science is excellent. The article on anger refers to the early Buddhist position as 'eliminatist', and says 'In any case, it is not as if the Buddhist thinks we can just will our way out of anger' (*The Moral Psychology of Anger*, p. xxii).

My chapter on anger in the present work is a response to three misunderstandings of anger made by critics in the West. The present book has an answer to some of these missing links with Buddhism. The book explores a new interdisciplinary study of the philosophy and psychology of emotions and the relevance of Buddhist practice for a world threatened with dramatic challenges to the environment and new forms of tension. The dominant focus is on counselling emotions. But this fact does not reduce the importance of the new series on the moral psychology of emotions. Emotion studies open up a new window to issues in applied ethics, where teachers are already using literary resources to generate a more authentic atmosphere, and where the logic of certain issues dominate to some extent. The issues are important but teachers are exploring some diversity of teaching techniques.

In spite of the neglect of the Buddhist tradition, the basic structure of this programme in moral psychology should be noted for its interdisciplinary flavour ranging from psychology, social psychology, neuroscience, anthropology, etc. As early as 1990 a group of very progressive philosophers in the West, Amélie Rorty, Owen Flanagan and David Wong introduced the notion of 'ethical realism', the relevance of empirical psychology for normative ethics. If I get the time and leisure to write a small monograph on 'Moral Psychology in Buddhism', it would be tempting to speak to a world in crisis—I have collected some material but this is currently only a possiblity.

Recent progress made in the 'moral psychology of emotions' is very encouraging. While the traditional stalwarts of ethics like Plato, Aristotle, Kant and the Utilitarians are important, as was evident from my deep study of these ethical traditions at the University of Hawaii, in the complex world of today we cannot afford to let ethics become isolated from the emerging challenges around the world, and so I have a special chapter on environmental ethics.

My training with the cross-cultural group was more on a Darwinian hypothesis developed by the world's foremost expert on emotions, Paul Ekman. Furthermore, the seminars were conducted by Ekman's student Jerry Boucher. Gradually my studies and reading became focused on Darwin, Freud and William James (de Silva 2017). The interdisciplinary flavour of emotion studies was a great attraction for me.

It was in Sri Lanka that I wrote my first book *Introduction to Buddhist Psychology* (1979). In those days I only had a typewriter to work with. The book had a chapter on emotions and by the time it reached the fifth edition in 2014, a completely new book *An Introduction to Buddhist Psychology and Counselling* had emerged (de Silva 2014). A study of excellent reviews and unbelievable sales confirmed that my writing was close to the hearts of the readers! Reviews acclaimed the book as a beautiful blend of 'clarity' and 'depth'.

By now I was living in Australia and passed through great upheavals in my life, reminding me of the African words of wisdom: 'one never knows what is around the corner'. One has to experience *dukkha* within the shattering upheavals of life. The chapters on sadness, grief and depression convey how I transformed the most shattering crises in life into resilience and deep spiritual transformation. One has to experience depression with maturity to transcend it, and for the first time, I felt the great enchantment of being one's own counsellor (see Chapter 26) and after three years of learning counselling, my dream was realized.

For six years at the Springvale Community Centre in Melbourne, Australia, I developed my own creation of *mindfulness-based emotion-focused theory.* Subsequently, a book with a number of case studies was published in 2008. It was dedicated to the memory of two wonderful women in my life, my mother Laura, and my wife Kalyani (Vishvalekha 2008). Above all, this service at the community centre was given free in memory of my mother and Kalyani:

> Grief counselling focuses on the ability to accept the loss and direct the pain into paths of emotional growth … Reflecting on grief enlarges one's notion of love and deeper spiritual transformation … The transformative power of grief over a loss to reach a deep reflective tone in life, added to by a wonderful resilience of the mind, are the result of the proper and mature management of life. (de Silva 2014, pp. 170–171)

This is a short entry into my interest in counselling in emotions and my way through life's upheavals. The complete narrative is provided in my book *Buddhist Psychology and Counselling* (de Silva 2014, pp. 171–174); my path through 'mindful counselling personal grief and sadness'. Counsellors who have gone through such existential crises have, in the words, of Irvin Yalom, 'the gift of therapy'. Philosophical studies of emotions today would certainly be enriched by a cross-fertilization with psychology, counselling and cross-cultural perspectives.

Six Emotional Styles Presented in Current Neuroscience

Most of the issues discussed on managing emotions have recently been backed by the groundbreaking research of Richard J. Davidson who worked with Sharon Begley (2012). As a preface to my book *Emotions in Counselling*, I present Davidson's findings.

This study gives both direction and confidence to counsellors.

1. *Resilience*: This reflects how quickly one recovers from adversity. In the analysis of emotions like anger and grief/sadness, resilience plays a central role.
2. *Outlook Dimension*: The capacity to remain upbeat and sustain positive emotions over time is the outlook dimension.
3. *Social Intuition Dimension*: Socially intuitive types have an uncanny ability to pick up on subtle non-verbal cues, to read other peoples' emotions on the face, body language, and vocal intonation. Acute sensitivity to the emotional state of others is a mark of empathy and compassion in the counselling and caring profession.
4. *Self-Awareness Dimension*: It refers to people who are acutely conscious of their thoughts and feelings and the messages they send to others through their body.
5. *Sensitivity to Context*: What we consciously regulate to context is largely intuitive, depending on special occasions.
6. *Attention Dimension*: Like resilience this is an important facet/or an enriching dimension for counselling clients who have problems. 'Can you screen out emotional distractions and stay focused in your daily tasks or work at the office without thinking of the fight you had with your spouse? Thus, those who have this "attention dimension" are not constantly pushed and pulled by emotional ups and downs' Davidson says, 'This is the kind of awareness that many forms of meditation cultivate.' Non-judgemental awareness has been measured in the lab by Davidson.

Regarding the *relationship of emotional styles to the brain*, Davidson makes a very significant observation:

> It is hardly surprising that where you fall on each dimension of Emotional Style is the result of specific patterns of brain activity since everything in our mental life is. What is surprising however, is that much of the circuitry underlying the six dimensions lies far from the brain's supposed emotion regions—the limbic system, and the hypothalamus. This emerged from the discovery that started it all: that the prefrontal cortex, site of such executive functions as planning and judgment, controls how emotionally resilient people are. (Davidson and Begley 2013, p. 68)

Neuroscience and Emotions

I am indebted to two recent reviews of the first draft of this book, regarding the need to clarify the relation of this study to the 'neuroscience of emotions'. This study focuses on works relating to Buddhist mindfulness practice, with a focus on emotions, often described as 'contemplative neuroscience'. Some of the excellent studies I have used are the following:

Daniel J. Siegel, *The Mindful Brain: Reflection and Attunement in the Cultivation of Well-Being* (New York and London: W.W. Norton & Company, 2007); Daniel Siegel, *Brain Storms* (Scribe Publishers, 2014); Daniel Siegel, *Mind Sight* (Random House, 2010); Richard Davidson, *The Emotional Life of Your Brain* (London, 2013); Rick Hansen, *Resilient* (New York: Harmony Books, 2018); Rick Hansen, *Buddha's Brain* (Oakland: New Harbinger, 2009).

My favourite book by Rick Hanson is *Resilient* (New York: Harmony, 2018). This is a beautiful presentation of integrating a meditative life into daily life. Day to day, like a diary, a constant companion that converts little movements of 'being hurt' (without anger, more sadness), when he says do not follow 'one dart by another back, making two'—suffering and stress increase, but convert into the royal paths of human understanding and empathy.

I have a poem in my personal 'random harvest', 'revolving forgiveness cycle' that deals with little movements of 'hurt' coming from innocent voices among the lovable people. These little poetry sketches will have to be digested and left for a future anthology. Moving away from academia now, in the true spirit of retirement, I embrace the spirit of the firefighters and the nurses, born to blush unseen. The nurses here at Regis herald a new morning for me with 'porridge and honey'; they are the greatest stalwarts, the heroes and heroines of our times. I have another poem on this theme, and one more on the animals and bushfires. As I indicate in the chapter on the environmental crisis, just as the Buddha predicted 2500 years ago if there are cracks in the lives of people, the four elements—air, water, earth and fire—will revolt.

We need to go beyond violations of 'rules of ethics' to deeper concerns, cracks and fissures in the lives of people that are spiritually debasing—but hidden from their awareness. The 'neuroscience of emotions' is a new field, with beautiful insights related to Buddhist practice. These helped me traverse through lost battles in academia. With plenty of softness on our side, we can manage little bits of innocent 'hurt', which can generate meaningless stress and tension in our lives. But neuroscience helps us to come back with a positive emotion of self-compassion, and mature forgiveness practised in disciplined stages.

For me, my *guru*—great monks like Venerable Dhammajīva of Mītirigala, a monk who approves recent neuroscience, and most Venerable Professor and Vice-Chancellor Phra Brahmapandit, who organized the last UN Day of Vesak Conference in Thailand, inviting me to give the keynote address—are all sending a deep spiritual message to uplift a collapsing world. Thus, this present book, with due humility, focuses on the potential of emotion studies to regenerate our emotional lives, to give some answers through both prose and poetry on how to rebuild our emotional lives at these difficult times around the world.

A new dimension to the present book is the use of poetry which emerged from both my pen and heart, in Chapters 29–31. It is a new experiment emerging from my regular participation in the Regis Poetry Club, and I am accumulating a rich harvest, which may inspire me to end up with a complete anthology, which of course will take time. Taking into account the stories of human distress, stress and tension around the world today, we need to construct new methods of communication. I am building a new milestone for Palgrave Macmillan in presenting emotion studies to people who will embrace a new message of 'stay calm', drawing from their 'own deep reservoir of a resilient heart'. In this Rick Hansen's writing has been a wonderful source of inspiration—his is a new and refreshing voice, and paradoxically, from the strong technical field of neuroscience. Crossing disciplines is a central need of the times we live in, so that all of us who write on emotions and ethics may develop a holistic ethos and go beyond the majesty of normative ethics, which is the fond possession of many teachers and also admirable, but which needs a more energizing contact with the outer world.

Counselling and the Buddhist Path of Liberation

What I write is based on my counselling experience; reflection on counselling emotions is based on my study of an extensive literature on emotions and my personal insight into the interaction of emotions in our lives. I have also helped a large number of clients, whose case histories I cannot reproduce, due to legal reasons, and would advise any teacher of counselling practice to use their own experience with clients based on their culture.

My practice on the 'liberation path' is a *personal matter*. But this has given me a more stable base and direction to what I write. I follow my own teachers like the Venerable Dhammajīva Mahāthero of Mītirigala, whose student I have been for over eight years. There are contexts, however, where I draw from my own reading and practice of meditation, which can be shared with others, such as managing the five hindrances of aversion, sensuality, restlessness and worry and remorse, sloth and torpor and boredom. In a more specific way, my exploration of anger management owes a great deal to the *Satipaṭṭhāna* and its penetrating presentation by Venerable Dhammajīva, including the insightful *Parābhava Sutta*. But regarding the higher reaches of meditation, I am still a student and a seeker of lasting peace and happiness. Furthermore, I am greatly inspired by Sayadaw U. Pandita (1921–2016), who in the words of Joseph Goldstein, is 'a spiritual warrior'. His lucid exposition in his book, *In This Very Life: Liberation Teachings of the Buddha* (1993), blends clarity with insight.

It is a paradox of the Buddhist spiritual path that when you are trodden down with anger and become melancholic with shattering grief (as happened in my life), or shamed when your narcissism (self-love) is broken—paradoxically, as Venerable Thích Nh'ât Hạnh (b. 1926) says, like converting rubbish into manure for generating flowers, anger may be converted into patience, forgiveness and equanimity; grief converted into reviving your love in commemorating a great life; writing beautiful poetry, or taking up counselling (without charging a fee) as I did. There is a beautiful poem on this theme (Chapters 29–31).

The Rhythms of the Body, Emotions and Life

Insight meditation and the body in emotional experience is one area where there has been some cross-fertilization between meditation practice and counselling. This is not only based on personal experience but is backed by an experienced therapist trained in Burmese Vipassanā meditation who is also a personal friend, Bruno Cayoun (de Silva 2017, p. 94). My book depicting the concept of 'somatic intelligence' (de Silva 2017) presents a complete philosophical and psychological background to the 'body-emotions linkage'.

To summarize his analysis: (1) Bodily sensations are in reality neither physical nor purely mental and are considered a link between the mind and the body. (2) He found in his regular therapy work, that *different patterns of bodily sensations and these emotions maps were culturally universal*. My writings on William James, Jesse Prinz and Paul Ekman, makes this a wonderful insight (de Silva 2017). (3) Objective observation indicates that emotions are made up of a combination of thoughts, bodily sensations and the need to react. As these patterns emerge so strongly, it is not easy for the untrained mind to separate the emotional event into its basic components. (4) The emergence of emotions starts at the preconscious level of emotions processing, and sometimes remains subconscious (or subliminal) if the emotion is very subtle. He also says that there are four basic characteristics of these bodily sensations: mass, from the lightest to the heaviest; motion from the most still to extremes of shaking, or agitation; temperature from the coldest to the hottest; and fluidity, better described as cohesiveness. The focus on four elements was a central facet of insight meditation as presented to us by Venerable Dhammajīva.

What is of great interest both for therapy and insight meditation is that anger tends to manifest with a predominance of heat and motion and increased heart rate and agitation. This is what the neuroscientist describes as 'reactivity'. Sadness is experienced with increase of mass—heaviness in the neck, head and shoulders, and constriction of throat. Fear tends to manifest with a decrease of fluidity, constriction in the chest and abdomen, increased heart rate and agitation. But we should not add personal meanings to these sensations (Cayoun 2015, Chapter 8).

My book takes its origins from the Ma Ma Charitable Foundation Lectures at the University of Hong Kong which I delivered in December 2018. These lectures provided an opportunity to initiate the new Buddhist Counselling Programme. I signed an agreement with the university to write *a student guide to emotion studies*, which may be used for a course on emotions in counselling. I recommend that the teaching staff use their own case studies *with a base in their own culture*, though the issues are common to academia and counselling work. Also at the time of these lectures occurred the launch of a Chinese translation of my book on Buddhist psychology, which took my writings to a distant land. This visit was an unforgettable chapter in my life.

Is Counselling a Technology or a Healing Art?

> [I]n a world of increasing alienation, fragmentation and disconnection, we need therapists who are true healers rather than mere technicians. (Bien 2006)

Today, therapy is becoming an impersonal technology, with volumes of evidenced-based research where the personality of the client gets drowned in minute forms of classification. Evidenced-base research is useful up to a point. But one can get drowned in this literature. The deep human relationship between the client and the therapist is based on a long tradition of therapists ranging from Sigmund Freud, Aaron Beck, Albert Ellis, Carl

Rogers, Rollo May, Irvin Yalom, Jon Kabat-Zinn, Mark Epstein, Marsha Linehan and Leslie Greenberg who inspired my personal counselling orientation, 'mindfulness-based emotion-focused therapy'.

My favourite therapists are Sigmund Freud (1856–1939), Mark Epstein, Jon Kabat-Zinn, Irvin Yalom and Leslie Greenberg. Their real personalities reverberate through their life and work. But there are a few exceptions like Bruno Cayoun who breaks up mindful awareness of the body and thoughts into different facets of the Buddhist doctrine. For instance, under 'targeted problems' he would include addictions, low-motivation issues, low self-worth, risk-aversion and anxiety. His writing is very close to some of my own reflections on the body and emotions. I correspond with him from time to time. He is probably the best out of the therapists using a mindfulness-based therapy orientation in their practice.

Sometimes, there are common-sense solutions that we miss due to overloaded theories of therapy. To cite a couple of examples, I had a client with addictions. He was provided with a common-sense solution: to have a rich daily agenda of music, gardening and an evening treat where his wife prepared coffee and cheesecake! This was to be followed by a few Sri Lankan videos and a small camping trip at the weekend for the family. Once he had undertaken that, he never looked for the 'bottle in the fridge'. I told him that there was no problem in having an occasional drink. He was also introduced to Venerable Thích Nh´ât Hạnh's wonderful essay, 'How to Eat a Mandarin'.

My subsequent book had a subheading, *The Magic of the Ordinary and the Elegance of Small Things*. Kindness and common sense are often great healers (de Silva 2008)! It is a simple therapy, where mindfulness has been used without labelling/calling the procedure as such. If a person can enjoy a mandarin and be fully mindful of the taste, he can enjoy life!

Even if one has the best methodology for statistics and classification systems in the world, then kindness, compassion, forgiveness, patience in adversity, humility, and contentment, such as the Buddha displayed, are the more important hallmarks of a caring profession. I am at the moment exploring a Buddhist contribution to the emerging field of moral psychology. Here the work on compassion, kindness, humility, patience, as well as regret, anger, disgust and conceit are being presented through philosophical analysis, psychology and literature.

I hope that these emerging interests will generate a wonderful cross-pollination with psychotherapy. Using literature and aesthetics for therapy is undertaken very effectively by Irvin Yalom. I sincerely wish that the poems in the last chapters of this book will open out a new window to people in distress today, all across the world. As Carl Jung said, 'True healing converts brass into gold'.

Emotions in Counselling

In this book about counselling emotions, I wish to refer to the methodology that I used, which was based on the five golden rules of emotional intelligence (EQ): knowing one's emotions, managing emotions, motivating oneself, recognizing emotions in others and handling relationships. First, I had to develop these skills for myself, and then to guide the client, at least in learning to know his emotions and how to manage them (Goleman 1996). In addition to these skills, I added *learning emotional skills the mindful way*. If you read my discussion of anger management, you will discover the very interesting relationship of anger to envy and jealousy.

Anger also has an indirect relationship to conceit of status, and an invisible relationship to depression and disgust. In the higher realm of Buddhist ethics, all five hindrances have a component of anger, excesses of sensuality, aversion, restlessness, worry, boredom and doubt. Also, anger is present in the subliminal, sleeping passions (*anusaya*). From a therapeutic point of view, anger was the most important issue. I sincerely hope that this venture into human emotions, while being a practical guide to the study of emotions in counselling, will also provide a useful base for integrating studies within counselling, and above all for adding new dimensions of meaning to an inspiring journey in life.

My *guru* Venerable Dhammajīva in Sri Lanka is working with a group who are being trained to integrate mindfulness practice in the daily lives of children, and at the moment I am helping him to develop a project on the 'education of the emotions' (EQ).

Melbourne, Australia Padmasiri de Silva

References

Begley, Richard J., and Sharon Davidson. 2012. *The Emotional Life of Your Brain*. New York: Penguin.

Bien, Thomas. 2006. *Mindful Therapy.* Boston: Wisdom Publications.

Cayoun, Bruno. 2015. *Mindfulness-Integrated CBT for Well-Being and Personal Growth*. Oxford: Wiley.

Davidson, Richard, and Sharon Begley. 2013. *The Emotional Life of Your Brain*. London: Hodder.

de Silva, Padmasiri. 1992. *Buddhist and Freudian Psychology*, 3rd ed.Melbourne: Shogam Publishers.

de Silva, Padmasiri. 2008. *An Introduction to Mindfulness-Based Counselling*. Ratmalana, Sri Lanka: Sarvodaya Vishvalekha.

de Silva, Padmasiri. 2010. *Buddhist and Freudian Psychology*, 4th ed. Melbourne: Shogam Publishers.

de Silva, Padmasiri. 2014. *An Introduction to Buddhist Psychology and Counselling: Pathways of Mindfulness-Based Therapies*, 5th ed. London: Palgrave Macmillan.

de Silva, Padmasiri. 2017. *Emotions and the Body in Buddhist Contemplative Practice and Mindfulness-Based Therapy*. London: Palgrave Macmillan.

Goleman, Daniel. 1996. *Emotional Intelligence*. New York: Bloomsbury.

Higgins, Kathleen, and David Sherman (eds.). 2012. *Passion, Death and Spirituality: The philosophy of Robert C. Solomon*. Heidelberg, New York, and London: Springer.

Solomon, Robert C. 2007. *True to Our Feelings: What Our Emotions Are Really Telling Us*. New York: Oxford University Press.

Stewart, Dianne. 2019. *Wisdom from Africa*. Cape Town: Struik Publishers.

U. Pandita, Sayadaw. 1993. *In this Very Life: Liberation Teachings of the Buddha*.

Acknowledgments

I wish to thank Professor Constant Mews and Maryna Mews for refining the text and updating the references. I am thankful to the Venerable Professor Mahinda Deegalle of Bath Spa University, for going through the full text and attending to the insertion of Pāli diacritical marks. I also thank Professor G. Somaratna of the University of Hong Kong for assistance given to me in my previous publications and for his timely assistance during my visit to the University of Hong Kong.

In my personal life, I have a new home at Regis in East Malvern, a wonderful place beaming with care, kindness and friendship, and I owe the people here the relaxed and peaceful hours for writing and pondering on 'emotions' and their place in our lives. My sons, Maneesh, Adeesh and Chandeesh have always been with me giving me confidence, and helping me ride through adversity to a wonderful life at my age.

In closing these acknowledgements, I pay due homage to my meditation *guru* Dhammajīva Mahāthero of Mītirigala, who is reaching the very pinnacle of a life's journey towards peace and wisdom, and therefore I wish him well with his current project—mindfulness for children—popularly known as '*Sati*' *Pāsal*'. For me, emotions in children is a wonderful theme for the future!

I wish to thank profusely two referees who read through the first draft of this book, revealing its central strengths, offering valuable contributions and ways in which some improvements could be made, and also suggesting new references. One of the referees particularly emphasized the need to present a clear analysis of the Western and Buddhist presentations of the concept of 'interoception'. I need to mention that though analysis in the Western presentations in neuroscience is valuable, a closer insight into Buddhist insight meditation as found in the authentic tradition and Buddhist *suttas* is necessary, according to me. But this is a difficult task for a practising meditator who has to keep within certain boundaries of humility and equanimity, which are important codes of practice for making deeper claims. Also, practice is a progressive journey where confidence grows as one continues, and I have found a very elegant and effective method to be the use of poetry—a somewhat innovative method.

Melbourne, Australia Padmasiri de Silva

Praise for *Mindfulness-based Emotion Focused Counselling*

"In this book, Dr de Silva integrates modern science of emotion with Buddhist psychological principles and philosophy with expertise and wisdom. It is rich in invaluable integrative ideas and practical descriptions of the phenomenology of emotions. The book guides us through an effective and compassionate integration of new insights in counselling. I highly recommend it!"

—Bruno A. Cayoun, *DPsych, Clinical Psychologist, Director of the Mindfulness-integrated CBT Institute, Australia, and Co-author of* The Clinical Handbook of Mindfulness-integrated Cognitive Behavior Therapy

"The Buddha's illuminating insights into human emotional conditions form the central core of Buddhist psychology. Such core Buddhist ideas have, however, received only limited attention in the West where for the past 5 decades we have witnessed notable advances in the delineation of both the behavioral and biological aspects of emotion. In this highly readable book, Padmasiri de Silva seeks to address this oversight, by demonstrating the relevance of Buddhist ideas on emotion to the areas such as affective neuroscience, moral psychology, and environmental counseling. Masterfully weaving together his personal experiences as a therapist and Buddhist notions, de Silva brings a fresh perspective to our understanding of a broad range of issues ranging from stress management to climate change. This is a must-read for a student who is interested in the Buddhist perspective on emotion."

—Piyadasa Kodituwakku, *Ph.D., Professor Emeritus, University of New Mexico School of Medicine, USA*

Contents

Abbreviations

A	*Aṅguttara Nikāya, Gradual Sayings*
D	*Dīgha Nikāya, Dialogues of the Buddha*
Dh	*Dhammapada*
M	*Majjhima Nikāya, Middle Length Sayings*
S	*Saṃyutta Nikāya, Kindred Sayings*

Part I

Architecture of Mind, Body and Emotions

1

Introduction

The study of emotions has been neglected for a number of reasons. This chapter gives an overview of the importance and the nature of emotion studies.

Emotions have been associated with subjective prejudices and are described as being a source of irrationality. Thus, they may be considered as antithetical to our cognitive skills, to think, reason and perceive. At the level of ethics, often ethically undesirable states figure in our daily conversation. Often emotions interfere with calm, voluntary, rational behavior. Psychologically, they are seen as states of agitation and imbalance sometimes leading to chaotic actions.

But a close study of emotions at an academic level, as well as the history of emotion studies indicate a different perspective. In novels, for example, emotions play a crucial role in understanding the diverse profiles of people portrayed in the stories and this feature adds depth. Since the writings of Aristotle, emotions in ethics has come down to contemporary times, as an important theme and illuminates various facets of moral philosophy. In our lives, both understanding other people and self-understanding is enriched through our emotions. In fact, moral psychology is emerging as an autonomous field and towards the latter

P. de Silva, *Mindfulness-based Emotion Focused Counselling*,
https://doi.org/10.1007/978-3-030-64388-1_1

part of the book, I shall present a dialogue between the contemporary moral psychology of compassion and Buddhism. Health care and ageing will also be covered and the book will conclude with a short chapter on the current interest in moral emotions. Thus, the coverage will be comprehensive and modern.

In the history of psychology, the dominance of behaviorism led to the neglect of emotion studies. Thus, the emergence of cognitive psychology in the 1960s was a veritable revolution. This initial phase was followed by new research in neuroscience, linguistics, molecular genetics and artificial intelligence. The relevance of these new interdisciplinary sciences for a dialogue between Buddhism and cognitive science was well articulated by Francisco Varela (1946–2001), whose work has been interpreted as a revival of William James (1842–1910). While the scientific study of consciousness achieved legitimacy, there were some obstacles to extending these trends to the development of a Buddhist psychology. I was fortunate to attend a conference in cognitive sciences organised by Varela, with a grant from the Sloan Foundation, at Naropa University, where I was a visiting professor for the summer. Buddhism and Cognitive Science conference was a trailblazer which helped Buddhist scholars to go beyond traditional Buddhist scholasticism. It paved the way for developing an experimentally based technology for meditation and the meeting of Buddhist psychology and current neuroscience, as could be seen in the ground-breaking studies of Richard Davidson and Daniel J. Siegel.

Emotion Studies Across Behaviourism and Cognitive Psychology

Behaviourism both in philosophy and psychology, changed theorizing about the mind in a radical way. Both had a strong focus on the 'objective' facet of experiencing, leaving out the 'subjective' side. Behaviourism moved from animal psychology to human psychology, at the same time keeping the same methods and goals. Reference to consciousness and the interior life was taboo. William Lyons says, that the one area where there was a lapse in behaviourist thinking was the study of emotions.

> The answer is, of course, that some aspects of our emotional life can be given the usual behaviourist treatment in terms of dispositions. An irascible person is disposed or prone to be angry at the drop of a peanut on the carpet. An affectionate person is someone who is disposed to frequent displays of loving behaviour such as hugs and kisses and compliments. Where the problem is for behaviourism, is in giving an adequate account of how we associate this sort of behaviour with anger, and that sort of behaviour with being in love and, more generally, in giving an adequate account of what anger or love or any emotion really is. (Lyons 1963)

The behaviourist attempts to explain emotions in terms of predispositions does not work, as an angry man may do many alternative things, pound the table, slam the door, bite the lips or pick a fight. Cognitive psychology maintains that it is the cognitions or thought patterns that can differentiate the different emotions.

The Pro-emotion Consensus

There was a veritable harvest in contributions to the field of emotion studies. These included the writings of Daniel Goleman, Antonio Damasio, Joseph Ledoux, Paul Ekman, and Robert C. Solomon. Taking her inspiration from stoic philosophy, a more recent latecomer to the scene is Martha Nussbaum with her voluminous book, *Upheavals of Thought* (2001). The Buddhist contribution on the subject is important and in the early writings of Rhys Davids (1914), it was said that there is an archaic silence on emotions in Buddhist psychology. I have over the years made amends to this deficiency in presenting the Buddhist psychology of emotions in a number of works: 1991–2014. More recently, I have done a highly concentrated study of the body and the emotions in Buddhist psychology (de Silva 2018). These writings will be integrated into the present book on emotions.

Western Theories of Emotion

After obtaining a comprehensive understanding of the Western theories of emotions, I will present a Buddhist theory of emotions. The most important entry point to understanding the Western view is to look at the current debate between physiological arousal theories and the cognitive theories of emotions: the former focused on the body and the latter on thought patterns, beliefs and appraisals. As an example, let us consider an emotion story from the writings of Joseph Ledoux. A man walking on a forest track stumbles on a bundle of dry twigs. Even before the central nervous system (CNS) tells him to examine what he has trodden on, he is alerted by the emergency bell, of fight or flight and he seeks to find the quickest way of moving away from what he thinks is a rattlesnake. In this context, the physiological arousal of the heartbeat and the invisible impact of the brain (Autonomic Nervous System/ANS) stands out as an emotion of fear. Let us take the example of a farmer who gradually sees the pattern in the severe drought. Since there has not been any rain for a while, some form of fear about the future will emerge. It may, however, be explained cognitively in terms of certain thought patterns in the farmer's mind.

There will be an impact on his physiology, which will be gradual. Or, he may think of shifting to another of his properties where the rainfall is very regular. In cognitive therapy for instance, the focus on thought patterns is followed by exercises for the body. If the person sees a rattlesnake a long distance away, he can collect himself and decide on an option: for instance, to move quickly to his van which is nearby. Physiological arousal of some degree is present in what are recognized as basic emotions like fear, sadness, and joy, and states like anxiety with a certain amount of stress.

Emotions range from physiologically colored ones to complex emotions with a cognitive structure. Let us take anger, which has both clear physiological and cognitive strands. Anger at an injustice involves feelings of potential retaliation or a feeling of moral indignation without a need to retaliate. One can rather talk to the person and correct him, or one can have conflicting feelings if one has some fear of the person who has wronged one. Thus, emotions emerge in a network. But I shall take the different dimensions of emotions separately: dimensions of feeling, physiology, motivation, and the cognitive orientation. A particular emotion can have both physiological and cognitive strands. This is important as these facets of emotions have emerged as rival theories and different philosophers have backed their own theories. In fact, more complex interdisciplinary facets of emotion studies like evolutionary biology, cognitive psychology, and neuroscience shed light on emotion studies. They are all important and are enriching facets of emotion studies.

The Feeling Theory of Emotion

What makes a condition an emotion, and what makes it the particular emotion, is the presence in consciousness of a particular felt quality which like sensory qualities (redness, the smell of burning wood) is completely accessible in no other way. 'The attraction of the feeling theory is that an emotion could occur without its typical overt expression and thus one could be angry or afraid without anyone noticing it' (Alston 1967). Also, if it is an inner mental state rather than a bodily state, it is based on an immediate infallible quality of one's thoughts and sensations that no one else has claims to know. However, in spite of this attraction, this feeling theory has limitations. If a person is so inclined and has sufficient control, the person should inhibit its possible overt manifestations, but yet the tendency to overt manifestation is strong. Also, it has yet to be proved that *someone can be angry without the activation of the internal bodily processes*. The second claim about infallibility has been disproved by psychoanalysis, and that is that a person could misidentify his or her own emotional states.

The feeling theory of emotions has been subjected to a critique of a more general nature by analytic philosophers under the influence of Wittgenstein. They say that terms that have reference only to private experience do not have a place in inter-subjective communication and thus do not function in the realm of public discourse. Philosophers have also said that the feeling theory does not help to grasp the finer distinctions between anger, fear, and sadness.

For these reasons, both philosophers and psychologists have developed a more physiologically oriented feeling theory of emotions: in particular, William James (1884). First, we will explain the nature of physiological theories of emotions and then attempt a comprehensive study of William James's theories, their classic importance and certain limitations presented by critics.

Physiological Approaches to Emotion Studies

Emotions have broadly two dimensions. The first is a blend of the cognitive and appraisal aspect: there is a snake and the snake is a threat and snake venom is poisonous. This facet has been described as the 'cold' aspect of emotions whereas the visceral side has been described as the 'hot' aspect.

The human nervous system has two dimensions, the central and the peripheral nervous system. The latter in turn is divided into the somatic and the autonomic nervous system. The somatic nervous system is in charge of the reception and conduction of information. The activation of the autonomic nervous system (ANS) is seen in the visceral muscles, the heart, veins, arteries, lungs and endocrine glands. It is in turn divided into the sympathetic and the parasympathetic systems. The activation of the former leads to excitement, dilation of the pupils to enhance vision, rising of skin hair, adrenal gland secretions, release of sugar from the liver, inhibition of digestive and excretory functions and constriction of the intestines. In general, the sympathetic system deals with the emergency reactions of 'flight' or 'fight'. The parasympathetic system moderates such arousal and results in secretion of tears and enhances digestive and excretory functions. William James, for instance, insisted that the quality of emotional experience depended on the *sensory feedback of the actual effects of the autonomic nervous system on the viscera.*

The importance of autonomic changes can be seen in the kind of metaphors used in routine life: 'red with anger', 'face looked pale and white', 'butterflies in the stomach', 'burning with fury'. Chapter 14 of the present work describes some emotion metaphors. Also, there are physiological changes in relation to emotions that are not necessarily upsets or disturbances. In emotions of joy, calmness and tranquility, there is empirical evidence of the working of the parasympathetic nervous system and this is very much seen in meditative experience and when listening to certain types of music. *Emotion metaphors have a physiological orientation*, as the body plays a central role in emotions in both upsetting and calm emotions.

Another important concern is the subject's awareness of these physiological changes. First, there are physiological changes of which we are aware and necessarily so: for example, dryness of the mouth and often increased constriction of the throat. Then there are changes that we are not necessarily aware of such dilation of the pupils and pallor. Other ones that we may not be aware of are increased pulse rate, increased respiratory rate, flushing, sweating, muscular tension, increased muscle tone and increased level of motility in the gastrointestinal tract. In general, we see that physiological changes are a necessary part of emotional experience. Regarding the question whether, 'different patterns of an ANS activity are associated with 'different emotions', there is considerable controversy over the issue. Experimental studies show that the face and the body have links with emotional experience. Paul Ekman's work on expressions on the face has demonstrated this facet of emotions, or what are called basic emotions, which have pancultural dimensions (Ekman 2003). However, the exact correlation of emotions and facial expression is a subject of further research.

Malcolm Gladwell in a fascinating study of Ekman on emotions and the face presents a useful review of Ekman's work for the general reader (Gladwell 2005).

The James-Lange Theory of Emotions

While William James is one of the psychologists who directed our attention to the role of physiology in emotions, in a more specific theoretical thrust, he suggested that 'an emotion is the feedback from bodily changes' (James 1884), a view he shared with the Danish psychologist C. G. Lange. According to James, certain stimulus situations generate specific bodily reactions such as the pounding of the heart and related visceral responses. *The perception of this physiological process is the emotion*:

> Common sense says, we lose our fortune, are sorry and weep; we meet a bear are frightened and run; we are insulted by a rival are angry and strike. The hypothesis here to be defended says that this order of sequence is incorrect… that the more rational statement is that we feel sorry because we cry… angry because we strike, afraid because we tremble. (James 1884)

Thus, for James, the feeling in emotion is an effect of bodily change and not their cause. We can, of course, think of a few examples that give some intelligibility to this theory. Imagine that you are walking down a long staircase and suddenly miss a step and you stumble and grab the handrail before you have time to recognize a state of fear. Then you feel that first sense, the pounding of the heart, rapid breathing and trembling in the arms. As an overall theory of emotions, James–Lange has had many critics, but over the years the theory has reappeared like the phoenix from the ashes. In fact, recently, this theory has re-emerged in a different form as the theory of somatic markers put forward by the neurologist Antonio Damasio and the philosopher Jesse Prinz, who describes emotions in terms of 'gut reactions'.

One of James's lasting contributions is that he was emphatic on the point that *physiological arousal is an important ingredient of emotions*, especially in basic emotions like anger, fear and sadness, while conceit, guilt and jealousy/envy are more complex, as to physiology. James presents his theory with the following, almost rhetorical remarks.

I now proceed to the vital point of my whole theory:

> If we fancy some strong emotion and then try to abstract from our consciousness of it all the feelings of this characteristic bodily symptoms, we find we have nothing left behind, no 'mind stuff' out of which the emotion can be constituted and that a cold and neutral state *of* intellectual perception is all that remains. (James 1884)

It is clearly found in this statement that, it is the experience of the bodily symptoms that gives *the emotional quality* to our consciousness. Many philosophers of the cognitive tradition of emotions have neglected this point, although Lyons is an exception, as he presents both the legitimate claims of the cognitive and the physiological theories.

Critics of the Jamesian Theory of Emotions

1. Gerald Myers, who has written an excellent study of the life and work of William James, observes: 'If James had worked out more clearly the link between an emotion and a feeling, he might have avoided the unfortunate conclusion not only in the elaboration of the James–Lange theory, but in this very formulation of it.' A similar criticism has been presented by Bennett and Hacker (2003). According to them, it is necessary to distinguish between emotion as an episodic emotional perturbation and a long-standing emotional attitude. The important point is that a person's judgment may be clouded not only by the distress and agitation of the moment but also by long standing resentments and jealousies. In the context of Buddhism especially, these dispositional dimensions are as important as episodic reactions of the moment. They also add that motivational patterns over time have a complex relation to emerging emotion and feelings.
2. The link between particular emotions and specific bodily feelings is a mystery that James did not resolve. Also, there is no single proto-type emotion, though Paul Ekman's concept of basic emotions certainly does illuminate many contexts. There are also instances like hope, remorse, guilt, pride, compassion and gratitude which offer complex conceptual features which are significant. From a cross-cultural perspective, I have shown that the emotion of 'disgust' has specific features of its own, not merely in the philosophy or psychology of Buddhism but also Buddhism as a contemplative tradition. In practical counselling dealing with facial expressions and emotions, Ekman's work has proved invaluable, as the language of the face is well understood by my clients and even by children.
3. Above all, emotions are linked to volition, agency and choosing, a point emphasized by the psychologist James Averill and the philosopher Robert C. Solomon (Averill 1980). It must be mentioned that

William James recognizes the importance of character and will in another context, though in his celebrated study of emotions, there was no place for the will. 'The faculty of voluntarily bringing back a wandering attention over and over again is the very root of judgment, character and will' (James 1950).

4. James's neglect of the cognitive dimension of emotions was another limitation.
5. The clue to understanding the apparently paradoxical claims of James is that perhaps there is an illicit logical movement from the position, 'the emotional quality of an emotion is caused by the bodily symptoms of emotions' to 'our emotions are caused by the bodily symptoms of emotions.'

Motivational Strands in Emotions

Human desires have strong links with emotions and have been neglected by cognitivists who are attracted by the thought patterns and appraisals that go to make an emotion. In fact, issues about desire lie at the heart of major controversies in contemporary theory of action and emotion. Yet this breath of attention has been matched by a shallowness of scrutiny given to the notion of desire itself. In most recent philosophical discussions of the nature of mind, we see a neglect of desire with belief showing as the paradigm of the intentional. Marks says that desire is 'intentional' but in an interestingly different from the way in which belief is 'intentional'. The term 'intentional' in this context may be described as 'directed towards', for instance, as an arrow released from a bow. Marks says that the preoccupation with cognitivism in emotion studies led to the neglect of the role of desire in emotion studies.

In the history of emotion studies, Aristotle and Spinoza recognized the role of desire in emotions and these linkages play an important role in Buddhist psychology, especially the nature of greed (*lobha*). While such greed is the basis of addictions, greed also feeds emotions like envy and covetousness. In my recent study of humour, a constellation of conceit, envy, anger work together to feed 'status anxiety' (de Silva 2018).

More recently, Anthony Kenny presents the linkage between desire and emotion clearly:

> For the connection between emotion and behaviour is made by desire: one emotion differs from another because of the different things it makes one do. Fear involves wanting to avoid or avert what is feared; anger is connected to the desire to punish or take vengeance on its object. Love of one kind is linked with the desire to fondle and caress the loved ones and shame with the desire to conceal. These, connections are not contingent: a man who was unaware of them would not possess the concept of emotions in question (Kenny. 1963)

Lyons also accepts the role of desire in emotions:

> Most though not all emotions contain desire as a part of their occurrent states, and with some emotions this appetitive aspect is part of their very concept. It is this aspect which explains how emotions can be cited as motives, and how behaviour can reveal the nature of emotions, for the desires generated by the evaluative aspect of behaviour are the causes associated with emotion. The appetitive aspect, while it does mingle with the evaluative aspect can be separated at the theoretical level. (Lyons 1980)

The Cognitive Orientation

What is today considered as a cognitive theory of emotions has been recognized since Aristotle. Being insulted by a person in front of an admirer and perceiving it as a bad action provides the cognitive element in anger: what Aristotle describes in his own way as 'the boiling of the blood' provides the physiological component of the emotion, and the desire for revenge would be the appetitive or the desire-oriented component of the emotion. Aristotle does not make a finer distinction between the purely cognitive aspect in recognizing the statement as an insult and evaluating it as a threat. Lyons defines a cognitive theory as follows: 'one that makes some aspect of thought, usually a belief, central to the concept of emotion' (1980). Such thought patterns help us to distinguish one emotion from another and that is one of the key values in this theory.

We also need to make a distinction between the factual component of an emotion and the evaluative facet: seeing a snake and considering it as dangerous. Out of the cognitive theories of emotions, Robert C. Solomon's theory that emotions are judgments has been a well-known and well-grounded theory (2004). Later in his writings, he did accept that physiology is important for locating the nature of some of the basic emotions.

Cheshire Calhoun says that only a small fraction of our beliefs is consciously articulated and that the greater portion is a 'darker cognitive area', an unarticulated cognitive set that interprets the world'. Her claim that we have a 'doxic' element that interprets the world ringing a familiar chord with Buddhism is an important point. In Buddhism negative emotions have a hidden cognitive core.

Critics of the Cognitive Theory of Emotions

A general point of criticism is that the cognitive theory of emotions, in spite of its variety, neglects other important facets of an emotion such as physiology and the role of desires in emotions. Joel Marks is critical of the cognitive theory of emotions as he considers belief over desires in explaining actions (1986). Neglect of physiology is also an important criticism of the cognitive theory, and in my recent studies on embodied cognition and emotions, I have cited recent trends regarding the place of the body in emotions. In the writings of Lyons on emotions, there is a very balanced outlook. Solomon, the most important pioneer of cognitive theories, also later in his studies became more receptive to a broader concept of emotions. Before his untimely death, he brought out an edited volume on thinking and feeling in which, he assembled the best minds in the Anglo–American tradition, which certainly is a landmark in the history of emotion studies (2004).

The Body and the Physiology of the Emotions

As mentioned earlier, while the cognitive theories of emotion have a focus on thought patterns and appraisals, the body-based physiological theories, first presented by William James, are now enjoying a revival through the work of the neurologist Antonio Damasio and the philosopher Jesse Prinz. It was William James who first described the body as the mind's sounding board, allowing the emotional signals to resonate as the sound of a guitar amplifies the sound of the strings. This means by suppressing some automatic bodily changes, and consciously making others, we gain emotional control.

In another chapter, when we discuss body-based therapies for pain management, it will become apparent that the body has acquired a new dimension of significance. In Buddhist mindfulness practice, the Buddha placed the body first, followed by feelings and thought patterns. And in this context, there is deep experiential/contemplative knowledge. The 'breath' is also a central pathway in Buddhist meditation. 'Knowing the body through the body' is also considered as a 'sixth sense' in deep meditation. Thus, the 'breath body' is an important pathway of Buddhist meditation.

References

Alston, W.P. 1967. Emotion and Feeling. In *The Encyclopedia of Philosophy*, vol. 2. New York: Macmillan.

Averill, James. 1980. Emotion and Anxiety: Sociocultural, Biological and Psychological Determinants. In *Explaining Emotions*, ed. Amélie Rorty. Berkeley, CA: California University Press.

Bennett, M.R., and P.M.S. Hacker. 2003. *Philosophical Foundations of Neuroscience*. Oxford: Blackwell.

Davids, Rhys. 1914. *Buddhist Psychology*. London: Bell and Sons.

de Silva, Padmasiri. 2017. *Emotions and the Body in Buddhist Contemplative Practice and Mindfulness-Based Therapy*. London: Palgrave Macmillan.

de Silva, Padmasiri. 2018. *The Buddhist Psychology of Emotions and Humour*. London: Palgrave Macmillan.

Ekman, Paul. 2003. *Emotions Revealed*. New York: Weidenfeld and Nicolson.
Gladwell, Malcolm. 2005. *Blink: The Power of Thinking Without Thinking*. London: Penguin.
Greenberg, Leslie. 2008. *Emotion Focused Therapy*. Washington, DC: American Philosophical Association.
James, William. 1884. What Is an Emotion? In *Readings in Philosophical Psychology*, ed. Cheshire Calhoun and Robert Solomon. Oxford: Oxford University Press.
Kenny, Anthony. 1963. *Action, Emotion and Will*. London: Routledge & Kegan Paul.
Lyons, William. 1963. *Philosophy Papers*. New York: Humanities Press.
Lyons, William. 1980. *Emotion*. Cambridge: Cambridge University Press.
Marks, Joel (ed.). 1986. *The Ways of Desire*. Chicago: Precedent.
Solomon, Robert C. 1977. *The Passions*. New York: Anchor Pressa and Doubleday.
Solomon, Robert C. (ed.). 2004. *Thinking About Feeling*. Oxford: Oxford University Press.

2

Emotion Profiles: Anger

Now that we have in very great detail looked at the nature of emotions, different chapters will explore the emotion profiles of anger, fear/anxiety, grief, sadness/depression, compassion and joy.

I shall first make a detailed study of the emotion of anger and then against that background, present the Buddhist perspectives on emotion studies. That will provide an ideal framework to portray other emotion profiles against the Buddhist background. I shall look at other emotion profiles on the way, as I develop the thematic setting of the present book.

Anger is an important emotion that has ramifications in our lives as well as in counselling and therapy. But as my meditation guru, Venerable Dhammajīva, of Mītirigala, Sri Lanka, observes in his discussion of the *Parābhava Sutta*, anger calls for a greater deal more of mindful observation than other emotions as it is often invisible, whereas greed is more visible. Also, anger may exist at a subliminal level (*anusaya*), and though greed may exist at a subliminal level, its voice is loud and visible. Anger may emerge in an outward acceptable form as moral anger but it is also a close cousin of envy, and there is a component of anger in envy: altogether an insidious emotion. Anger is also a very volatile

P. de Silva, *Mindfulness-based Emotion Focused Counselling*,
https://doi.org/10.1007/978-3-030-64388-1_2

emotion and may enter in a disguised form as a hindrance in the practice of meditation, as aversion, lethargy, boredom and agitation. Anger is greatly mixed up with envy, jealousy and sadism. In my book on humour, I have shown that while there is the presence of very refined humour, I have said that humour may degenerate into sarcasm and laughter at another's foibles (de Silva 2018). A very important facet of anger is anger as a moral emotion and the last chapters of the book will highlight the moral psychology of anger.

Anger has a clear facial expression. The normal physiological correlates are increased heart rate, blood pressure, and levels of adrenaline and non-adrenaline. It also manifests in body language. Our main concern, in keeping with the counselling orientation in this book, is anger management. Jayatunga, in her study of mindfully managing anger makes a pointed analysis:

> Detached watching of anger in routine events; Mindfully pointing out the fault-finding nature of the mind; Mindfully pointing out the mistakes of others. Overcoming deeply rooted anger with mindfulness; Dealing with hatred at the communal level. Seeing the ownerless nature of anger; Going beyond good and bad; Significance of developing divine abodes; Developing forgiveness and patience; Apologizing; Making a team effort; Accommodating criticism; Recollection of death; Contemplation on the reality of the body. (Jayatunga 2012)

What is important is the non-judgmental and non-reactive stance we need to take in a situation that normally causes anger.

Six Perspectives on Managing Anger

Anger is a paradigm of negative emotion and Buddhist psychology accepts that emotions have a great impact on our lives. The afflictive negative emotions are reactive. Such ingrained states are sticky and restrictive, locking us into old patterns of neural firing, tying us to previously *learned* information and priming us to react in rigid ways. Non-reactivity reveals an important facet of resilience that of managing afflictive emotions. Buddhist mindfulness practice helps in developing resilience towards an emotion like anger. Richard Davidson says that both resilience and emotional outlook need to be developed. What is described as outlook is the *capacity to sustain positive emotions over time* and that is a key measure of the 'outlook dimension' of your emotional style. The outlook reflects how long and how well you can sustain positive emotions (Davidson 2018).

I shall present six perspectives for managing negative emotions with a special focus on anger. *The initial technique of Buddhist mindfulness practice is not to repress or suppress such afflictive mental states, but to identify the rise and experience of these states, creating an open space.* Here the focus is on acceptance instead of experiential avoidance. The Buddha says, 'see anger as anger and 'lust as lust' without judgment and self-identification. Especially in the context of guilt and remorse, adopt a posture of curiosity and tolerance without judgment and self-identification. The *Satipaṭṭhāna* clearly emphasises the following: not to oppose unwholesome states but to be receptively aware and to recognise the states of the mind; not to ignore those states that go against your ego and not to use deception (*vañcaka dhammā*).

Managing Anger and Aversion in Vipassanā Meditation

Compared with the management of anger in routine life, in your special hours of mindfulness practice or at a retreat, as you identify the five hindrances, it is necessary to be aware of the subliminal state of anger (*paṭighānusaya*), as the five hindrances may obstruct a meditator in a very subtle way. Sense desires arise due to unwise reflection and generate aversion in the meditator. In general, sense control, meditation on ugliness, decay and decomposition, moderation with food and having a wise friend are recommended. Regarding restlessness, worry and remorse; it is said that if you are immersed in mindfulness, it is like a good pair of spectacles, so that you see things clearly, but when the mind is agitated, you need to replace it with patience, clarity and discernment. In a meditation setting, physical and mental comfort is the antidote to restlessness.

Boredom is a natural part of a meditator's life, and it is a kind of attention crisis; mindfulness done with joy and rapture may deal with boredom. One can also shift to walking mediation, which some enjoy practicing. Csikszentmihalyi, an expert who conducted experiments with hill climbers, athletes, musicians, meditators and people doing varied types of jobs, presented the concept of 'flow experience': different types of meditation work towards a peak experience. The attraction of mindfulness as a flow experience has been described as a new model for education (Hassed and Chambers 2014). In Vipassanā meditation, sloth and torpor and other defilements indicate the need for a deep reflective mind, and a sense of joy, upliftment and complete absorption in one's practice of meditation. I shall discuss at length the emotion profile of boredom in a later part of the book.

The second strand in the management of anger is a point on which I have published a full book: the theme of 'somatic intelligence' (de Silva 2017). The *Satipaṭṭhāna* itself is divided into the sections on the body, feelings, thought patterns and the psycho-physical complex, where the body comes first. Cognition is embodied when it is dependent on the body at a deeper level, a fact that was ignored by the existing cognitive sciences till the ground-breaking work of Varela emerged: *The Embodied Mind* (Varela et al. 1999). Based on this paradigm, there was an emerging interest in the inner experience and contemplative practices which had been blocked by the followers of behaviourism in psychology. Another new strand that has given a boost to contemplative studies is the field of neuroscience. In psychology and neuroscience, the linkages between the body and the brain have given a new direction to emotion studies. Antonio Damasio has presented a new interpretation of William James which stands out as direct evidence for the bodily basis of emotions:

> Think of the muscles in the face adopting the configurations of joy, sorrow or anger, or of the skin blanching as a reaction to bad news or flushing in a state of embarrassment or bodily postures that signify joy, defiance, sadness. (Damasio 2000)

The third strand is of interest to meditators with experience in the practice of Vipassanā and I am drawing on many years of learning under Venerable Dhammajīva. The technique of developing the sixth sense (*anindriyapaṭibaddha viññāna*), non-sensory consciousness needs explanation. Our normal consciousness is connected to the body through the six doors of the senses: seeing, hearing, tasting, smelling, touching and mind door (*mano dvāra*). But as we develop our meditative sittings and refine our consciousness, we move into a form of consciousness that is not related to the senses (Dhammajīva). Neurologist Daniel Siegel describes this experience as *interoception* (Siegel 2007). The tranquilization of the 'breath body', leads to the experience of the contemplative emotions of joy and rapture. In the Western emotion tradition, there is hardly any mention of contemplative emotions. The fourth strand comes from the meditative practice of *dhammānupassanā*, where defilements are converted into objects of meditation. We do not throw away our defilements but as Venerable Nyānaponika says, with a little magic these may be converted into powerful insights. He quotes the following lines from *The Little Locksmith* (2000) by K. B. Hathaway:

> I am shocked by the ignorance and wastefulness with which persons who should know better throw away things that they do not like. They throw away experiences, people, marriages situations, all sorts of things because they do not like them—almost all, those things which get thrown away are capable of being worked over by a little magic into just the opposite of what they are.... (Nyānaponika 2014)

A fifth dimension is the initial safety and security from negative emotions preserved at the level of *sīla*. The celebrated fourfold methods of dealing with defilements are the following: taking necessary steps through restraint (*saṃvara*); abandoning them once they have emerged (*pahāna*); developing positive emotions (*bhāvanā*); stabilising them once they have emerged (*anurakkhanā*). Thus, we see the emergence of a coordinated sensibility to deal with defilements (negative emotions) and to develop positive ones. This sensibility is captured through some graphic metaphors used by the Buddha: the watchfulness of a doorkeeper; instilling discipline like a horse trainer; the persistence of an army defending a fortress; the balance and vigilance of an acrobat.

The sixth perspective is both literally and metaphorically taken from medicine. This is the use of specific antidotes to deal with a specific malady: for the malady of ill-will, the remedy is the development of forgiveness, patience and loving kindness; for sensuous lust, the remedy is impermanence, decay and disgust. The Jewish philosopher Spinoza (1632–1677) says, 'an emotion cannot be restrained or removed unless by an opposed and stronger emotion' (Spinoza 1963). He also considers the importance of the body: 'An emotion, in so far as it is related to the mind, cannot be removed unless by the idea of a bodily modification opposed to that which we suffer and is stronger than it' (Spinoza 1963).

Spinoza also says, 'Hatred has to be conquered by love or generosity, and is not to be met with hatred in return' (1963). Spinoza says that vanity is pursued by a man who pursues glory too easily. Spinoza's analysis of good and bad emotions presents interesting similarities to Buddhism. In the Buddhist context remembering the good within us and others mingled with *mettā* removes any trace of self-hate or anger towards others. *Karuṇā* (kindness) is a powerful ally to deal with grief and when joined with gratitude to those who have been separated, adds a reflective and dedicatory quality to grief. Taking pleasure in the happiness of others (*muditā*) is hard to cultivate but is the best antidote to envy and jealousy; and equanimity (*upekkhā*) steers clear of undue elation and conceit (*māna*) as well as steering clear of dependency and dejection.

The sixth technique is that of the Tibetan Buddhist tradition. But as some of these facets found in Tibetan and Zen Buddhist tradition may be shared with the early Buddhist tradition (Theravāda), this dialogue is very important and I shall attempt a balanced study.

Working with Emotions (Rinpoche 1992), is an elegant monograph which cites five techniques centered round the graphic metaphor of the Great Peacock, where the negative emotions are described as poisons. Though the peacock eats the poison, this process generates the resplendent feathers of the peacock. The techniques are described as abandoning, remedying, controlling, transforming, recognizing their true wisdom nature, and taking emotions as the path. Negative emotions are generated by clinging to the ego: giving them consideration as attractive (desire), unattractive (anger) neutral (ignorance). Overemphasizing one's experience is pride; judging our position in relation to others is jealousy.

To abandon emotions is not to suppress them but to understand their unattractive side. Distancing oneself from them gives us space to work with them.

Anger may be abandoned by not building up enmity and desire but by appreciating the value of contentment. Mental dullness has to be cleared by clearly distinguishing the ethics of good and bad. Those who are virtuous should not inflate themselves by comparing themselves to others, as pride may emerge in virtuous people. The most important result of abandoning negative emotions is our readiness to let go of negativities and of developing spaciousness and flexibility at the level of *our emotions.*

Remedying involves working with antidotes. There is the remedying of desire by contemplation on the body's impurities; love and patience are the antidotes for anger and hatred. In general, loving kindness (*mettā*) is one of the most powerful antidotes for anger and hatred. The demolition of pride is done by reflecting on our predicament in the *saṃsār*ic round of existence. Pleasure at the success of others counteracts jealousy. Tibetan Buddhism also uses the technique of *visualizatio*n for transformation of emotions.

Zen and the Emotions

Zen Buddhism is a large reservoir of apparently disconnected insights with an underlying unity. Zen masters turn things upside down and unify them when wisdom emerges, as was evident in the words of the legendary Thai monk, Ajahn Chah (1918–1992), who said you need a transparent mind to see the subtleties of desire in your very attempt to rid yourself of desire: 'Buddhism teaches us to make earnest efforts in the things we do, but our actions should not be mixed with desire. They should be performed with the aim of letting go and realizing non-attachment.'

The Zen perspective has its own style of dealing with emotions. Rinzai Zen, as presented by Parkes (1990) in an illuminating study, was critical of the 'stultifying dogma and rigidity of conventional Buddhism'. Above all Zen was open to the emotions, a point which Nietzsche (1844–1900) noted, as he was very critical of the Platonic tradition that was trying to 'annihilate the passions and desires simply because of their stupidity'. One of the interesting parallelisms between Nietzsche's philosophy and Zen is that he does 'reverse and undercut the distinction between positive and negative emotions' (Parkes 1990). It is a kind of non-judgmental perspective on emotions. The following illuminating lines from Parkes best describes his perspectives on emotions and the body:

> Of the forces that move our souls, the emotions are among the most significant, with the closest ties to the body. They also have a special connection with pathology, being capable themselves of engendering illness as well as participating in its cure. The similar estimation of the importance of sickness on the part of Hakunin and Nietzsche may be grounded in a similarity of physical and psychical make up; like Nietzsche's, Hakunin's bodily constitution was initially weak. (Parkes 1990)

Together with certain truths about the human condition, Nietzsche gave the emotions an important cognitive and hermeneutic role. Some of these insights may be shared with Zen Buddhism and early Buddhism at a certain level of depth.

Prejudices of Psychologists and Philosophers in the West

In contemporary times, there has been great interest in Buddhist psychology, mindfulness-based therapies and Buddhist contemplative practice. Furthermore, neuroscientists have been working on the brain. But there have been prejudices and mis-information regarding Buddhist practice. I shall present a few of these observations among well-recognized scholars. For example, Aronson says:

> A new series of issues arose for Western Buddhists who entered psychotherapy. Buddhist teachers counsel to abandon anger, develop patience, give up attachments, and understand the absence of Self. This is taught in a context of disciplined communal practice—the Sangha. Therapists encourage those who are emotionally shut down to experience feelings of anger, and they facilitate the request for relationship and intimacy, this is done in a context that supports self-assertion and individuality. How are we to follow both approaches? (2004)

Similarly, Owen Flanagan says that in the West, anger is a basic emotion but the Buddha says it is to be eliminated from one's basic emotional constitution (Flanagan 2000). Jack Engler provides a similar refrain: 'The labelling of aversive emotions as "defilements" or as "unwholesome" in Buddhist Practice can lead to thinking that the goal is not to feel and disturbing emotions, and then feel guilty if you do' (Engler 2006).

All Buddhists and non-Buddhists need to understand that this is a basic distortion of how we manage anger using the *Satipaṭṭhāna.* My detailed study of anger here clearly indicates that Buddhism does not tell people to eliminate anger but transform it into a liberating insight. While agreeing with the recent mindfulness-based therapies and appreciating their work has drawn the best from the Buddhist practice of mindfulness, and aware that Buddhism is a liberation-oriented message for those suffering from depression, a few qualifying comments need to be made. Apart from considering anger from a non-judgmental point of view, we also discern anger related emotions conveyed from Pāli terms such as *kodha* and *kopa* as mental defilements; *dosa* as an unwholesome root; *vyāpāda* as a hindrance; and *paṭighānusaya* as subliminal anger—at the level of morality. But in sitting for meditation there is a contextual change—where anger is neither good nor bad, neither yours nor mine, and is a process which emerges, stays for a while and then passes away.

As I have already clarified, in *dhammānupassanā*, the meditator makes anger an object of meditation; in *cittānupassanā*, as in Mindfulness-based Cognitive Therapy (MBCT) the meditator becomes aware of the thought processes, the thought components of the emotion and the auto-pilot processes that feed anger; in *vedanānupassanā* one 'puts on the breaks', at the initial emergence of disagreeable feelings (*dukkha vedanā*), and does not let them develop into anger. In tranquility meditation (*samatha),* the development of bodily and mental calm may temporarily push the anger aside, but may not radically deal with the roots, though it helps the meditator to move around in daily life with calm and composure. In *kāyānupassanā* which is focused on the body and is the preliminary section of the *Satipaṭṭhāna*, the focus is on the body and here we are able to focus on the central features of negative emotions. Body sensations are the earliest indications of emotions like anger, fear and sadness. Thus, you will see, how Western commentators like Aronson, Flanagan and Engler have distorted the Buddhist perspective on negative emotions.

Cognitive therapists like Jon Kabat-Zinn were on the right track and their wonderful work is recognized, though the Buddhist liberation path goes beyond psychotherapy. Thus, it is wrong to say that the Buddhist is advocating destruction of anger but rather, that the Buddha offers *several ways of managing anger and converting it to a transforming experience of insight*. Tantric Buddhism and Zen also have techniques to transform anger into insightful experience.

We shall explore the subject of 'embodied emotions' and William James in a separate chapter.

There are three other emotion profiles which I need to contextualise in different chapters: *sadness* in the chapter on exploring the logic of depression; *fear* in the section on Freud and anxiety; *human greed* has to be charted in a new chapter towards the latter part of the book within socio-political and environmental issues—and there will be a new chapter on environmental counselling—a ground-breaking horizon for expanding the field of counselling.

References

Aronson, H.B. 2004. *Buddhist Practice on Western Ground*. Boulder, CO: Shambhala Publications.

Damasio, Antonio. 2000. *The Feeling of What Happens: Body and Emotion in the Making of Consciousness*. London: Vintage.

Davidson, Richard, and Sharon Begley. 2013. *The Emotional Life of Your Brain*. London: Hodder.

de Silva, Padmasiri. 2017. *Emotions and the Body in Buddhist Contemplative Practice and Mindfulness-Based Therapy*. London: Palgrave Macmillan.

de Silva, Padmasiri. 2018. *The Buddhist Psychology of Emotions and Humour*. London: Palgrave Macmillan.

Engler, Jack. 2006. Promises and Perils of the Spiritual Path. In *Buddhism and Psychotherapy Across Cultures*, ed. M. Unno. Boston: Wisdom.

Flanagan, Owen. 2000. Destructive Emotions. *Consciousness and Emotion* 1 (2): 67–88.

Hassed, Craig. 2008. *The Essence of Health*. Sydney, NSW, Australia: Random.

Hassed, Craig, and Richard Chambers. 2014. *Mindful Learning*. Gosford, NSW: Exisle.

Jayatunga, Ruchira. 2012. Mindfully Managing Anger. In *Let Us Be Mindful*. Ganemulla, Sri Lanka: Printwell Printers.

Nyānaponika Thero. 2014. Managing Anger. In *An Introduction to Buddhist Psychology*, ed. Padmasiri de Silva, 182–183. London: Palgrave Macmillan.

Parkes, Graham. 1990. The Transmutation of Emotions in Rinzai Zen and Nietzsche. *The Eastern Buddhist* XXIII: 1.

Rinpoche, Lama Glendun. 1992. *Working with Emotions*. Carlton North, VIC: Zambala.

Siegel, Daniel. 2007. *The Mindful Brain*. New York: Norton.

Spinoza, B. 1963. *Ethics*. New York: Hafner.

Varela, Francisco, Evan Thompson, and Eleanor Rosch. 1999. *The Embodied Mind: Cognitive Science and Human Experience*. London: MIT Press.

3
Emobodied Cognition and Emotion: Somatic Intelligence

I have already looked at anger as a negative emotion and wish to expand the findings of the last chapter to the more current climate of research into somatic intelligence—the wisdom of the body. If there is an element of repetition coming from the last chapter, it does not matter, as the new research both in the emotions studies area as well as my personal contemplative practice illuminate the important difference between reactive emotions and resilient emotions.

You will eventually realize that this is an important dimension of the *Satipaṭṭhāna* in managing emotions: not to oppose or suppress negative emotions like anger or sensations like pain but to be receptively aware of the state of the mind and thought patterns and more subtle bodily reactions. In contemporary neuroscience non-reactivity is a central concept and especially well articulated in a recent work by Rick Hanson (2018). Non-reactivity is also a central technique in mindfulness-based cognitive therapy. These insights are also a kind of response to the Western critics of Buddhist anger management.

Somatic learning has been described as the art and practice of 'embodied mindfulness' or in simple terms, 'the wisdom of the body'. Cognition is embodied when it is deeply dependent on the features of

P. de Silva, *Mindfulness-based Emotion Focused Counselling*,
https://doi.org/10.1007/978-3-030-64388-1_3

the physical body, when, a person's body beyond the brain plays a significant role from a causal or constitutive stand in cognitive processing. Earlier, cognitive science looked at cognition in a very narrow sense in abstraction from the bodily mechanism of sensory processing and motor control. But with the publication of the book, *The Embodied Mind* by Varela, Thompson and Rosch, there was a major paradigm shift: 'One of the major realizations over the last few years in science has been to understand that one cannot have anything close to a mind or mental capacity without it being completely embodied, enfolded with the world' (Varela et al. 1999). Against this background emerged a new dialogue between cognitive psychology, Buddhist contemplative practice and mindfulness-based therapy (de Silva 2017). Following the work of Varela and others, my recent publication is to some extent a pioneer work on Buddhist somatic intelligence. Also, this work expands into applied work in the fields of pain and trauma management. *Body and emotions will have a central place in the present book.*

Body, Mind and Resilience

This book will present the timely psychology of resilience as developed by Rick Hanson in his recent book, *Resilient: How to Grow an Unshakable Core of Calm, Strength and Happiness* (2018). Daniel Siegel presents a similar thesis as does Richard Davidson:

> Resilient people are somehow able not only to withstand but to benefit from certain kinds of stressful events and turn adversity to advantage. This in a nutshell is the puzzle that has driven my research... The answer that has emerged from my own work is that different people have different emotional styles. These are constellations of emotional reactions and coping responses that differ in kind, intensity and duration. (Davidson and Begley 2013)

The Resilient Brain

At one end of the spectrum we find that when struck by adversity and setbacks, they either recover very slowly and others who will fight back with a quick recovery. Davidson's research brings out a very important point that *resilience is marked by greater left versus right activation of the prefrontal cortex, while a lack of resilience comes from right prefrontal activation.* When we feel anxious, threatened or fearful, the amygdala is involved (Siegel 2007).

Anger mobilizes energy and shines a bright light on whatever is at issue. Nevertheless, anger also comes wrapped with tension, stress and threats to relationships. Frequent or chronic anger is fatiguing; like hot acid, it eats away physical and mental health. Of all the emotions we express to each other, anger usually compels the most attention, like a red-light flashing danger. Then we react to the other person's anger with our own anger, creating vicious cycle in relationships.

Cooling down anger does not mean enabling injustice or turning into a patsy. You can still be strong and forceful. Think of the times when you or others were determined, passionate, or assertive while not being swept away by anger.

This study will first present the significant position of the body both in cognition and emotion and then focus on the distinction between reactive emotions and resilient emotions: in general, what may be described as the *philosophy of resilience* which is also a feature of Buddhist psychology. I shall specifically focus on anger as a reactive emotion, and Western scholars who have misunderstood the Buddhist analysis. In making this extension to anger analysis, I am of course repeating some of the material in the earlier chapter but it does not matter, as the context is different. I refer to Flanagan, Aronson, and Engler. It must be emphasized that in a Buddhist meditation setting, anger is an impersonal process which emerges, stays for a while and passes away—it has a *hermeneutical* role underlying the processes of impersonality and impermanence. Cultivation of the positive emotions of patience, kindness and compassion strengthen the path towards resilience. My intention in taking anger at the top of part one before other emotions is that the management of anger provides a beautiful model which brings the Buddhist and neuroscience perspectives together.

Emotions and the Body: Embodied Emotions

The subject of 'embodied emotions' has received much attention in a different lineage from Buddhism. Jesse Prinz has revived William James's thesis that emotions are perceptions of changes in the body and they allow us literally to perceive danger (fear) and loss (grief). 'The core idea I will defend is that *emotions are perceptions* (conscious or unconscious) *of patterned changes in the body* (Prinz 2004). William James presented the paradox: 'first you run and then feel the fear; first you cry and then feel sad'. Though this sounds paradoxical, that was James's way of emphasizing the place of physiology in emotions. Also, Antonio Damasio's ground-breaking research on the emotions, the body and neurology, brings out well the physical transformation of emotions in the body:

> Think of the muscles in the face adopting the configurations that are typical of joy, sorrow, or anger; or of the skin blanching as a reaction to bad news or flushing in embarrassment; or consider the body postures that signify joy, defiance, sadness or discouragement; or the sweaty and clammy hands of apprehension, the racing of heart associated with pride; or the slowing, near stillness of the heart in terror. (2000)

The most significant research on emotions and the face has been by Paul Ekman, in his work *Emotions Revealed* (2007). We have looked at anger from ethical and therapeutic perspectives but I wish to look now at anger in its features as an embodied emotion. Ekman looked at anger closely, like an artist looking at the intricate patterns of the body and face. As one of the recurring themes of the book is on emotions and the body, the physiology of emotions is important. I have already looked at anger in relation to the misguided criticism of the Buddhist position by three Western philosophers. But I wish to explore this profile of anger as an embodied emotion and to examine recent work on the subject. Two questions which are important are anger as an embodied emotion and the difference between emotional resilience and reactivity.

The Role of Physiology in Emotions

This is a central concern of this book as it is being discussed from different perspectives. It also includes an introductory chapter on the nature of emotions. There is at present a great deal of technical and statistical work on the emotions and related subjects, but as a counsellor, especially with a Buddhist background, I have adopted a perspective close to ordinary life. I draw on the insights of Ekman, Damasio, Richardson and Siegel in the way that they may be applied to routine life as well as to counselling issues. For six years I offered my services as a counsellor at the Springvale Community Centre, which was within walking distance from my home. My services were offered basically free of charge as a life-time commitment in order to come close to the lives of others: both my clients and their families. This is important as much academic research issues in counselling need to be kept in their proper place—the sense and sensibility of the client is crucial.

Most of the Buddhist teachings on anger in traditional studies have been on their ethical overtones. Though it is very important if you shift to a meditative setting, the concept of non-reactivity is a central concern. From the modern neurological findings, it is evident that the pre-frontal cortex plays a significant role in: developing non-reactivity; the regulation of the body system; balancing emotions; attuning to others; modulating fear; responding flexibly; and showing empathy for others. In fact, they say that *'morality' has links with the pre-frontal region of the brain.*

Paul Ekman, the world's outstanding scholar on emotion studies says:

> When we are in the grip of an emotion like anger, a cascade of changes (without our choice or immediate awareness) occurs in split seconds in the emotional signals in the face and voice; pre-set actions; learned actions; the autonomic nervous system activity that regulates the body,

> the regulatory patterns that continuously modify our behaviour… these changes are involuntary and we do not choose them. (Ekman 2003)

But if we can make a choice and become conscious of what we feel, then he says, that is close to what the Buddhist call 'mindfulness'. Mindfulness is able to break through impulsive actions reflected in the body, the automatic appraisals (auto-pilot) seen in our thought patterns, and the causes of anger through which we can identify emotional triggers. What the Buddhists offer is the systematic practice of the *Satipaṭṭhāna.*

Emotions and Body Reactivity

There is a new theory of emotions associated with different patterns of body sensations and thoughts: termed co-emergent. Bruno Cayoun who developed the theory of mindfulness-integrated CBT (i) considered thoughts and body sensations in a co-emergent process, that strikes new ground in the relationship between emotions and the body; and he considers them as a link between the body and mind. (ii) He found in his regular counselling that different emotions were associated with different patterns of body sensations and these emotion maps are culturally universal. Also, observations indicated that emotions are made up of a combination of *thoughts, bodily sensations* and the *need to react.* As these patterns emerge so rapidly, it is not possible for the untrained mind to separate the emotional event into its basic components.

I am delighted that Cayoun says:

> [T]here are four basic characteristics of these bodily sensations: mass: from the lightest to the heaviest; motion: from the most still to the extremes of shaking, or agitation; temperature from the coldest to the hottest experience; fluidity also called cohesiveness from the most diffuse to the dense. (Cayoun 2015, pp. 119–121)

Cayoun says, **anger** *will tend to maintain itself with predominance of increased temperature (heat) and motion, increased heart rate and agitation.* **Sadness** is usually experienced with an *increase of predominant mass* (*heaviness in head and shoulders)* and perhaps decreased fluidity (*constriction of the throat*). The emotion of **fear** manifests with a predominance of decreased fluidity (*constriction in chest and abdomen, increased heart rate, agitation*). To perceive emotions in an objective way means focusing on the sensory perception aspects of the emotion (mass, motion, temperature and fluidity). This analysis by Cayoun has great similarities to the *Vipassanā* tradition of focusing on the four elements, as presented by Venerable Dhammajīva, which forms a central part of my regular meditation practice.

References

Cayoun, Bruno. 2015. *Mindfulness-Integrated CBT for Wellbeing and Personal Growth*. Oxford: Wiley.

Damasio, Antonio. 2000. *The Feeling of What Happens: Body and Emotion in the Making of Consciousness*. London: Vintage.

Davidson, Richard, and Sharon Begley. 2013. *The Emotional Life of Your Brain*. London: Hodder.

de Silva, Padmasiri. 2017. *Emotions and the Body in Buddhist Contemplative Practice and Mindfulness-Based Therapy*. London: Palgrave Macmillan.

Ekman, Paul. 2003. *Emotions Revealed*. New York: Weidenfeld and Nicolson.

Hanson, Rick. 2018. *Resilient: How to Grow an Unshaken Core of Calm, Strength and Happiness*. New York: Harmony.

Prinz, Jesse. 2004. *Gut Reactions: A Perceptual Theory of Emotions*. Oxford: Oxford University Press.

Siegel, Daniel. 2007. *The Mindful Brain*. New York: Norton.

Varela, Francisco, Evan Thompson, and Eleanor Rosch. 1999. *The Embodied Mind: Cognitive Science and Human Experience*. London: MIT Press.

4

The Buddhist Architecture of the Mind

I have already presented the Western theories of emotions in detail; then I have presented the theory of embodied emotions and the pathways of resilience in Western theories, and in the light of these studies presented a comprehensive study of Buddhist anger management, along with a critique of Western critics. Now, it is time to look at the Buddhist theory of emotions. The Greek philosopher Aristotle first presented the architecture of the tripartite division of the mind. In this light, there is (i) cognition/perception (*saññā, viññāna*); feeling, the affective dimension (*vedanā*); conative or volitional dimension (*saṃkhāra*).

Four Mental Aggregates and the Body

i. Perception (*saññā*)
ii. Consciousness (*viññāna*)
iii. Feelings (*vedanā*)
iv. Volitional activity (*saṃkhāra*)
v. The Body (*rūpa*)

P. de Silva, *Mindfulness-based Emotion Focused Counselling*,
https://doi.org/10.1007/978-3-030-64388-1_4

Even though this traditional picture of the mind is useful, we need not place absolute reliance on it, as all four mental aggregates and the body may be present at the very minutest level in states of consciousness. A significant point about Buddhist psychology is already illustrated in a previous chapter: the reciprocal relationship between body and mind. Further, it avoids any Cartesian dualism, or reductionism: reduction of the mental into the physical or the physical into the mental.

The causality of what is described as 'dependent origination' gives some insight into the emergence of different psychological factors; for instance, sensory contact conditions feeling, feeling conditions craving and craving conditions clinging. Thus, in addition to the structural perspective of the mind and the body, there is also a dynamic facet of the interplay of sensations, feelings, desires, volitions and dispositions. This dynamism helps us to uncover the patterns of human behaviour in anger, sadness and compassion, and in general the whole changing patterns of human behaviour.

Another central perspective is that the Buddhist concept of the mind is supplemented by an analysis of mental activity at a *subliminal level*. Threshold consciousness is open to six sense doors through which stimuli reach us: as seeing, hearing, smelling, tasting, touching; and via the mind door, conceptual and ideational activity, including memory. The ability to control the senses help a person to stay unaffected by the inroads of sensory stimuli, but the mind is subject to subliminal pressures. In an earlier edition of *Buddhist and Freudian Psychology* (de Silva 1992), I developed the idea of an unconscious in Buddhism that was influenced by Freud's theories and clinical studies, but recently, I discovered that there is a difference beyond this similarity.

Buddhism accepts the traumatic unconscious in Freud, but there is a more significant layer of activity that lies in an area closer to routine life, which is important. Closer to our everyday life is what I describe as the 'subliminal', and this change is duly recognized in a later edition of the book (de Silva 2010). I have moved away from the archaeological metaphor of 'digging' in the inaccessible and often traumatic layers of the psyche to a metaphor of 'opening up' thoughts and affects close to ordinary life/threshold consciousness.

Today, in mindfulness-based cognitive therapy (which is different from Freud's psychotherapy), the focus is on the moment-moment flow of thoughts, which is described as the 'auto-pilot' of mechanical responses. New research in neurology by Joseph Ledoux (1996), explains how our normal rational consciousness may be hijacked by the amygdala, the instigator of impulsive activity. He cites the example of a man walking on a forest track, and his boots crush a bundle of dry twigs while walking and he is about to run, thinking that it is a rattlesnake. In the context of Buddhism, the concept of *anusaya* (subliminal tendency) explains how amygdala activity is possible. Regular mindfulness activity is able to access these levels of subliminal activity, as it is closer to our consciousness: the subliminal tendencies of anger, fear and greed. This dormant level is referred to in Buddhism as *anusaya bhūmi*; and these sleeping passions may also lie at the level of thoughts and thought patterns described as *pariyuṭṭhāna-bhūmi* or become fierce and ungovernable and result in impulsive activity (*vītikkama-bhūmi*).

The Archaeological Metaphor

The archaeological metaphor was one of Freud's favourites. Once disowned intentions are brought to consciousness, it would be possible to take responsibility for them, and in that process, we could be free of their tyranny over us.

The Opening Metaphor

However, in Buddhism—and even in recent psychoanalysis—a different model has emerged, one that is less about digging and more about opening (Oatley 2004).

At the root of this difference lies an alternative view of the unconscious. These two contrasting metaphors convey the new perspectives on the 'subliminal' that I have developed instead of the Freudian unconscious.

A Buddhist Perspective on Emotion Theories

It is very strange that there is no Pāli word for the term emotion and this is also true of the Tibetan tradition as the Dalai Lama has indicated in a dialogue with Matthieu Ricard. In teaching psychology in Sinhalese, at the University of Peradeniya, I had a problem and in fact I used a technical term, *cittavega*, a term rarely used in ordinary conversation. In early Buddhist psychology, greed (*lobha*) provides the basis for addictions and attachment; hatred (*dosa*) provides the basis for emotions of aversion/reactive and for delusion/identity confusion (*moha*) is what may be described as a 'doxic ailment'.

Emotion concepts in Buddhism first has a focus on '*vedanā*', translated as 'feeling' which represents the initial affective dimension or a hedonic tone.

Such feelings may be pleasant, unpleasant and neutral (indifferent). It should be made clear that, in Buddhist psychology, 'feeling' is the bare sensation noted as pleasant, unpleasant (painful) and neutral (indifferent). Hence, it should not be confused with emotion, which though arising from the basic feeling, adds to it, likes and dislikes of varying intensity, as well as other thought processes.

In Buddhist psychology, an emotion may be considered as an interactive complex or construct emerging within the causal network of the five Aggregates.

Thus, within this network, it is possible to distinguish feeling, bodily sensations, desires, beliefs and appraisals as variables that go to make anger, fear, sadness and so on. Though there are differences within the Tibetan Buddhist tradition regarding the number of emotions, they agree that negative emotions are afflictive, causing suffering, and they are also described as defilements. The concept of *saṃkhāra,* translated as volitional activities provides the notion of intention and accountability, crucial in the context of moral accountability and the ethics of emotions. Negative emotions are fed by the cognitive distortions rooted in egoism and greed along with anger/reactivity. Emotions such as conceit and pride are more clearly rooted in the delusions of the ego and a later chapter will be devoted to such emotions.

Feelings

Feeling arises when there is a meeting of three factors: the sense organ, object and consciousness. This interaction is described by the Pāli term *phassa*, which means 'contact'. It is six-fold and it is conditioned by the five physical sense organs and the mind. According to the law of dependent origination, contact conditions feeling, feeling conditions craving. Pleasant feelings, if not properly understood and managed, may turn into lust, greed and infatuation. Painful feelings if not properly understood and managed, may manifest as anger, destructive forms of fear, and depression; neutral feelings if not properly understood lead to boredom. Pleasant feelings which result in attachment to pleasant objects may arouse subliminal tendency towards greed (*rāgānusaya*) and painful feelings may arouse the subliminal tendency towards anger and hatred (*paṭighānusaya*) and the delusions of the attachment to the ego arouse the latent tendency towards ignorance and conceit (*manānusaya*).

> This therefore is a crucial point in the conditioned origin of suffering, because it is at this point that feelings give rise to passionate emotions of various types, and it is here that one may be able to break that fatuous concatenation. If in receiving a sense impression, one is able to pause and stop at the phase of feeling and make it in its first stage of manifestation, the object of Bare Attention, Feeling will not be able to originate Craving. It will stop at the bare statement of 'pleasant', 'unpleasant' or 'indifferent'. (Nyānaponika 1983)

By the processes of bare attention, the possible transition from feelings to negative emotions is watched with great vigilance. It must be emphasized that 'feeling' is in fact a part of a synthetic process and it is only by abstraction that one can isolate feelings. However, in meditation practice, conscious awareness is kept on the primary object by noting and labelling and thus any transition that takes place in the stream of consciousness is noted. Thus the 'slowing down' process helps one to focus on feelings in their unalloyed form in meditative practice. Though in a sense, sensory consciousness, feeling are inseparable, the meditator understands the patterns as having dependent origination: visual consciousness arises because of eye and material shape; the meeting of the three is sensory impingement and because of sensory impingement arises feeling (M.I.111).

It was a characteristic feature of the 'contextual wisdom of the Buddha' that he did not convert these distinctions into an unending metaphysical issue but through a pragmatism and the importance of meditative practice, developed an insight into the different stages in the flow of experience, which is the one way of understanding the components of meditative experience.

The Buddha's pragmatism and contextualism may be illustrated by how he intervened in a celebrated controversy among the monks regarding the exact number of feelings. The Buddha said that one way of analysis of feelings is to speak of two feelings (bodily and mental); three feelings in another way: pleasant, painful and neutral; five types of feeling: the pleasure faculty, pain faculty, joy faculty, displeasure faculty and the equanimity faculty; six feelings, related to the five organs and the mind; eighteen feelings: six accompanied by joy, six by displeasure and six by accompanied by equanimity; thirty six types of feeling: six joys of household life, six joy on renunciation, six types of displeasure in household life, six on displeasure in renunciation, six accompanied by equanimity in household life, six on equanimity in renunciation; or a hundred and eight feelings: the above thirty six into the past, present and future (S II, 232–3). Thus, they are designations to be used in appropriate contexts. The Buddha brought a sense of sanity and pragmatism to these debates.

For those immersed in the psychology of the West would find it difficult to understand and absorb the Buddhist concept of the arahant (perfected one). He is a person with a refined sensibility going beyond the attachment-reaction circuits found in the ignorant world ling (*puthujjana*). The perfected one is free from the 'aroma of subjectivity': the appropriation of things as 'mine'. The arahant may experience a painful feeling, as in the case when a bamboo splinter injured the Buddha but he only experiences the physical impact without a psychological reaction. This does not mean that Buddhist detachment is free of human emotions of compassion and care for other beings both humans and animals. The Buddha experiences a wide range of positive emotions.

Desire and Craving

As Joel Marks claimed, the nature of desire has been neglected in current emotion studies in the West. He also says, desire is also *intentional*. In fact, this point makes the Buddhist analysis of desire and craving doubly interesting. In fact, in the moral criticism of emotions, the motivational bases of actions are very crucial. According to the discourses of the Buddha, a person feels attraction (*sarajjati*) for agreeable objects and feels repugnance for disagreeable objects (*byāpajjati*). An individual thus possessed of likes and dislike approaches pleasure-giving objects and avoids painful objects. Strong craving gets fixated as clinging (*upādāna*) and such clinging goes beyond craving (*taṇhā*). Not merely a desire to possess but also a desire to destroy and unpleasant object is a form of clinging. Desires like sexual/sensual desires are temporarily satisfied, but they incessantly emerge, and it is this hedonic treadmill that the Buddha described as *kāmasukhallikānuyoga*. Sensuality also implies an incessant change for different types of pleasure (*tatta tattābhinandinī*). The pleasure lover also is subject to boredom and emptiness.

It must be noted that desire (*chanda*) is virtuous or vicious depending on context. For instance, a desire is a vice that generates evil, partiality, enmity, stupidity and fear. When we take up issues pertaining to emotions and ethics or morality, we need to look at the springs of human behaviour: the six roots, including greed (*lobha*), which may manifest as the craving for sensuous gratification or the craving for egoistic pursuits; hatred (*dosa*) which manifest in aggressive and self-destructive behaviour; and delusion (*moha*) which may be rendered in the present context as the existential regard for the self. These bases of craving provide a framework to plot the negative emotions: attachment emotions such as greed, covetousness and addictions; emotions of aversion such as anger, indignation, resentment, self-hate, malice; and emotions of delusion such as conceit, pride, vanity, shame and the emotion of jealousy. In the context of the liberation path, we find hindrances: sensuous desire, ill-will, dullness, boredom; restlessness and worry. On the positive side equanimity (*upekkhā*) provides emotional balance.

Emotions and the Cognitive Orientation

Buddhism has a strong cognitive orientation and this is exemplified in a celebrated sermon, the *Vitakkasanthāna Sutt*a (M.I.118–122). There are interesting parallels between techniques used in contemporary cognitive therapy and this *Sutta*, which I have used in developing mindfulness-based cognitive therapy. This sermon presents five techniques of dealing with intrusive thoughts and perhaps as an ancient predecessor of contemporary cognitive therapy is focused on the 'autopilot' of repetitive thinking:

1. First is the method of getting the mind to focus on a 'different object'. Ideational activity associated with desire, aversion and delusion is to be eliminated by reflecting on a wholesome object. This is compared to a carpenter driving out a large peg with a small peg.
2. The second aims at scrutinizing the perils of the harmful thoughts. This is compared to a man in the prime of life, who is fond of the adornment of the body seeing the disgusting sight of a carcass round his neck.
3. The third is 'not attending' to the thoughts.
4. The fourth: uncovering the causal roots of the bad thoughts.
5. The fifth: if these techniques fail, use your will power. Repeated practice makes a person succeed.

There is the possibility of 'cognitive distortions' at a deeper level. Our cognitive life is not limited to clear, fully conceptualized, articulated beliefs. Instead, beliefs constitute a small illuminated portion of that life. The greater portion is rather dark, an articulated framework for interpreting our world which if articulated, would be an enormous network of claims.

The Body and the Physiology of Emotions

> Bhikkhus, just as various winds blow in the sky, winds from the east, winds from the west, winds from the north, winds from the south, dusty winds and dustless winds, cold and hot winds, mild winds and strong winds; so too various feelings arise in the body: pleasant feelings arise, painful feelings arise, neither pleasurable nor painful feelings arise. (S IV, 218)

Leslie Greenberg, the founder of emotion-focused therapy says:

> People need to attend to whether the emotional experience felt in their bodies as hot or cold, a big ball or a small knot…Thus if you begin to label the quality of and location of your feelings as a 'hot sensation in my chest' to notice its intensity as 'moderate' and its shape as a 'round ball', then the torrents of emotion will subside. (2008)

While the cognitive theories have a focus on thought patterns and appraisals, the body-based physiological theories, first presented by William James, are now enjoying a revival through the work of neurologist Antonio

Damasio and the Philosopher Jesse Prinz

As the present book is basically devoted to emotion studies, I have designed a special chapter on Darwin and James. Also, recently, I have been working on the concept of 'somatic intelligence', which in simple language is the wisdom of the body.

It is against this background that I wish to present the revival in Darwinian studies and also the writings of William James.

References

de Silva, Padmasiri. 1992. *Buddhist and Freudian Psychology*, 3rd ed. Melbourne: Shogam Publishers.

de Silva, Padmasiri. 2005. *An Introduction to Buddhist Psychology and Counselling*, 4th ed. London: Palgrave Macmillan.

de Silva, Padmasiri. 2010. *Buddhist and Freudian Psychology*, 4th ed. Melbourne: Shogam Publishers.

Greenberg, Leslie. 2008. *Emotion Focused Therapy*. Washington, DC: American Philosophical Association.

James, William. 1950. *The Principles of Psychology*. New York: Dover Publishing.

Ledoux, Joseph. 1996. *The Emotional Brain*. London: Weidenfeld & Nicolson.

Nyānaponika, Mahāthera. 1983. *Contemplation of Feelings*. Kandy, Sri Lanka: Buddhist Publication Society.

Oatley, Keith. 2004. *Emotions: A Brief History*. Oxford: Blackwell.

5

Somatogenic vs Ideogenic Theories of Emotions: James, Darwin and Freud

During the last two decades, there has been a remarkable emergence of research in emotion studies and on the body and brain. Their historical roots are found in William James and Charles Darwin and more recently in applied counselling fields like pain and trauma management. The research indicates the importance of somatic psychology. I have discussed the concept of somatic psychology in a recent work (de Silva 2017). Further, Joseph Ledoux's work, *The Emotional Brain* heralds a new era in emotion studies. To appreciate the enriching focus in emotion studies of Joseph Ledoux (1996) Antonio Damasio (2000) and Richard Davidson (2013) on neuroscience and Daniel Siegel (2007) with his focus on the body and brain, one has to probe the historical roots in Charles Darwin (1872, 2015) and also in William James (1890, 1918, 1950). I have referred to this tradition as the somatic tradition in my recent work (de Silva 2017). *Awakening Somatic Intelligence* is the title of a book by Risa Kaparo (2012). My recent book (de Silva 2017) develops a complete perspective on emotions and the body in Buddhist somatic psychology.

This chapter focuses on the body in Darwin and James and the work of contemporary neuroscientists.

P. de Silva, *Mindfulness-based Emotion Focused Counselling*,
https://doi.org/10.1007/978-3-030-64388-1_5

Antonio Damasio presented the early research and the philosophical groundwork for neuroscience while Joseph Ledoux wrote a ground-breaking study of the emotion of fear. Richard Davidson introduced the celebrated concept of neuroplasticity and Daniel Siegel presents useful studies with their philosophical implications. Paul Ekman (2007) rediscovered the work of Darwin while Jesse Prinz, in his work *Gut Reactions* (2004) remains as the best philosophical expositor of William James. Thus, it is very necessary to appreciate the historical roots of current writings in Darwin and James. I have used the term 'somatic intelligence', meaning wisdom of the body following Howard Gardner's epoch-making work, on the theory of multiple intelligences (1983), where he refers to eight types of intelligence and describes what he calls body kinaesthetic intelligence, a neglected concept. This concept will have a central role in the course content of the present book designed for the new programme of Buddhist counselling at the University of Hong Kong with its rich sources in Buddhist and Chinese philosophy. In the area of counselling for pain management, Risa Kaparo's brilliant study, *Awakening Somatic Intelligence* (2012), presents the role of the body in counselling for pain management.

It is against this background that I wish to present the revival in Darwinian studies and of William James.

Charles Darwin on Emotions

Darwin's, *The Expression of the Emotions in Man and Animals* was published in 1872 but a modern edition was reissued recently (2015). Thus, it was not until hundred years had passed, that a systematic study of the autonomic changes in the basic emotions of anger, disgust, fear, joy, sadness and surprise was made (Ekman 2008). Darwin had developed his emotion studies against the background of the theory of evolution. Paul Ekman's thesis on the universality of facial expressions depicting different emotions, however, was to a great extent influenced by Darwin's research on emotions:

> Species-constant learning also cannot account easily for our recent findings that anger, fear, sadness, and disgust are marked by different changes in the heart rate, sweating, skin temperature, and blood flow... I was forced by these findings to the conclusion that our evolutionary heritage makes a major contribution to the shaping of our emotional responses. If that is so, it seems likely that evolution would also play a major role in determining the universal themes that trigger emotions. (Ekman 2007)

Darwin integrated his work on emotions in the light of the theory of evolution and Ekman, in developing his own theory of emotions and facial expression feels that this background needs recognition. It was not until hundred years had passed after Darwin's seminal work that Ekman initiated a systematic study of the autonomic changes in the basic emotions of anger, fear, disgust, joy, sadness and surprise (2007). This remarkable somatic heritage was passed on through William James and led to the more recent and sophisticated studies by Damasio. Darwin treated emotions as separate discrete modules: as anger, fear, disgust, joy, sadness and surprise.

My personal interest in Darwin's emotion studies was first aroused when Jerry Boucher, a student of Ekman invited me to join a cross-cultural study group coordinated by the Culture Learning Institute of the East West Center in Hawaii. The project which lasted two years collecting emotion words and emotion stories in different cultures, including Sri Lanka and a study of Darwin and emotions across nearly ten cultures was so stimulating that emotion studies became my hobby and inspired me to engage in research and present a number of publications. The University of Hong Kong (2018) provided an opportunity to present some of my work in emotion studies and to integrate them into the present book. The basic theme of the lectures is Emotion *Studies and Buddhist Counselling*. Paul Ekman's research, exploring the emotional cascade across our face, reinventing Darwin on emotions in a masterly study, *Emotions Revealed* (2007) has been a great resource for me.

This revival of Darwin on emotions has made Ekman the world's foremost expert on emotions and facial expressions. Darwin used photographs and engravings, taking for granted that he could obtain the greatly needed information when the facial expression was displayed.

According to Ekman, facial expression begins and then reaches an apex of the muscular contraction that is going to occur. The muscular contraction is held for a few seconds with a little variation during the apex. Any time slice within the apex carries information regarding which emotion is signified. These are the snapshot expressions that are different from aggregate signals—which incorporate a sequence of expressions. The extent of the muscular contraction provides information about the intensity of the emotions signaled.

Another important point about what are called *basic emotions* is that the facial expression of these emotions is universal and pan-cultural. Basic emotions include sadness, happiness, anger, fear, wonder and disgust. Darwin's study of emotions was greatly related to animal behaviour who have the same biological heritage as the humans. Emotions like anxiety, guilt, shame, pride, jealousy and envy are often described as cognitive emotions. The emotions which attracted the attention of Freud, whom I will discuss in a separate section, may be described as 'ideogenic' as different from the 'somatogenic' emotions described by Darwin.

While Darwin did not find a method for measuring facial expressions, this has been the great mission of Ekman. Malcolm Gladwell (2005), the best-selling author, makes a close description of Ekman's contributions to the study of emotions and facial expressions. Ekman worked on the study with Frierson. Gladwell says:

> They combed through medical books that outlined the facial muscles, and identified every distinct muscular movement that the face could make. There were only forty-three such movements. Ekman and Frierson called them action units. Then they sat across from each other, for days on end, and began manipulating each action unit, first locating the muscles in their minds and then concentrate on identifying it, watching each other closely as they did, checking their movements in a mirror, making notes how the wrinkle patterns on their face would change with each muscular movement and videotaping the movement for their records. (2005)

Later they assembled all these combinations and produced the, 'Facial Action Coding System'.

William James

William James was greatly indebted to Charles Darwin (1808–1882), but I shall first present the Jamesian theory of emotions and then explore the clear Darwinian impact on James. James introduced a stimulating rider, which made us have a second look, different from our ordinary accepted views: 'Common sense says we lose our fortune, are sorry and weep; we meet a bear and are frightened and run, we are insulted by a rival, are angry and strike'. However, he defends the idea, that we feel sorry because we cry, angry because we strike, afraid because we tremble. This hypothesis looks as if he is putting the cart before the horse. This thesis has been discussed, debated, criticized over and over again in the history of psychology, and in modern times, rises again like phoenix from the ashes!

In fact, this theory emerged with new life and in a new form with modern thinkers like Antonio Damasio, the neurologist, and Jesse Prinz, the philosopher. Damasio was breaking new ground and he bemoans the neglect of Darwin, James and Freud to emotion studies:

> By the end of the nineteenth century Charles Darwin, William James, and Sigmund Freud had written extensively on different aspects of emotion and given emotion a privileged position in scientific discourse. Yet, throughout the twentieth century and until quite recently, both neuroscience and cognitive science gave emotion a very cold shoulder. Darwin had conducted an extensive study of the expression of emotion in different cultures and different species. William James had seen through the problem with his characteristic clarity and produced an account that, in spite of its incompleteness remains cornerstone. As for Freud, he had gleaned the pathological potential of disturbed emotions and announced their importance in no uncertain terms. (Damasio 1988)

But as will be seen in the contemporary writings there has been a great revival of interest in the neuroscience of emotions.

The Buddhist Perspective

The mind-body relation in Buddhism has different approaches and by *contextualizing* each approach we get a more comprehensive understanding. The interaction of body and mind, as well as mind interacting with body is a theory I have upheld over the years. James defined the *body as the mind's sounding board*, 'allowing the emotional signals to resonate, much as the sound box of a guitar amplifies the sound of the strings' (Evans 2001). Though James's theory sounds somewhat narrow, his lasting contribution was that it is *the experience of the bodily symptoms that gives the emotional quality to our consciousness*:

> If we fancy some strong emotion, and then try to abstract from our consciousness, of it all the feelings of its characteristic bodily symptoms, we find we have nothing left behind, no 'mind stuff' out of which the emotion can be constituted, and that a cold and neutral intellectual perception is all that remained. (James 1884)

What is of special importance in Evans's analysis is that, 'in meditation and relaxation the calming effects are achieved by the feedback from the body'. The rhythmic breathing and the relaxed state of the muscles are interpreted by the brain as conducive to a calm frame of mind (Evans 2001). Also, by deliberately suppressing some of our automatic bodily changes, we can have some measure of control over our emotions, like raising one's fist when about to get angry. Thus, while emphasizing the body, we leave room for a two-way relationship between the body and the mind:

> James was pointing to the fact that the relationship between the mind and the body is not just one way. There is a feedback mechanism by which the body can affect the mind just as the mind can affect the body. As with any feedback loop, this allows for amplification. James described the body as the mind's sounding board allowing the emotional signal to resonate much as the soundboard of a guitar amplifies the sound of the strings. (Evans 2001)

James makes a classic reference to the activation of the body. 'Everyone knows how panic is induced by flight and how giving way to grief increases those passions themselves. Each feat of sobbing makes the sorrow more acute…'.

The notion that some measure of control over our emotions can be exercised by suppressing some automatic bodily changes is a key point that calls for recognition.

James's indebtedness to Darwin is seen in Darwin's description of fear and hatred which James quotes:

> Withdrawal of the head backwards, withdrawal of the trunk, projection forward of the hands, as if to defend oneself against the hated object; contraction or closure of the eyes; elevation of the upper lip and closure of the nose—these are all elementary movements of turning away. Next threatening movements as: intense frowning; eyes wide open; display of teeth; grinding teeth and contracting jaws; open mouth with tongue advanced; clenched fists; threatening action of arms; to stamping with teeth… (Darwin, quoted in James 1884)

Darwin on fear says the following:

> Widely opened eyes and mouth, raised eye brows dilated nostrils, stiff posture, motionless, a racing heart, increased blood supply to the body, pallor of the skin, cold perspiration, piloerection, shivering and trembling, hurried breathing, dry mouth, faltering voice, fists that are alternatively clenched and opened… (Darwin, quoted in James, 1884)

James's theory generated lot of controversy among the cognitive theorists of emotions from Walter Canon to more contemporary cognitivists like Robert C. Solomon, where focusing on 'thought patterns' help us to distinguish fear, anger, sadness and other emotions. There was a concern with envy, jealousy and guilt where there was no clear physiological boundary. These emotions like jealousy, envy, guilt, melancholy had a clear focus of study and analysis in the work of Freud.

Critical Evaluation of James

James's great contribution was taking Darwin's work as a springboard, he focused on the physiology of emotions. Even contemporary neuroscientists like Damasio and Ledoux and the philosopher Prinz are aware of drawing on the background of the Jamesian revolution in emotion studies.

One of the weak points raised by Bennett and Hacker (2003), is that it is necessary to make a distinction between an emotion as an episodic perturbation and a long-standing emotional attitude or disposition as for example, jealousy towards a rival. Some of these emotional patterns may emerge at a subliminal level, which both Ledoux, Buddhism and Freud accept. They are sleeping passions which are excited by a trigger. Ledoux cites the case of a man walking on a forest track who stumbles on a bundle of dry twigs. He is about to run, thinking it is a rattlesnake. In this context, the central nervous system has been hijacked by the amygdala.

Robert C. Solomon focuses on the importance of the will and intention in emotions and this is also a crucial dimension in Buddhist psychology. Though James did not give attention to intention in emotion, he does so in another context. There is a memorable line often quoted by Jon Kabat-Zinn:

> The faculty of bringing back a wandering attention over and over again is the very root of judgment, character and will. (James 1884)

James's overall philosophy has a richness and complexity of its own.

Sigmund Freud and the Ideogenic Revolution

Sigmund Freud started his professional life as a neurosurgeon but he was disappointed with the progress that he made in studying the brain of frogs. So, searching for a fresh lease of life, he went to France to work with Charcot and Joseph Breuer. The work *Studies in Hysteria* written by

Freud and Breuer heralded a new era for Freud. The psychological character of posthypnotic suggestion played a key role in tracing repressed ideas in the unconscious.

Jon Deigh says that the Freudian revolution stands in marked contrast from the Jamesian revolution. According to Deigh (2004), Freud's ideas are the source of the view that emotions transmit meanings or purpose to the feelings and behaviour that manifest them. Though Freud often described emotions as flows of energy, his view of them as transmitters of meaning, or purpose was nonetheless implicit in his notion of an unconscious emotion and he used to make sense of feelings, behaviour and physical maladies that otherwise seemed inexplicable. Thus, he showed that studying the emotions helps to see feelings, behaviour and bodily conditions as meaningful products of the mind.

The case study of Anna where the patient could not move her arm but did not have any physical defect, is a case where through hypnotic treatment the patient did recover. It is after Anna's recovery that Freud made the classic statement that 'hysterics behave as if anatomy does not exist'. Later, Freud developed a therapeutic system of his own as 'The Method of Free Association', where unlike hypnotism the patient was able to develop insight into his or her own problems. He also went to explore the unconscious in the normal mind in *The Psychopathology of Everyday Life* (SE, Volume 6) and *Dream Interpretation* (SE Volume, 4). It is remarkable that Freud's work cut across the normal and abnormal mind.

Buddhist Mindfulness and Freud's Psychoanalysis

Mark Epstein says that in the popular mind Freud's work is associated with the traumatic unconscious, but Epstein says that Freud's work underwent several stages from the deeply buried unconscious to the ever-present subliminal levels: (i) The first is the cathartic view, where he used hypnotism for re-enacting and re-living traumatic experience. (ii) The second was when he gave up hypnotism and used the method of 'free association' to recall memories without inhibition. (iii) The third is the stage where Freud moved from forgotten memories to the immediate present. Epstein says that many interpreters have missed the third stage embodied in the paper. 'Remembering, Repeating and Working Through' (Freud 1958).

This insight of Epstein was so great that I changed the translation of the Buddhist concept of *anusaya* to 'subliminal' rather than the 'unconscious'. Buddhism refers to subliminal lust (*rāgānusaya*), subliminal anger (*paṭighānusaya*) and subliminal conceit (*manānusaya*). Epstein says that in looking at the subliminal, one has to give up the archaeological metaphor. 'It is less about digging and more about opening'. Epstein says 'it is a root difference' (2007).

Sigmund Freud and the Ideogenic Passions: Jealousy, Anxiety and Melancholy

> If I imagine that an object beloved by me is united to another person by the same or closer bond of friendship than that by which I myself alone had the object, I shall be affected with hatred towards the beloved object itself, and shall envy that other person. (Spinoza 1963)

Jerome Neu says that there is a rich internal complexity in the emotion of jealousy with its conceptual surroundings which are very rich, a wealth of discrimination such as envy, resentment, begrudging, malice, spite, ill-will, hatred, ingratitude, revenge, hostility and so on.

I draw my reflections from two very insightful articles: 'Jealous Thoughts', by Jerome Neu and 'Jealousy, Attention and Loss', by Tov-Ruach in an anthology, *Explaining Emotions* (Tov-Ruach 1980). Neu says that the presence and persistence of jealousy has more to do with self-identity than with the possession of others. He also observes that an underlying fear may move us into even pathological forms of jealousy; jealousy on many occasions may be tied to genuine love. Regarding envy, there can be healthy emulative envy and selfish envy that borders on avarice.

For Tov-Ruach, jealousy is an emotion that has perceived danger to the self at its centre, generating variety of defence, as some jealousies are attended by depression/withdrawal, some by anger, and still others by the intensification of the original attachment or frenzied competitive behaviour. All the varieties of jealousy depend on a contextually determined state of the ego.

In summary, the essential point about jealousy found in Freud and discussed by other philosophers like Spinoza, Neu and Tov-Ruach are as follows:

1. One's position as a favoured individual is threatened.
2. Jealousy may be understood in terms of possessive behaviour.
3. Jealousy may be understood as a crisis in personal identity, as a wound to self-esteem and self-love
4. Self-love as contained in Freud's celebrated paper on 'narcissism'. When there is disappointment, the innate sense of narcissism suffers. Such ego injury results in 'secondary narcissism'.

In the face of disappointment, the innate sense of narcissism suffers setbacks. Thus, with a sense of ego injury the pride of a person manifests in the form of secondary narcissism. Primary narcissism is the original libidinal ego-cathexis, part of which normally persists while the rest gets transformed into objects. Freud defines secondary narcissism as that which arises when the *libidinal cathexis* is withdrawn. The next important landmark in Freudian theory is the 'ego as the seat of anxiety', which I will take up as we proceed. To come back to jealousy:

> Jealousy is over which what one possesses and fears to lose, while envy may be over what one has never possessed and never hope to possess. Going further with this, the focus of envy is typically the other person, rather than the particular thing or quality one is envious over... In jealousy there is always a rival believed or imagined, but who may not know that the focus of concern is the valued object. (Tov-Ruach 1980, p. 433)

What is special about jealousy is the fear, fear of the loss connected with fear. But the immediate focus of envy isn't oneself and one does not expect to get anything. Robert Solomon says jealousy may indicate a profound sense of love, unlike envy.

Buddhist Perspectives on Envy and Jealousy

In the Tibetan Buddhist tradition, it is said that the multifaceted emotions may be reduced to five: hatred, desire, confusion, pride and jealousy. In this context, jealousy is described as 'an inability to rejoice in the happiness of others'. The definition comes close to the definition of envy. In the early Buddhist tradition, selfishness/envy is associated with the Pāli word *macchariya*, meaning that the other person may not prosper. Stinginess is just attachment to money and property (*lobha*), but envy does not want another person or even a group of persons to have wealth, houses, money, fame, rich relatives: and extends even to those with learning and beauty.

The Buddhist analysis of jealousy falls in line with Freud and the interpretations of Neu and Tov-Ruach, and is also similar to the clear analysis of Ernest Jones, the celebrated biographer of Freud: according to him, three elements make up jealousy: fear at losing loved ones, hatred of the rival, and the wound to self-esteem (narcissism). The latter point indicates diminished self-worth. Spinoza adds the mechanism of ambivalence, which is also a Freudian concept: the vacillation between love and hatred, and directed to the beloved; and also the sadness of losing the beloved. In the Buddhist analysis, it is a kind of emotion blend of fear, anger, love, ambivalence, sadness, prestige, humiliation and self-love (narcissism) The Buddhist also use the term *issā* as a defilement of the mind (*upakkilesā*) and a form of entanglement (*upādāna*).

Identity Issues in Buddhism

It is of very great interest that Freud gradually came to recognize that the ego is the actual seat of anxiety. As a result, his work on narcissism acquired a new meaning for him, and the probing of the emotions of anxiety and jealousy gave him a dimension of the applied value of narcissism in emotion tangles. With my own research project on Freud and Buddhism, his paper on narcissism was one of the richest and illuminating papers that I read. But equally challenging and fascinating of the Freudian projects was his essay, 'Beyond the Pleasure Principle' (Freud 1953, SE 39), where he presented the notion of a death instinct.

According to Jacobson, 'when we probe identity problems in Buddhist perspective, at a deeper level, we see the indeterminacy, ambiguity and formlessness at the centre of their lives' which we may describe as 'secondary narcissism', and their tendency to fix their identity upon some cluster of transient identifications with which they become involved in learning to live in a particular time and place (Jacobson 1966, p. 61). Jacobson concludes: 'the Buddha's brilliant and unique grasp of this predicament is found in his teaching of *anattā* (egolessness)'.

Freud on Anxiety

Gradually Freud came to realize that the ego is the seat of anxiety and not the re-emergence of repressed libido. Realistic anxiety is part of the ego's self-preservative instinct. Freud's analysis of melancholia and depression is very profound but discussion of that will come in a separate chapter which is on depression and grief.

References

Bennett, M.R., and P.M.S. Hacker. 2003. *Philosophical Foundations of Neuro science*. Oxford: Blackwell.

Damasio, Antonio. 2000. *The Feeling of What Happens: Body and Emotion in the Making of Consciousness*. London: Vintage.

Darwin, Charles. 2015 [1872]. *Expression of Emotions in Man and Animals*. London: HarperCollins.

Davidson, Richard. 2013. *The Emotional Life of Your Brain*. London: Hodder.

Deigh, J. 2004. Primitive Emotions. In *Thinking About Feeling*, ed. R.C. Solomon. Oxford: Oxford University Press.

de Silva, Padmasiri. 2017. *Emotions and the Body in Buddhist Contemplative Practice and Mindfulness-Based Therapy*. London: Palgrave Macmillan.
de Silva, Padmasiri. 2018. *Ma Ma Foundation Lectures*. University of Hong Kong (available on the Internet).
Ekman, Paul. 2003. *Emotions Revealed*. New York: Weidenfeld and Nicolson.
Epstein, Mark. 2007. *Psychotherapy Without the Self*. New Haven: Yale University Press.
Evans, Dylan. 2001. *Emotion*. Oxford: Oxford University Press.
Freud, Sigmund. 1953. *Beyond the Pleasure Principle*, Standard ed., vol. XVIII. London: Hogarth Press.
Freud, Sigmund. 1958. *Remembering, Repeating and Working-Through*, Standard ed., vol. 12. London: Hogarth Press.
Gardner, Howard. 1983. *Frames of Mind: The Theory of Multiple Intelligences*. New York: Basic Books.
Gladwell, Malcolm. 2005. *Blink: The Power of Thinking Without Thinking*. London: Penguin.
Jacobson, Nolan Pliny. 1966. *Buddhism: The Religion of Analysis*. New York: Humanities Press.
James, William. 1884. What Is an Emotion? In *Readings in Philosophical Psychology*, ed. Cheshire Calhoun and Robert Solomon. Oxford: Oxford University Press.
James, William. 1950. *The Principles of Psychology*. New York: Dover Publishing.
Kaparo, Risa. 2012. *Awakening Somatic Intelligence: The Art and Practice of Embodied Mindfulness*. Berkeley: North Atlantic Books.
Ledoux, Joseph. 1996. *The Emotional Brain*. London: Weidenfeld & Nicolson.
Neu, Jerome. 1990. Jealous Thoughts. In *Explaining Emotions*, ed. Amélie Rorty. Berkeley, CA: University of California Press.
Siegel, Daniel. 2007. *The Mindful Brain*. New York: Norton.
Spinoza, B. 1963. *Ethics*. New York: Hafner.
Tov-Ruach, L. 1980. Jealousy, Attention and Loss. In *Explaining Emotions*, ed. Amélie Rorty. Berkeley, CA: University of California Press.

Part II

Practical Issues in Counselling

6

Will, Conation, Volition and Intentionality

In the Buddhist philosophy of mind, there are three important dimensions, the *cognitive*, *affective* and the *conative*. So far, I have been concentrating on the cognitive dimension, especially 'embodied cognition'. Then through the affective dimension of emotions, I focused on sadness and depression, along with anger management. Now, I explore the nature of will and *conation*. In the following chapters, following this exploration of 'intentionality', I shall have a chapter on *mindful emotions,* linking our meditative experience to the management of selected emotions and their place in Buddhist counselling.

A very important affective realm of activity originates with feeling (*vedanā*) which is also a base related to the emergence of human emotions. Cognitive processes are related to the functions of *saññā* and *vitakka.*

Conative activity is more difficult to chart out and has also been neglected in emotion studies. The concept of *saṃkhāra* may be rendered as *motivated and purposeful activity*. A neglected dimension of activity is the role of will/conation. I have briefly discussed this facet in an earlier chapter on emotions but this chapter is fully focused on the nature

P. de Silva, *Mindfulness-based Emotion Focused Counselling*,
https://doi.org/10.1007/978-3-030-64388-1_6

of human volition and intention, a topic neglected in psychology and philosophy and neuroscience:

> The capacity for voluntary action is seen as essential to human nature. Yet, neuroscience and behaviorist psychology have traditionally dismissed this topic as unscientific, perhaps because the mechanisms that cause actions have long been unclear. However, new research has identified a network of brain areas, including the parietal cortex that underlie voluntary action. These areas generate information for forthcoming actions and cause the distinctive conscious experience of intending to act and then controlling one's actions. Volition consists of a series of decisions regarding whether to act, what action to perform and when to perform. (Haggard 2008)

In Buddhist psychology, the will is not a faculty as such but rather a quality of the potential and actual manifestation of human behaviour. It may be described as the dispositional potential of qualities cultivated over a period of time as seen in one of the strands of meaning in the term *saṃkhāra.* If we use an analytical approach, there are different conceptual strands that illuminate the Buddhist perspective on will and volition. In the lives of exceptional people intentionality raises them above the average run of humanity. This involves a tremendous generation of energy and purpose, all welded together in contributing to humanity: a creative and liberating energy as may be found in the Buddha as well as the personalities of those like Jiddu Krishnamurti (1895–1986) and Rabindranath Tagore (1861–1941).

Different Dimensions of the Concept of Will

The most important ingredient in the context of the concept of the will is the *weighing of alternative courses of action and taking deliberate action* that seems the best, which of course will be goal directed. There can be decision making from a long-range perspective or decision making which is greatly specific and context oriented, as in fixing goals dependent on abstract values which are important but need contextual application. A further facet related to goal setting is to take stock of desires, impulses and habits that obstruct and distract attention. The most important ingredient, however, is perseverance against obstacles in the pursuit of goals, a feature emphasized greatly in the Buddhist path of spiritual development. Buddhism also looks at moral weakness in the context of goal seeking that may obstruct a person: as the Buddha focuses on *sīla*, moral development. In the final analysis, the Buddha emphasizes the central value of a teacher. As a therapist, I find that generating confidence and strength in the client at critical times is a wonderful context for exercising one's will.

Due to the writings of Arthur Schopenhauer (1788–1860), the Buddhist concept of will has been misunderstood and identified with craving (*taṇhā*). A very crucial dimension for Buddhism is the practice of meditation where the will grows through transparency: developing mindful attention.

A Phenomenology of the Will: A Note from My Personal Life

Most of the graphic descriptions of the exercise of will may be seen in narratives and I will illustrate this point with a slice from my personal life. Going through a personal crisis with its drama of discontent, mild depression and final mastery and happiness was a great turning point in life. It is against this background that in addition to being a professional philosopher I was trained as a therapist, illuminating the lives of migrants for six years. In 2008 my monograph was published: *The Magic of the Ordinary and Elegance of Small Things* (de Silva). This book has been described thus: 'The author himself does channel the momentum of a personal life crisis to a journey of self-awakening and paths of emotional growth'. The book is an introduction to mindfulness-based counselling.

The Education of Emotions Through Their Narrative Structure

The best philosophical study of the 'intentionality of emotions' has been presented by Peter Goldie. His basic theme is that emotions can be understood through a narrative structure:

> Our lives have a narrative structure—roughly speaking, they comprise an unfolding, structured sequence of actions, events, thoughts and feelings, related from the individual's point of view ... with emotional experience, it is the notion of narrative structure which ties together and makes sense of individual elements of emotional experience. (2002)

Goldie's thesis is very useful in giving a new dimension to emotion studies as it ties into a deep *dimension of human intentionality* while feeling, bodily changes and cognitive factors are important. Furthermore, the way that individual emotional episodes relate to the emotion is important. They are also linked to the character and character traits which help us to understand the three-cornered setting of jealousy or how jealousy differs from envy. According to Goldie, a narrative is not merely an interpretive framework, it displays the nature of life as it is.

The Buddha used narratives as a part of his pedagogy. To understand a Buddhist perspective let us look at the story of Aṅgulimāla. It is the development of a narrative that generates remorse, forgiveness and re-building of character. Equally so is the story of Kisāgotami and the mustard seed, which spells out the radical transformation of a desperate person who has lost a child.

A Contemporary Perspective on Intention and Mindfulness Studies

The best research on intentionality has recently emerged from mindfulness studies:

> Two of the essential elements of mindful awareness practice appears to be an awareness of awareness itself and a focus on attention on intention. We have examined the metacognitive process of self-monitoring and have seen that it is associated with the activation of the pre-frontal region. But how do we pay attention to intention. We can imagine that intention, as a mental state of the internal world, is likely to be associated by the self-reflective middle frontal region. (Siegel 2007, p. 176)

> Why would intention be so pivotal in our lives? Intentions tie a given movement of life together, link action now with the action of the next movement, creating the underlying 'glue' that directs attention, motivates action, and processes the nature of reactions. (Siegel 2017)

An important question is how to distinguish reflex actions from intentions. Patrick Haggard clearly observes that voluntary actions involve two distinct subjective experiences that are absent from reflexes. These are the experience of intention—that is the planning to do something—and the experience of agency, which is the latter feeling that one's actions have caused a particular event (Haggard 2008). Volition matures later in the development of an individual, whereas reflexes can be present before or after birth. Thus, the capacity for voluntary action is an essential quality of humanity, though the earlier behaviorists dismissed the topic as unscientific. However, new research has identified networks of brain areas, including the pre-supplementary motor area, the anterior pre-frontal cortex and the parietal cortex that underlie voluntary action.

These insightful observations from neuroscience may be confirmed by our routine lives, where most adults have a strong feeling of voluntary control over their actions, making choices and acting accordingly. In crime and punishment, the possibility of voluntary action and even current projects of prison reform have developed a concept of mindful changes and reform. When people become habituated to alcoholic addiction, they cloud their vision, though they are responsible for the gradual erosion of the skills for voluntary action.

Right Intention in the Buddhist Path

In the Buddhist eightfold path, we discern the spiritual facet of right intention, which is preceded by right view. It is *sammā saṅkappa* that is translated as right intention. Right view presents the cognitive facet of the eightfold path and right intention the conative aspect. Emotions or affectivity also have links with conative activity. Basically, effort and direction need to be combined with deep reflection and investigation.

The Buddha explains right intention as threefold: the intention of renunciation, the intention of good will, and the intention of harmlessness. These three are opposed to three parallel kinds of wrong doing: intention governed by desire; intention governed by ill-will; and the intention governed by harmfulness. The good intentions counter the bad intentions. Desire in this context has reference to craving, but unfortunately there has been a variety of translation terms for desire, and as Thomas William Rhys Davids (1843–1922) says, one English word is used to do the work of seventeen Pāli words (1914). In some contexts, the word refers to lust and attachment. The term *chanda* often refers to wholesome desires.

As Bruce Matthews points out, the interpretation given by Schopenhauer was responsible for associating the Buddhist concept of will with craving:

> The impression that willing in Buddhism is always associated with thirst or desire, and that desire in turn is deleterious was reinforced by early translations of the Pāli texts into European languages. (1983)

Matthews says that Rhys Davids's essay (1914) on the will in Buddhism is a comprehensive study, illustrating how Western thinkers like Schopenhauer distorted the Buddhist concept of will with craving, thus missing a central ethical dimension associated with the term. While Schopenhauer's writings on compassion are valuable, Schopenhauer is misled with regard to the concept of will.

Buddhist conative psychology in its highest ethical and liberation quest is seen in the thirty-seven qualities associated with awakening (*bodhipakkhiyā dhammā*). Of these, two most important facets which illuminate the Buddhist concept of will are the four right exertions (*sammāpahāna*) and the seven factors of awakening (*bhojjhaṅga*).

In the Psychological Dimension

Saṅkhāra refers to the conative facets of volition/will in Buddhism: motivated and purposeful activity which has moral consequences. There are three facets of this concept: deliberation, volition and dynamism. The term *cetanā* which is also synonymously used suggest the notion of *volition*. The term *abhisaṅkhāra* indicates a more focused dynamism: 'The wheel kept rolling so long as the impulse that set it moving lasted, then it circled round and fell' (A I, iii). Right intention, effort, energy and persistence are necessary to withstand the strength of defiling impulses. It is said that there are four kinds of effort necessary: the effort to restrain the senses, the effort to abandon evil thoughts, the effort to develop spiritual skills; and the effort to watch over and concentrate on repulsive objects that would destroy any emerging lust and greed.

References

Davids, Rhys. 1914. *Buddhist Psychology*. London: Bell and Sons.

de Silva, Padmasiri. 2008. *The Magic of the Ordinary and the Elegance of Small Things*. Ratmalana, Sri Lanka: Sarvodaya Printers.

Goldie, Peter. 2002. *Emotions: A Philosophical Exploration*. Oxford: Clarendon Press.

Haggard, P. 2008. Human Volition: Towards a Neuroscience of Will. *Nature Reviews Neuroscience* 9: 934–966.

Matthews, Bruce. 1983. *Craving and Salvation: A Study in Buddhist Soteriology*. Waterloo, ON, Canada: Wilfrid Laurier University Press.

Siegel, Daniel. 2007. *The Mindful Brain*. New York: Norton.

7

The Elegance of Being Your Own Therapist

Irvin Yalom, in his delightful book, *The Gift of Therapy*, refers to two models of therapists. Drawing a tale from Herman Hesse's Master Ludi, Yalom refers to two types of therapists represented by two renowned healers who lived in biblical times. The younger healer Joseph, healed through quiet, inspired listening:

> Pilgrims trusted Joseph. Suffering and anxiety poured into his ears vanished like water on the desert sand and penitents left his presence emptied and calmed. On the other hand, Dion the older healer, actively confronted those who sought his help. He divined their unconfessed sins. He was a great judge, chastiser, scolder, and rectifier, and he healed through active intervention. (2003)

They worked as rivals but later discovered that they needed each other's help for healing themselves. Often the therapist has to delve into a client's problems, analyze and break them into manageable sections, and deal with them one by one. But it also becomes necessary to follow the path of 'deep listening'.

What is 'deep listening'? We have developed a whole culture of techniques based on speed, accuracy, rigour and certainty, and this aspect

P. de Silva, *Mindfulness-based Emotion Focused Counselling*,
https://doi.org/10.1007/978-3-030-64388-1_7

exercises a strong hegemony on all aspects of our education. *When someone comes for therapy and counselling, there is a new paradigm working as we slow down, relax, listen, and respect the flow of life*. We need a less deliberative, slow and intuitive approach to deal with situations that are intricate, shadowy and chaotic. We work with a new educational model, that of 'flow'; it is a state in which people are so involved and absorbed that nothing else matters.

The hurrying syndrome: people who are subject to such time pressures are not good listeners, interrupt other people and become impatient. When confronted with difficult situations they fail to discern the options and solutions before them. The passionate therapist does not try to control the clients and dissect their problems but likes to sit and relax, to let the client live or relive the problems (Claxton 1977). Like the tortoise laying the eggs, we sit on our anger, impatience and fear, we do not destroy them—but contain them, taking in their disorganised form, and see them with the gift of listening that calms and energizes. As I have asserted in Chapter 2, we do not throw away or destroy anger but with a little magic, we transform anger into forgiveness, patience and self-congratulation.

This is a process that Carl Jung described as *emotional alchemy* an approach I have combined with mindful emotions and used in my practice as a therapist in my own counselling centre, 'Viveka' at the Springvale Community Centre. I described this as 'emotional alchemy', and later this approach was converted into mindfulness-based emotion focused therapy (EFT). While I was inspired by Leslie Greenberg, the pioneer of EFT, I used my own mindfulness-based EFT. To me both the therapist and the client work with the imagination of an artist. I was inspired by the following words of Rainer Maria Rilke: 'Being an artist does not mean reckoning and counting, but ripening like the tree which does not force its sap, and stands confident in the storms of spring without the fear that after them no summer may come. But it does come' (Rilke 2001). In my notebooks I wrote the following observation:

> When a client leaves the room of the therapist after an hour of therapy, often I feel that the client has touched a deep part of himself, a part that has witnessed the shock and crisis of the existential challenges in life.

Such a dimension of human empathy, along with deep compassion, and positive regard for the client helps to heal the client, as well as the therapist. Carl Rogers's three great virtues for the therapist were—accurate empathy, unconditional positive regard for the client and the therapist's own genuineness. Something equally important occurs, as Sigmund Freud observes in his work, *Analysis Terminable and Interminable*: when the client leaves the consulting room. After completing a series of successful sessions, the journey of self-exploration has just begun and the client has become qualified to become an analyst of his own mind (de Silva).

Sigmund Freud says:

> [B]ut we reckon on the stimuli that he has received in his own analysis not ceasing when it ends and on the processes of remodeling the ego spontaneously in the analyzed subject and making use of all subsequent experience in this newly acquired sense. This does in fact happen, and in so far as it happens, it makes the analyzed subject qualified to be an analyst himself. (1966)

The path of continuous self-exploration that is mentioned here, has attracted some contemporary therapists like Anthony Storr. Writing on the concept of 'cure', he observes that psychoanalysis offers something more than relief from symptoms, for which clients want to be treated; they rather seek the processes of analysis as an end in itself. *Thus, analysis becomes more than a form of treatment; it becomes a way of life* (Storr 1966). This thesis has two important correlatives: the first is that in Buddhism, the *practice of mindfulness is a way life* and when it is seen in this manner, the greater the effect on the integration which becomes very holistic.

The second point needs more elaboration. Though Western psychology and psychotherapy consider psychological health as normal and psychological suffering abnormal, this assumption is fading away. Contemporary changes have led to congested and over-crowded living, especially in urban areas and long working hours under difficult conditions. It comes on the heels of an acquired workaholism; people working without rest and necessary recreation and experiencing long-distance travel from home to workplace. Workaholism is not limited to the poor who are trying to make ends meet, but can occur even in the very bosom of the affluent corporate executive immersed in the routine bundle of files, who has prospects of a higher income.

In fact, it is a multi-faceted crisis, well described in Tibor Scitovsky's book, *Joyless Economy* (1986). Erich Fromm (1900–1980) has a graphic description of this predicament of submerged human suffering. 'All the misery that is experienced by many lies to a great extent not in the fact that they are sick but that they are separated from everything that is interesting in life, that is exhilarating, that is beautiful in life' (2013).

Over the course of a year, over thirty percent of the population in the world suffers from recognized psychological disorders: depression being the fourth biggest. According to available records in 2002, it was deemed to be the second biggest. Drug and alcoholic addiction are a recurrent concern with increasing numbers falling prey to large drug sales directed by big underground businesses. As I will also illustrate in my chapter on depression, the near allies of depression are boredom, alienation, meaninglessness and loneliness. There are other major concerns like self-esteem, which is the thematic focus of Alain de Botton's television documentary and book, *Status Anxiety* (2014), which I have utilized in my own recent work (de Silva 2018). All this means that all 'normal people' may benefit from having counselling, especially mindfulness-based counselling. This is now offered as a non-religiously affiliated educational venture for both students and staff at Monash University, Melbourne by Craig Hassed and Richard Chambers (2014).

For students, mindful learning reduces stress and improves brain performance for effective learning.

Our central focus in this book is the emotional dimension of our lives and in the area of education, recent neurological studies have focused on the importance of what may be described as 'emotional learning'. The higher executive centre, working through the prefrontal cortex of the brain is that part of the brain directed to the use of reason and rationality. The middle part, is related to the limbic system, which is the centre that deals with emotions, as well as what I described as 'intentionality' which is related to courage, determination and resolution. There is also the lower (mesolimbic reward system), the appetite centre: and, if there is no guidance from the higher centre, our hedonic pleasure drives obstruct our plans for mental and bodily health. Buddhism emphasizes these ethical guidelines in order to have mental health and a holistic lifestyle. It is a central thesis of the present book that the education of the emotional dimensions of life through mindfulness practice and moral rigour contributes to lifestyle enhancement.

According to the clinical practice and selection of clients I followed as a counsellor, most of the clients I encountered in my practice (with a few exceptions) were not people who were subject to severe clinical disorders but through the neglect of routine they experienced stress and strain, tensions, anxieties and mild depression. They were not looking at their concerns with an open mind, but were shutting down their minds with denial and repression and were finding escape routes that converted ordinary concerns to debilitating psychological issues. Some of these issues generated undue pressure on other members of the family and they made attempts to drown out these issues by addiction to alcohol, which makes things worse—it is virtually a vicious circle! Most of the clients who have these types of problems fear any attempts to open up to a counsellor.

In the Buddhist perspective, we do not get rid of symptoms but either transform the apparent demons in our lives or see with insight and perspective the self-made load of pseudo-suffering: and experience their gradual cessation (*nissaraṇa*). I had clients who were devout Buddhists as well as Christians, Hindus and followers of Islam, but as they grasped the meaning of 'contentment', they discovered that *false self-images stood in the path for contentment and happiness.* De Botton says:

> When inequality is the general rule in society, the greatest inequalities attract no attention. But when everything is more or less level, the slightest variation is noticed and that is the reason for the strange melancholy often haunting inhabitants of democracies in the midst of abundance and for the disgust with life sometimes gripping them even in calm and easy circumstance. (2004)

Today stress and strife among those who are fortunate and paradoxically those who are affluent has increased. Current research on suicide studies indicate a very sad situation. De Botton's television documentary and book on status anxiety reveals this.

But once the clients who came to me, managed to keep the demons of discontent, stress and anxiety away- They were able to enjoy an evening walk and have a homely meal. I often recommended that my clients have *coffee and cheesecake* as part of their evening meal. This is a metaphor that I use for the enchantment with small things in life, which Thích Nh'ât Hạnh (b. 1926), the great Vietnamese philosopher described as experiencing the magic of the ordinary while enjoying the flavour of a mandarin. Prescribed drugs can often assist a person deal with depression, but they can only *assist* and it is in this context that mindfulness practice will play a crucial role in recovery.

By using the technique of mindfulness awareness meditation, we bring conscious awareness to the here and now, and we do this with openness, interest and receptiveness.

Richard Harris says:

> There are many facets to mindfulness, including living in the present moment; engaging fully in what you are doing rather than getting lost in your thoughts; and allowing your feelings to be what they are; letting them come and go rather than control them. When we observe our private experiences with openness and receptiveness, even the most painful thoughts, feelings and sensations and memories can seem less threatening or bearable. In this way mindfulness can help us to transform our relationship with painful thoughts and feelings, in a way that reduces their impact and influence over our lives. (2006)

In recent times, there has been an important attempt to extend mindfulness practice to what may be called contemplative education. Tobin Hart says the following:

> However, how we know is just as fundamental to teaching and learning. Contemporary schools emphasize both rational and sensory knowing. The rational involves calculation, explanation, and analysis; the sensory lives off observation and measurement. Together they form the rational-empirical approach that has set the standard of knowledge across most disciplines. However, another way of knowing—contemplation—has been recognized over time, culture and disciplines as essential to the pursuit of knowledge and wisdom yet it remains absent from today's

curriculum and pedagogy. Contemplative knowing is a missing link, one that affects student performance, character and depth of understanding. (2004)

Concluding Thoughts: Two Pieces from My Counselling Diary That Inspired Me

Rainer Maria Rilke says:

> Have patience with everything unresolved in your heart and try to love the questions themselves as if they were locked rooms or books written in a very foreign language. Don't search for answers, which could not be given to you now, because you would l not be able to live them. And the point is to live everything. Live the questions now. Perhaps then, someday, far in the future, you will gradually, without even noticing it, live your way into the answer. (2001)

The Guest House
This being human is a guest house
Every morning is a new arrival.
A joy, a depression, a meanness,
some momentary awareness comes
As an unexpected visitor
Welcome and entertain them all!
Even if they're a crowd of sorrows,
who violently sweep your house
empty of its furniture,
still treat each guest honorably.
He may be clearing you out
for some new delight.
The dark thought, the shame, the malice,
meet them at the door laughing and invite them in.
Be grateful whoever comes,
because each has been sent
as a guide from beyond. (Rumi 1995)

Therapists as Healers

Thomas Bien writes:

> [I]n a world of increasing alienation, fragmentation, and disconnection, we need therapists who are true healers rather than mere technicians. To become true healers, we therapists might consider trying to see ourselves in the context of the ancient roles of shaman, guru, and healer. While we may not be able to adopt these models wholesale into our twenty-first-century role, we can nonetheless find inspiration in them that goes beyond our technical training. (2006)

References

Bien, Thomas. 2006. *Mindful Therapy*. Boston: Wisdom Publications.

Claxton, Guy. 1977. *Hare Brain, Tortoise Mind*. New York: Eco Press.

de Botton, Alain. 2004. *Status Anxiety*. Camberwell, VIC: Hamish Hamilton.

de Silva, Padmasiri. 2018. *The Buddhist Psychology of Emotions and Humour*. London: Palgrave Macmillan.

Freud, Sigmund. 1966. *Analysis, Terminable and Interminable*. Standard Edition, vol. XXIII. London: Virago.

Fromm, Erich. 2013. *To Have or to Be?*. London: Bloomsbury.

Hart, Tobin. 2004. Opening the Contemplative Mind in the Classroom. *Journal of Transformative Education* 2 (1): 28–46.

Harris, Richard. 2006. Embracing Your Demons: An Overview of Acceptance and Commitment Therapy. *Psychotherapy in Australia* 12: 2–8.

Hassed, Craig, and Richard Chambers. 2014. *Mindful Learning*. Gosford, NSW: Exisle.

Rilke, Rainer Maria. 2001. *Letters to a Young Poet*, ed. Amélie Rorty and trans. Stephen Mitchell. New York: Modern Library.

Rumi, Jalaluddin. 1995. *The Essential Rumi*, trans. Coleman Barks. San Francisco, CA: Harper.

Scitovsky, Tibor. 1992. *The Joyless Economy: The Psychology of Human Satisfaction*. Oxford: Oxford University Press.

Storr, Anthony. 1966. The Concept of Cure. In *Psychoanalysis*, ed. C. Rycroft. London: Constable.

Yalom, Irvin. 2003. *The Gift of Therapy*. London: Piatkus.

8

Counselling for Depression

Man must become ill before he discovers the truth.
Sigmund Freud (1917).

Looking at anger deeply, as I have illustrated in an earlier chapter, generates a new level of mindfulness and depth and in this chapter, we are looking at sadness and depression.

Among psychologists, depression is considered along with mania and anxiety as *affective* disorders. Certain forms of depression may be considered as pathological, while others may be considered as exaggerations of normal affective responses. A recent study points out that due to a strong tendency to medicalize depression, sadness over loss and grief, which is an inherent part of the human predicament, is being converted into a depressive disorder. Lewis Wolpert says that depression, which is an exaggeration of a normal response, when neglected, gets converted into 'malignant sadness'.

Very often what I call 'pedestrian' depression, which all of us are subject to, needs mindful attention: temporary setbacks to health; accumulated bills; a child falling ill failure at several job interviews; and so on. In my counselling experience, failed job interviews need mature and sane responses like for instance suggesting that the client gets trained in

P. de Silva, *Mindfulness-based Emotion Focused Counselling*,
https://doi.org/10.1007/978-3-030-64388-1_8

a new field. In some of my clients expressing a heavy dose of anger with the employer is counterproductive. It would be better to have a friendly meeting with one's employer and obtain a certificate from him and turn towards alternatives. Bringing sanity to family life when there are conflicts may be well handled by talking to a counsellor. There are many such signposts in life: temporary challenges that need to be managed with patience, equanimity resilience and self-compassion. Sigmund Freud, in a beautiful study on melancholy (1957) focuses on grief and sadness as distinct from clinical depression. My own observations in this context are that grief and sadness are a kind of traffic junction on the path to depression.

Freud's is perhaps the earliest study in psychiatric literature that focuses on the importance of grief and sadness, as distinct from clinical depression, though it must be mentioned that Karl Abraham's collaborated with Freud on the subject Radden (2000) says that there is an interesting tension in Freud between, on the one hand the belief that melancholic propensities are rare and pathological and, on the other hand, that they are common, and even a part of the human condition. The notion of considering melancholy as a part of the human condition is something that Freud owed to the tradition exemplified in Burton's *Anatomy of Melancholia* (1927). Radden also notes that melancholy was associated with genius, exalted moods and creative energy. As a way of resolving this tension, I have identified two strands of melancholia, one a positive facet of existential angst and the other a negative one of pathological depression.

Regarding grief, it is of great interest that *grief is subject to a self-healing process where the mourner will return to normality.* There are delicate boundaries through grief, depression and melancholia and the sensitive therapist will see the clinical boundaries with care, mindfulness and empathy.

Boredom and Depression

Today whole cultures are swayed by a near ally of depression, which is boredom. As depicted by Erich Fromm; the misery that many people experience lies to a large extent, not in the fact that they are sick, but rather in their separation from everything that is interesting or beautiful in life. They need an enlargement and intensification in life (Lutz 1995). Tibor Scitovsky's writing on the joyless economy also presents another dimension of a culture without joy. Cultures play a role in shaping the lives of individuals. In contrast, is the Ifaluk culture in Micronesia. It is well portrayed by Catherine Lutz, where based on the strong roots of compassion, the suffering of one person is nurtured by others, and there is a natural shock absorber for depression. There is 'sadness without depression' in this culture where a strong sense of compassion pervades human relationships. Traditional Sri Lankan culture had similar features. I provide a separate chapter on 'compassion' later in the book.

Mindfulness-based cognitive therapy offers an elegant and innovative method for breaking through the cycle of recurrent depressive episodes. It also illuminates the relationship between cognition and emotion. It is a clinically proven methodology focused on the mechanisms that lie behind the changes in thinking and feeling that accompany depression. The relation between thinking and feeling and the related mechanisms play a central role in this therapy. It is a therapy, which within a mindfulness approach emphasizes holding thoughts and feeling in awareness rather than trying to change them. In depression, sad moods can reawaken negative thoughts, symptoms of depression, guilt, remorse, and negative, self-critical thinking. What is important on the path to recovery is that there is a change in the patient's relationship to negative thoughts and feelings.

As the present chapter has a central focus on grief counselling and depression as it relates to normal life, I shall go into more detail on Mindfulness-based Cognitive Therapy (MBCT) in the chapter on pain management, where MBCT, as used by Vidyamala Burch has been very effective.

The Lost Art of Sadness

In his book, *The Gift of Therapy*, Yalom says: 'The therapist and the client are fellow travellers. There is no therapist and no person immune to the tragedies of existence (2003).

Bien says something similar: 'True healers do not stand outside of the struggle of those they help. Healers know themselves as wounded, know their own suffering as a part of the human condition' (2006).

The dominant psychiatric traditions have failed to comprehend clearly that sadness is a basic facet of the human predicament and not a psychiatric disorder. Let us take grief first which in some contexts generates depressed feelings. It is true that grief and mourning are grave departures from routine life, but it is not a morbid condition and there is no need to hand over the mourner for medical treatment. In grief counselling, some of the richer facets of grief are seen: grief being the contribution of the lost one that makes one's love alive. It is also a time for deep reflection and the meaning of life and commemorating the contributions of the lost one. In response to Irvin Yalom's insight, my personal story of grief and depression ultimately inspired me to spend three years learning the skills of counselling, and six years of practice as a counsellor, at the Springvale Community Centre. Extreme cases of depression are somewhat different from the depression that overtakes normal people and in such a context, 'over-pathologizing depression', is to mishandle many people with quite legitimate sadness in the face of adversity (Biegler 2011). Thus, we may agree with Sigmund Freud that:

> Although grief involves grave departures from the normal attitude to life, it never occurs to us to regard it as a morbid condition and hand over the mourner to medical treatment. We rest assured that after a lapse of time it will be overcome, and we regard any interference with it as inadvisable and even harmful. (1957)

I add that in certain cases of depression, psychiatric advice is necessary along with any ameliorating medicine and tablets recommended. They may be combined with counselling:

> Sadness is an inherent part of the human condition, not a mental disorder. Thus, to confront a psychiatrist's invalid definition of depressive disorder is also to consider a painful but an important part of our humanity that we have tended to shunt aside in the modern medicalization of the human problems. As science allows to gain more control over our emotional states, we will inevitably confront the question of whether

> normal intense sadness has any redeeming features or should be banned from our lives. Such a momentous scientific and moral issues should not be spuriously resolved by using a semantic confusion in the DSM that mistakenly places states of intense sadness under the medical category of disorder. We can only adequately confront the complex and important concerns involved if we clearly differentiate normal sadness from mental disorder. (Horowitz and Wakefield 2007)

The Buddha emphasized the pervasiveness of human suffering and Freud presents a similar sentiment:

> Freud showed profundity when he stated that the aim of psychoanalysis was to replace neurotic unhappiness by normal unhappiness. A psychiatry based on a purely hedonistic ethics, a psychiatry that does not recognize that periods of anxiety and periods of melancholy are a necessary part of human life, such a psychiatry will be no more than a superficial affair. Our task is not merely to relieve but to interpret. (Drury 1973)

There are also many forms of psychological disorders that do not constitute clinical disorders, like for instance, loneliness, alienation, boredom, meaninglessness and low self-esteem. Normal people gain by psychological counselling, being close to normal life. This was the case with a majority of my clients: people unexpectedly losing jobs; failing an examination in spite of high expectations; the breakdown of an emerging romance; temporary disposition towards alcoholism which can be cured. During the time of the Buddha there was no clinical concept of abnormality but people driven by excessive craving, addictions and reactive behaviour.

In certain contexts, I used my own version of emotion focused therapy (EFT). This is not to reify depression as a thing, but to see it as an emotion constructed out of a number of components—perception of a situation, body sensations, feelings, thought patterns and intentions to act. I call this the 'componential approach' breaking an emotion into the ingredients that produce it, which would help us to isolate sadness from clinical depression and as Wolpert says in his book, *Anatomy of Depression,* very often depression is mishandled sadness (1999).

In fact, Paul Ekman sees depression in terms of emotion blends, which is also a useful perspective as they can be applied to therapy:

> If sadness dominates depression, we speak of retarded depression, if agony is more prominent, it is agitated depression. People who are depressed not only feel helpless to change their lives, they feel hopeless. They do not believe it will ever get better. In addition to sadness and agony, guilt and shame are strongly felt, for depressed people feel they are worthless… anger directed inwards or out, and fear are often manifest. (2003)

Ekman adds to my componential theory, that other emotions like agitation, guilt, remorse and worthlessness may be at the base of depression. Someone who has led a life of sexual pleasures or has been sexually exploited by an older person may experience worthlessness and shame and in the case of the perpetrator they may feel remorseful.

My own practice of mindfulness-based emotion focused therapy had good results, as the study of emotions has been my hobby as the present book will prove. Also, Ekman's work on emotions and facial expression led to my discovery of illuminating contexts for anger, fear and sadness. If you discover one or two emotions at the base of depression, then there are clear lines for therapy to proceed.

Social Dimensions of Depression: Depression and Its Near Allies

Erich Fromm refers to the challenges of meaninglessness and boredom in the lives of people as 'alienation' from the most human qualities of finding life interesting and meaningful. Fromm had a regular correspondence with the German-born Sri Lanka-ordained Theravada monk, Venerable Nyānaponika and was greatly interested in Buddhism. Venerable Nyānaponika edited a volume of articles on Erich Fromm to which I contributed. In the case of Fromm, instead of seeing depression and boredom in individual clients, he observed that whole cultures were caught up by a malady, '*la malaise du siècle*': a state in which there are no specific symptoms except an unhappy feeling that life has no meaning.

He says that the misery which many people experience lies to a large extent not in the fact that they are sick but lies in their separation from everything that is interesting.

They need an intensification and enlargement in life and he considered 'boredom' as a sickness of our times. There is a sense of isolation and lack of connection, a point also true of clients who are depressed. Erich Fromm's *To Have or to Be* (2013), and *The Art of Listening* (1994), present this deep study of alienation. Tibor Scitovsky's *Joyless Economy* (1976) focuses on the point that people should do activities for their own sake: activities, which they enjoy. Mihaly Csikszentmihalyi in searching for a way out of this predicament worked on a research project with artists, mountain climbers, athletes, musicians, chess players and manual labourers as well as surgeons. He found that the sheer enjoyment of the activity was the principal incentive:

> Research into states of peak experiences or 'flow states', which athletes refer to as 'being in the zone' shows that these share a strong relationship with mindfulness. (Hassed and Chambers 2014)

Joseph Goldstein described boredom as an attentional crisis:

> To realize that boredom does not come from the object of attention but rather from the quality of attention is truly a transforming insight. Fritz Pearls one of those who brought psychotherapy to America, said, 'Boredom is lack of attention'. Understanding this brings profound changes brings profound changes in our lives. (Goldstein 1993)

If you have an ability to get intensely interested in something that is exhilarating and beautiful in life, there is no room for the infiltration of boredom into your life. Whatever the object is, it is the subjective state of exhilaration that is within you—it may be music, art, gardening, cooking or reading. In fact, art therapy is often used for people with depression, allowing their imagination to take interesting routes. One needs to have values and goals that inspire you. In my personal life, I found the following words of Tolstoy inspiring: 'Only people who are capable of loving strongly can also suffer great sorrow, but this same necessity of loving serves to counteract their grief and heals them': cited in Worden (2018).

Boredom has many varieties and these belong often to whole cultures, as Fromm points out. There is a kind of boredom which emerges out of the manic quality of life, paradoxically, with all the 'time compression effect': increased stress at work, sleep deprivation, burnout and workaholism.

Recent clinical studies on 'attention' deficit throw more light on boredom. An *attentional deficit* is characterized by the inability to focus on a selected object. The mind becomes withdrawn and disengaged even from its internal processes. *Attentional hyperactivity* occurs when the mind is extremely aroused, resulting in compulsive distraction and fragmentation. An *attentional dysfunction* occurs when we focus on things in an afflictive manner, not conducive to the welfare of oneself or others (Wallace and Shapiro 2006). These defective psychological states are counter to our health and wellbeing. However, there are people who are genuinely immersed and enjoy whatever they do, as indicated by Mihaly Csikszentmihalyi, the expert on 'flow' experiences has demonstrated. Those who enjoy life and work, have curiosity and interest in life, persistence and low self-centredness, find creative and meaningful ways of spending their life.

Understanding and Managing Grief

Some element of 'depression' as a passing state does emerge in the loss of someone dear to you, but it can be converted into a journey of self-exploration: of love and compassion. One needs a great deal of resilience or non-reactivity. Denial, anger and mild depression often follow. Then follows acceptance and working through with love and compassion:

> In other words, with mindful awareness of grief, you can move closer to the people in your life who matter most, and change habits or ideas that have been keeping you away from living fully. Full awareness, especially in grief, of your patterns of feeling, and behaviour can take you from

living with misery and discontent to living with openness and passion. (Kumar 2005)

As Kumar observes in this manner, one can channel the momentum of grief into a journey of self-awakening. As Tolstoy observes, grief may be seen as an extension of one's love. Reflecting on grief enlarges one's notion of love and deeper spiritual transformation, in terms of issues pertaining to the meaning of life. The transformative power of grief over loss produces a deep reflective tone in life. Furthermore, the wonderful resilience of the mind results in the mature management of grief.

In the work, *The Lost Art of Compassion*, Lorne Ladner says that in dealing with grief and love one needs to move away from an exclusive focus on pathology for many years (Ladner 2004). Ladner refers to the words of Martin Seligman, a former president of the American Psychological Society: 'the exclusive focus on pathology that has dominated so much of our discipline results in the model of the human being lacking in positive features that make life worth living' (Ladner 2004). Ladner also says that according to this disease model, we try to repair damage rather than aim at positive mental health but now a veritable change is taking place in the West with the new revolution of the importance of mindfulness techniques for therapy. In fact, the impact of mindfulness-based stress reduction therapy along with mindfulness-based cognitive therapy indicates a radical transformation in current conceptions of therapy. Later chapters will deal with mindfulness-based pain management and mindfulness-based cognitive therapy for depression.

Catherine Lutz, the anthropologist who worked with the Ifalik/Ifaluk culture, says that in this culture, there is a durable and automatic link between the suffering of one person and their nurturing by others. It was more than cushioning but there was the emergence of positive emotions of compassion and empathy. Traditional Sri Lankan culture had similar features. I have a separate chapter on compassion and this study of Lutz shows the importance of culture for a very natural and humane expression of compassion.

The Story of Kisāgotami and the Mustard Seed

This story is very rich as a dramatological model for Buddhist reflections on the theme of death and grief. It is a story that is staged from time to time for children in Sunday school. Kisāgotami was struck by tragedy when her infant died. She went all over to find a medicine to bring the child back to life. Kind people in the village advised her to talk to the Buddha with her request. There was a large crowd listening to the Buddha when she came into his presence. The Buddha displayed great compassion to her. Her dress was in disarray and the people gave her clothes to cover herself. The Buddha requested her to go back to her village and to bring back a mustard seed from a family that had not lost anyone. She came back to the Buddha but was not able to come back with a mustard seed. By that time a sense of realization had dawned on her. A profound process of healing emerged within her and she was on the path to liberation. As a story for children which is often told by the teacher in the Sunday school, I wish to recall the words of Martha Nussbaum, a celebrated Western philosopher:

> [A]n education in common human weakness and vulnerability should be a profound part of the education of the children. Children should learn to be tragic spectators and understand with subtlety and responsiveness the predicament to which human life is prone. Through stories and drama, they should learn to decode suffering of others and this decoding should deliberately lead them into lives both near and far, including the lives of distant humans and lives of animals. (Nussbaum 1991)

Therapies

I shall be devoting a separate chapter to MBCT (Mindfulness-based Cognitive Therapy for depression). Briefly, MBCT was developed as a targeted approach for people who have a history of depression and are therefore vulnerable to future episodes. I shall also devote a part of the chapter to mindfulness-based emotion focused therapy.

References

Biegler, Paul. 2011. *The Ethical Treatment of Depression*. Cambridge, MA: MIT Press.
Bien, Thomas. 2006. *Mindful Therapy*. Boston: Wisdom Publications.
Burton, Robert. 1927. *The Anatomy of Melancholy*. New York: Farrar and Reinhart.
Csikszentmihalyi, Mihaly. 1978. *The Psychology of Optimal Experience*. New York: Harper and Row.
Drury, Maurice O'Connor. 1973. *The Danger of Words*. London: Routledge and Kegan Paul.
Ekman, Paul. 2003. *Emotions Revealed*. New York: Weidenfeld and Nicolson.
Freud, Sigmund. (1957). Mourning and Melancholia, Standard Edition, vol. 14. London: Hogarth Press.
Fromm, Erich. 2013. *To Have or to Be?*. London: Bloomsbury.
Fromm, Erich. 1994. *The Art of Listening*. London: Constable.
Goldstein, Joseph. 1993. *Insight Meditation*. Boston: Shambhala.
Hassed, Craig, and Richard Chambers. 2014. *Mindful Learning*. NSW: Exisle.
Horwitz, Allan, A.V., and Jerome Wakefield. 2007. *Loss of Sadness*. Oxford: Oxford University Press.
Kumar, Samit. 2005. *Grieving Mindfully*. Oakland, CA: New Harbinger.
Ladner, Lorne. 2004. *The Lost Art of Compassion*. New York: HarperCollins.
Lutz, Catherine. 1995. Need, Nurturance and the Emotions on a Pacific Atoll. In *Emotions in Asian Thought*, ed. Joel Marks and Roger Ames. New York: State University of New York Press.
Nussbaum, Martha. 1991. Compassion and Terror. *Daedalus* 132: 20–26.
Radden, Jennifer. 2000. Love and Loss in Freud. In *The Analytic Freud, Philosophy and Psychoanalysis*, ed. Michael P. Levine. New York: Routledge.
Wallace, Alan B., and Shauna Shapiro. 2006. Mental Balance and Well-Being. *American Psychologist*, October.
Wolpert, Lewis. 1999. *Malignant Sadness*. London: Faber and Faber.
Worden, J.W. 2018. *Grief Counselling and Grief Therapy: A Handbook for the Mental Health Practitioner*, 5th ed. New York, NY: Springer.
Yalom, Irvin. 2003. *The Gift of Therapy*. London: Piatkus.

9

Stress Management

We shall do well to look at stress and strife in daily life. Furthermore, there is a clear distinction between the alertness that comes with the practice of mindfulness and stress:

> High stress is associated with poor executive function and hence poor performance, whereas being mindful is associated with better executive function and better performance... An overactive stress centre in the brain (amygdala) hijacks executive functioning making functioning effectively difficult if not impossible. (Hassed and Chambers 2014)

There has been important research on mindful learning and the relationship between stress and poor learning in stress situations. There is also research linked to brain functioning. The context of stress in daily living is very much related to what I described as 'pedestrian depression' in the last chapter. In fact, it has been said that stress is an unavoidable aspect of being alive. Hence, how people respond to stress determines to a large extent, the impact of stress upon their lives. Hans Selye who first popularized the term in the 1950s opted to define stress as a response, and a stressor to describe the stimulus. It is basically an adaptation to

P. de Silva, *Mindfulness-based Emotion Focused Counselling*,
https://doi.org/10.1007/978-3-030-64388-1_9

the pressure of experience, and how we respond becomes crucial. Sometimes, a minor event can make us overreact or a major emergency may be managed with care and grace. Jon Kabat-Zinn who is the creator and founder of the Stress Reduction Clinic and the Center for Mindfulness at the University of Massachusetts observes:

> [I]t stands to reason that by becoming conscious of our options in stressful situations and being mindful of the relevance and effectiveness of our response to these situations, we may be able to exercise control over our experience of the stress and thereby influence whether or not it will lead to disease. (1990)

In general, stress management looks at four important facets:

i Physiological level: cardiovascular system, musculoskeletal system, nervous system, immune system. Symptoms are alarm reactivity, bodily tensions, headaches, backaches and high blood pressure.
ii. Emotional level: stress responses, anger, irritation, annoyance, irritation, indignation, sadness-depression spectrum, worry, fear and anxiety.
iii. Behavioural level: poor concentration and weak attention to work, inability to maintain interpersonal relations, fall in productive work and lack of flexibility.
iv. Cognitive level: weak self-confidence and lack of self-assurance, lack of enthusiasm, pessimism. Moderate levels of stress are believed to give some exercise to the brain, so that all stress is not bad.

A Case Study

Wilson is a student who is seventeen, is studying at university and has completed three years of engineering studies. He is an only child and his parents are fond of him. They are somewhat conservative, however, and the boy does not discuss issues pertaining to his personal life with his parents. Wilson is by nature a very shy person. He is also very reserved and does not mix much with the girls. Wilson had taken a great liking to Amy who is also in his class and this feeling grows into an infatuation without Wilson being aware of it. With one more year to go before his finals, Wilson gets a bit forgetful about completing his class assignments. In addition, the shopping that he usually does for his mother is not done regularly. Further, for a period, he stops working at his part-time job. When having morning breakfast together, his parents gradually discern that their son looks stressed and absent-minded. His father intuits that Wilson has fallen love and thinks that a quiet, frank conversation may reveal what he is keeping from his parents.

During an evening walk, Wilson's father, John, opened up the conversation in a playful mood. In a light-hearted way he said to Wilson: 'After you complete your finals, are you going to go on a treasure hunt, I mean find a nice girl? First, Wilson's face turned red and he tried to deny things. But, after some more cross-questioning he opened up like a cascade in a waterfall. He then described frankly what he had been going through during the past few months. John now had some words of wisdom to pass on. 'I am glad that you have opened up your heart towards someone. Go slowly and see what sort of person Amy is. You don't have to do this in a week or two. Now that your heart is warm, go back to your studies with a new gusto and self-discipline. It may be Amy or someone else—keep the field open and the choice is yours'. In a week or two Wilson was back to his normal self.

Young people are often difficult to handle if they are not approached in the right way. Family tensions with children need to be handled with calmness and wisdom, and when the context permits, with good humour. In my personal life, from my wife Kalyani, I learnt to treat the children like friends and to share a bagful of humour with her, some of which she brought back from the school where she was teaching. She was a very versatile cook and dinner time was very lively. Good counselling is not always dealing with some psychosomatic disorder. The problems my clients had like that of Wilson were very close to real life. Lively and mature families may develop a mini-therapeutic culture of their own, which is the golden path to good counselling (de Silva 2008).

Recent Work on Stress Management

Craig Hassed, in a recent study of stress management and health, says that stress is sometimes described as a perceived inability to cope. If we are confronted by certain challenges but do not have the ability to deal with them, and this is continuous, it is described as chronic stress. We need to realize that the management of stress is in our own hands. To begin to take control of our lives requires clear awareness, practice, discernment and courage. It is also necessary to realize that it is not merely a medical condition (Hassed and Chambers 2014).

I shall conclude this chapter with mentioning a few benefits from mindfulness-based stress therapy: improved immunity, reduced anxiety, reduced distress and depression, increased empathy and spiritual experience, increased knowledge about stress, decreased sensitivity towards oneself and the development of positive coping skills (Hassed and Chambers 2014).

References

de Silva, Padmasiri. 2008. *An Introduction to Mindfulness-Based Counselling*. Ratmalana, Sri Lanka: Sarvodaya Vishvalekha.

de Silva, Padmasiri. 2017. *Emotions and the Body in Buddhist Contemplative Practice and Mindfulness-Based Therapy*. London: Palgrave Macmillan.

Hassed, Craig, and Richard Chambers. 2014. *Mindful Learning*. Wollombi, NSW: Exisle.

Kabat-Zinn, Jon. 1990. *Full Catastrophe Living*. New York: Delacorte.

10

Pain Management and Trauma

Foundations of Mindfulness

There has been a radical transformation of the Western psychological tradition which has during modern times, accepted the Buddha's perennial insight that the severity of human suffering depends largely on our attitude to it.

Our relationship to emotional pain is a key factor in how much we suffer. For example, the latest wave of cognitive behaviour therapy understands that trying to change our thoughts directly is less effective than creating a wide, openhearted space for our experience—a less resistant, less avoidant relationship to our thoughts and feelings. This view is expressed in the mindfulness-based cognitive therapy maxim: 'thoughts are thoughts and not facts'.

Thus, firstly, opening up and creating a space is important. Secondly, acceptance, curiosity, tolerance, willingness and the ability to embrace pain with friendship as presented in acceptance commitment therapy (ACT) can be helpful. ACT draws a distinction between *pain* and *suffering*. When we encounter painful content within ourselves, we want to do what we always do, fix it up and sort it out, so that we can get rid of it. ACT emphasizes the danger of experiential avoidance and invites

P. de Silva, *Mindfulness-based Emotion Focused Counselling*,
https://doi.org/10.1007/978-3-030-64388-1_10

people to perceive that acceptance is not a heavy, sad, dark, thing—it is an active vital embrace.

Thirdly, the Buddhist perspective, while endorsing the first two strands, also considers that capacities like attention, compassion and empathy are skills that can be learned, rather than a product of good genes and a fortunate childhood. Christopher Germer offers an insightful path for befriending painful feelings (2009).

The following three points are at the heart of *Satipaṭṭhāna* according to a recent commentary.

1. The contemplation of the mind does not involve active measures to oppose unwholesome states of mind, like anger or lust.
2. The mind has to be receptively aware by clearly recognizing the state of mind that underlies a particular train of thought: as the Buddha says, see lust as lust and anger as anger. This is necessary as there is a tendency to ignore that which goes against the grain of one's self-importance.
3. There is also a tendency to use techniques of deception (*vañcaka dhammā*) and these are also fed by (unconscious) subliminal tendencies (*anusaya*) of lust, anger and conceit. Such hidden motives may be clearly seen at three levels: (dormant level (*anusaya*); as emerging thoughts (*pariyuṭṭhāna*); or result in ungovernable impulsive actions (*vītikkama*) or physiological pressure. Of these the subliminal anger emerges as negative thoughts, self-critical, unable to respond to pain with calm. In MBCT, this is referred to as *rumination*:

> Rumination is a particular style of self-critical, self-focused, repetitive, negative thinking. It is preoccupied with and driven by the desire to 'solve' the emotional challenge of unhappiness or lowered mood.
>
> Experiential avoidance is the attempt to remain out of contact with the direct experience of challenging thoughts, emotions and body sensations. (Crane 2009)

While these observations are directly relevant to pain management, these insights emerged in the MBCT programme for depression management.

Fourthly, if we look at anger/aversion of pain as a negative emotion to be destroyed, we lose sight of the fact that for Buddhism such an emotion has a *hermeneutic*al role, where the cognitive meaning is important: the message that this pain is impermanent. Immediate anger at pain needs some reflection. The Buddha said that instead of considering them as defilements as such, one could see them as impermanent processes (*dharmas*). This attitude, which emerges in a meditative setting, where anger is neither good nor bad but an impersonal process, which helps to ward off resentment, remorse and guilt, and thus leads one to develop resilience instead of reactivity (in neurological terms). Thus, both Western MBCT and Buddhist contemplative practice are twin pillars to emotional healing. I also wish to emphasize this from my personal experience both as meditator and therapist.

Fifthly, Venerable Nyānaponika says, 'Do not throw away your negative emotions as they can be transformed by a little magic and converted into their opposites. With patience and forgiveness towards yourself and others they can also be made into objects of meditation *(dhammānupassanā*). Liberation by insight; the method of remedying one emotion by another is advocated by the Spinoza. For example, one can change aversion by showing compassion and kindness towards oneself. The philosopher Friedrich Nietzsche (1844–1900) and the Tibetan Buddhist tradition recognize that there is a vital power in some negative emotions.

The Structure of the *Satipaṭṭhāna* and Mindfulness-Based Cognitive Therapy

To bring awareness to the body (*kāya*), feelings (*vedanā*), and thoughts (*citta*) are facets covered in the Buddhist *Satipaṭṭhāna* and also MBCT. *The body scan in MBCT involves, direct experience of physical sensations, being with the body in the present moment; being intentional about where and how the attention is placed, deliberately engaging and disengaging as we move through the body; relating skillfully to the wandering of the mind and thoughts without judging them; allowing things to be as they are; encouraging relaxation instead of restlessness.* The range of emotions we experience is vast.

Similarly to Buddhism, MBCT focuses at the experiential gut level: *we constantly register our internal and external experiences as feelings, pleasant, unpleasant and neutral. Aversive reactions are triggered by unpleasant feelings, and their impact on the body is seen.* Tuning in and befriending feelings helps to see the linkages between the body and feelings. In Buddhist practice, in using the technique of bare attention, any transition from painful feelings to negative emotions is triggered by subliminal anger. Likewise, a transition to pleasant feeling is triggered by subliminal lust. It has been emphasized that *knowing* that our experience is made of body sensations, thoughts and feelings is different to *experiencing* them.

Auto-Pilot Thinking According to MBCT

Our skills with practical activity have become our automatic repertoire, and this way of habitual problem solving has become automatized. Often, beyond our conscious awareness, the normal thinking mind is engaged in automatic activity of judging and monitoring. But this habitual turn of mind that takes place automatically makes the person incapable of making conscious choices in responding to experience, and this narrowed activity may have a catastrophic impact on our emotional lives as thought and emotion are integrally related. *Unlike feelings, our emotions are guided by our thought patterns.* This pattern is described as the 'doing mode' which leads to repetitive automatic thought patterns rather than the 'being mode', which is mindful of what is happening. For example: 'I thought that this time I would get the job, but I failed. I am a failure. I just cannot see any alternatives. I have no one to help me.' This is how the auto-pilot works. In depression and anxiety, this sort of perspective dominates. One alternative would be to get trained and pass exams in a field where the prospects are good. But the automatic thought patterns get in the way. In pain management too such negative anxiety emerges.

Rumination, as described earlier is an attempt to solve emotional problems in a destructive way. The extra dose of our suffering is of our own making.

In pain management, pain is inevitable but suffering is our own creation. Those who take to blocking pain by smoking, getting addicted to alcohol or compulsive eating add an extra layer of suffering. This is very much true of pain management. Mindfulness training helps us to see these habitual 'avoidant patterns', of running away from the problem. In depression, unlike pain management the setting is more complex but whatever the context, experiential avoidance makes the condition worse, as reservoirs of unprocessed material accumulate.

Icons of Pain Management

Vidyamala Burch suffered from chronic back pain for over thirty years due to congenital weakness, a car accident, and multiple surgeries. She was trained by Kabat-Zinn and she underwent a complete systematic program and emerged strong. She then used the rest of her life to helping others. She has become known all over the world with the Breathworks 8 steps program (Burch 2008).

Risa Kaparo is well known for the work, *Awakening Somatic Intelligence: The Art and Practice of Embodied Mindfulness* (Kaparo 2012). She has a remarkable story too. She says: 'Somatic learning is not something I learnt from books or teachers but from my own body.' She was originally an artist who was given an assignment by the government to build a fibre art playground. It was to be built on rock, but she imagined the rock was soft and that it would be possible to handle it with a jackhammer.

However, the rock proved to be very hard, and while trying to use the jackhammer, it rebounded on her body causing severe injuries. The injuries were so severe that it is only in reading her story that one realizes that the method that she worked out to heal herself was near miraculous. While teaching sculpture to a group of blind students, she found that they had remarkable insight into 'body vibrations'. She made this a paradigm experience to explore what she called the wisdom of the body. She created a kind of eclectic philosophy, blending the thinking of Krishnamurti, yoga and Buddhist meditation, but it was an original philosophy and therapy. She also integrated the most recent insights from neuroscience into a holistic philosophy. Reading her book was a great inspiration when writing on pathways to somatic intelligence in my recent book (de Silva 2017). She wrote this inspiring thought:

> The willingness to pay deep attention to the inner wisdom and the movement of your body is a fully sufficient teacher to move you into a state of utter wholeness and aliveness. (Kaparo 2012)

Theory of Pain Management

Traditional sensory neurophysiology that dominated pain research was influenced by a Cartesian dualism that the brain detects and perceives pathological bodily processes passively and mechanically. The body and mind were seen as separate entities. According to the new view, pain is subjective and physical pain is invariably tied to our emotions:

> Pain refers broadly to describe any unpleasant experience that has a physical dimension, whether caused by disease, injury, stress or emotion. (Burch 2008, pp. 56–58)

> Pure pain is never directed as an isolated sensation. Pain is always accompanied by emotion and meaning unique to the individual. (Burch 2008)

There is a difference between primary pain and secondary pain. *Secondary pain is beyond mere physical sensation, adding both physical and emotional responses.* A well-known medical practitioner and academic from Monash University, Melbourne, who has also integrated mindfulness practice into his teaching, Craig Hassed, points out that along with mental and physical pain, the second layer of physical pain may be described as stress (Hassed and McKenzie 2012). (i) Stress increases the output of inflammatory chemicals: we have poured fuel on fire; (ii) we may be physically tensed when stressed, which may add to the muscle spasms that are present at the site of pain; (iii) when we become hyper-vigilant for the pain (always looking for it), we sensitize the pain circuits of the brain. Hassed observes that, this may be an important reason why mindfulness is so therapeutic as it helps to unhook attention from the preoccupation with pain and reduces emotional reactivity when noticed. (iv) Stress seems to change the chemical composition of the nerve endings, making them more liable to fire off pain messages. Hassed observes that mindfulness practice has the potential to change and reverse the unconscious processes and the way in which we anticipate, react and respond to pain.

Buddhism and Mindfulness Practice

The Buddha is saying that instead of trying to eliminate suffering, the wise person learns to change the relationship to suffering. The celebrated *Sallekha Sutta* (M.I.40), presenting the man who is struck by two arrows sums up the Buddhist position:

> When an ordinary person experiences a painful bodily feeling, they worry, agonize and feel distraught. Then they feel two types of pain, one physical, the other mental. It is as if a person was struck by an arrow and then immediately afterwards by a second arrow, and thus he experiences the pain of two arrows. Having being touched by the painful feeling, he resists and resents it—sorrows, grieves, laments, beating his breast he becomes distraught. (*Sallekha Sutta*)

Here we see that his pain is nourished by subliminal anger (*paṭigha anusaya*) and he knows no other alternative to anger except sensual pleasures diversions. As Vidyamala Burch says, he is *blocking out pain* by recreational drugs, shopping, chocolates, work, talking, sleeping, etc. If he follows such unprofitable routes he may get depressed.

According to Buddhist psychology there is a three-faceted base of craving at work. The first is *kāma taṇhā*, the drive for sense pleasure through the body, and when pain emerges, the escape routes to sensuality are sought; the second is *bhava taṇhā*, wanting to become 'this and that' and thus find escape routes, as the attachment to the body is strong; the third is the *vibhava taṇhā*, the desire to get rid of things or even destroy what is painful, emerging in self-destructive behaviour like addiction to alcohol.

As presented by Venerable Sumedho (b. 1934), letting go is the way to move out of a vicious circle of grasping without letting go: holding on to your pain. This is different to attempting to destroy things you do not like:

> It is important to know when you have let go of desire: when you no longer judge or try to get rid of it; when you recognize that it is the just the way it is. When you are really calm and peaceful, then you will find that there is no attachment to anything. You are not caught up trying to get something or get rid of something. Wellbeing is just knowing things as they are without feeling the necessity to pass judgments upon them. (Sumedho 1998)

Post Script

During the last six months, I have moved away from Lexington Gardens Retirement Village, where I lived for a wonderful fifteen years with a very active life. This was due to a fall and problems with the right knee. But about six months back I shifted to REGIS which provides a new home for me, where regular group exercises by experts, walking, musical evenings and an active participation in the newly formed poetry club and most important, a new lease for my meditative life. Though time to time, I use a walker or a four- wheeler, tremendous change in a physical, emotional and spiritual transformation has taken place. The collection of poems in this book is a poetic expression of inner calm, and physically a very relaxed body. I will need lots of time to write on such a holistic approach to pain management and also make new discoveries on the way.

References

Burch, Vidyamala. 2008. *Living With Pain and Illness*. London: Piatkus.
Crane, Rebecca. 2009. *Mindfulness-Based Cognitive Therapy*. London: Routledge.
de Silva, Padmasiri. 2017. *Emotions and the Body in Buddhist Contemplative Practice and Mindfulness-Based Therapy*. London: Palgrave Macmillan.
Germer, Christopher K. 2009. *The Mindful Path to Self-Compassion*. London: Guilford Press.
Hassed, Craig, and Stephen McKenzie. 2012. *Mindfulness for Life*. NSW: Exisle Publishing.
Kaparo, Risa. 2012. *Awakening Somatic Intelligence: The Art and Practice of Embodied Mindfulness*. Berkeley: North Atlantic Books.
Sumedho, Ajahn. 1998. *Four Noble Truths*. Taiwan: Amaravati Publications.

Part III

Emotional Life

11

Disturbing Emotions

Emotions in the Western Philosophical Traditions

In the Western philosophical tradition emotions were more focused on morality or ethics. Studies on the emotions were dominated by epistemological and ethical concerns rather than a having clear therapeutic stance. Interesting exceptions were Spinoza and to some extent the Stoics. Spinoza and the Stoic, Seneca, upheld the view that *philosophical therapy can free us from the bondage of emotions.* The Buddhist path combined ethical, epistemological and therapeutic facets of analyzing emotions. But in a deeper sense, as Matthieu Ricard says: 'The Buddha was concerned with the alchemy of human suffering' (2006). He also indicates that a part of the causal network of human suffering is caused by disturbing emotions:

> Why can't we simply allow the negative emotions to wear themselves down? Experience shows that, like an infection that goes untreated, the disturbing emotions gain in strength when allowed to take their course. Unleashing anger whenever it arises, for instance creates trends to creating psychological instability that only increases irascibility. The results of

P. de Silva, *Mindfulness-based Emotion Focused Counselling*,
https://doi.org/10.1007/978-3-030-64388-1_11

> various psychological studies contradict the notion that giving free rein to the emotions temporarily relieves bottled up tensions. By systematically allowing our negative emotions to express themselves, we develop habits to which we are vulnerable every time the emotional charge reaches the critical threshold. In addition, the threshold will gradually become lower and anger will erupt more easily. The result will be what is commonly called a bad temper, accompanied by chronic suffering. From the physiological point of view, arterial tension diminishes if we prevent anger from openly expressing itself, but it increases when we fly into rage. (Hokanson 1962)

Ricard also observes that behavioural studies indicate those who balance their emotions are also more open to others. *Suppressing emotions creates problems as they need to be mindfully recognized.*

As we have already mentioned in an earlier part of this book, one way of distinguishing between different emotions is examining the *motivational roots* as for instance in Buddhism, greed, hate and delusion of the self are the roots of unwholesome emotions, like covetousness, anger and conceit. Ricard considers the consequences of negative emotions as leading to suffering. He accepts moral indignation directed at an injustice as wholesome, as does Aristotle: though we need to be sure that moral indignation does not arouse one's anger. In contrast to Aristotelian ethics, Buddhism rejects the view that all emotions are healthy, as long as they are not excessive or inappropriate to time and place. Rather, Buddhism maintains that some mental states are afflictive regardless of their degree or the context in which they arise.

Rather than focusing on increasing consciousness of one's inner state, as Buddhism does, the emphasis in psychology has instead been to reappraise situations, or control (regulate emotional behaviour and expressions. But reappraising situations and controlling anger, for instance, may have benefits for a Buddhist. This is specially the case with moral indignation which due to certain complexities calls for deep reflection. Identifying the emotions that lead to mental wellbeing would be a positive Buddhist value. Ricard says that introspection and self-observation or what is now popularly rendered as, 'mindfulness' is crucial in managing emotion. My earlier discussion of MBCT and pain management proves this point.

Three Remedies for Disturbing Emotions

Ricard recommends greater familiarization with emotions:

> The three principle ways are antidotes, liberation and utilization. The first consists of applying a specific antidote to each emotion. The second allows us to unravel or 'liberate' the emotion by looking straight at it and letting it dissolves as it arises. The third uses the raw power of an emotion as a catalyst for inner change. (2006)

The first method consists of neutralizing afflictive emotions with a specific antidote, in the manner we neutralize the destructive effects of poison with anti-venom. The other point is that two diametrically opposed mental processes cannot emerge simultaneously. We may fluctuate between love and hatred but they cannot exist together. By habituating one's mind to altruism one may eliminate hatred. The Jewish philosopher Spinoza, in a study of emotions which sounds very Buddhistic says, 'hatred has to be conquered by love or generosity and is not to be met with hatred in return' (1963). He also says: 'in order that we may always have this prescript of reason in readiness whenever it will be of service, we may think over and often meditate upon the common injuries inflicted by men, and consider how and in what way they may best be repelled by generosity (1963). This sounds like the Buddhist concept of *mettā*/loving kindness.

Spinoza's antidote to fear is also that one should be aware of the common dangers in life and develop presence of mind and courage. His prescription for 'vainglory' or vanity is also very Buddhistic as Buddhism considers conceit (*mana*) a kind of measuring oneself against others, as a defilement of the mind and conquered only in the higher reaches of a meditative mind. Vanity is pursued by a man who pursues glory too eagerly. He advises people to think of its proper use, the ends and means to be followed, and the inconsistency of what people do. It is in this manner that ambitious people torment themselves, when they despair of obtaining honours for which they are striving. The interesting point is that those who covet glory, are the loudest in disclaiming its abuse and the vanity of the world. This is also not limited to those who are ambitious but common to all to whom fortune is adverse and who are also impotent in mind. Some who are both poor and also avaricious would talk of the abuse of money and the abuses of the rich, and are unable to bear with equanimity the wealth of others. A man who is not well received by his mistress may talk of the fickleness of women and their faithlessness. Spinoza concludes: 'He, therefore, who desires to govern his emotions and appetites from a love of freedom alone will strive as much as he can to know virtues and their causes, and to fill his mind with joy which springs from a true knowledge of them: least of all while he desires to contemplate the vices of men, and disparage men, or to delight in a false show of freedom'. This last point sounds like the Buddhist concept of equanimity.

The Use of Antidotes

The Tibetan Buddhist tradition use antidotes to deal with negative emotions. The peacock eats poison and this generates resplendent feathers. In the same way negative emotions may be transformed. The techniques used in the Tibetan tradition are described as: abandoning negative emotions, controlling, transforming, remedying and recognizing their wisdom. *Remedying involves the use of antidotes*: remedying of desire by contemplation on the body's impurities; replacing love and patience with anger and hatred; demolishing pride by reflecting on our predicament in the wheel of samsara.

Freeing the emotion (for instance anger), is liberating anger at the moment it arises by seeing its emptiness, and the lack of its own existence (Ricard 2006). It is at the very moment anger arises that we must see its emptiness and free it from its hold on us. This method can be used for all other defiling emotions.

Using emotion as a catalyst is the third method, where we recognize that *some apparent negative emotions have some positive ingredients:*

> Anger rouses us to action and often allows us to overcome obstacles. It also contains aspects of clarity, focus and effectiveness that are not

> harmful in and of themselves. Desire has an element of bliss that is distinct from attachment; pride has an element of self-confidence that can be firm without lapsing into arrogance; envy, a drive to act that cannot be confused with the unhealthy dissatisfaction it entails.
>
> Once we learn to avoid that fixation, we do not need to bring in antidotes from outside: the emotions themselves act as catalysts for freeing ourselves from their baneful influence. (Ricard 2006)

In the final analysis, the source of the emotional disturbance is our attachment to the self.

References

Hokanson, J.E., and M. Burgess. 1962. The Effects of Three Types of Aggression on Vascular Processes. *The Journal of Abnormal and Social Psychology* 64(6): 446–449.

Ricard, Matthieu. 2006. *Happiness: A Guide to Developing Life's Most Important Skill*. New York: Little Brown.

Spinoza, B. 1963. *Ethics*. New York: Hafner.

12

Fear and Anxiety

Psychological Dimensions

I have already discussed the Buddhist perspectives of the emotions of anger, and the sadness/grief/depression dimension. Like anger and sadness, fear is a central emotion in Buddhist psychology, ethics and counselling. In the psychological dimension of fear, ground-breaking research has come from Joseph Ledoux's work, *The Emotional Brain* (1996).

Ledoux's central contribution which has relevant implications for Buddhist psychology is the notion of the subliminal unconscious, which is different from the Freudian concept of the traumatic unconscious. As mentioned earlier, according to Buddhism, the subliminal proclivities towards (*anusaya*), lust, anger, and conceit are more like sleeping passions that may wake up due to certain triggers and invade us in a quick impulsive manner. Joseph Ledoux's research into the emotion of fear indicates this point. A man walking on a lonely forest track tramples on a bundle of dry twigs, hears a crackling sound and is subject to the fight or flight response, where he is about to run, thinking it is a rattlesnake. In a context of this sort, the central nervous system has been hijacked by the amygdala and then impulsive action follows. In

P. de Silva, *Mindfulness-based Emotion Focused Counselling*,
https://doi.org/10.1007/978-3-030-64388-1_12

normal contexts, the CNS (central nervous system) provides the information and this provides the basis for action. Such tendencies to fear or anger may lie at a subliminal level (*anusaya bhūmi*); or they may emerge as thought processes (*pariyuṭṭhāna bhūmi*); or become fierce and ungovernable (*vītikkama bhūmi*).

Seven *anusaya*s are mentioned in the Dialogues of the Buddha:

1. Sensuous craving/lust (*kāma-rāga*)
2. Anger (*paṭigha*)
3. Conceit (*māna*)
4. Erroneous opinion (*diṭṭhi*)
5. Scepticism (*vicikicchā*)
6. Craving for existence (*bhava-rāga*)
7. Ignorance (*avijjā*).

The Low and the High Road

The fact that emotional learning can be mediated by pathways that bypass the neocortex is intriguing, for it suggests that emotional responses can occur without the involvement of the higher processing system of the brain, systems believed to be involved in thinking, reasoning, and consciousness:

> Although the thalamic system cannot make fine distinctions, it has an important advantage over the cortical input pathway to the amygdala. That advantage is time. In a rat it takes about twelve milliseconds for an acoustic stimulus to reach the amygdala … The thalamic pathway is thus faster. It cannot tell the amygdala exactly what is there, but provides a fast signal that warns us that something dangerous may be there. It is a quick and dirty processing system. (Ledoux 1996)

According to Ledoux, the crackling sound brought out by trampling on a dry twig is a fast message, though our brain cannot tell that it is a dry twig. This study has significant messages for human interaction. For example, where a person is carrying a sickle to his paddy field, what is seen by another person may be quickly interpreted by the amygdala as a danger signal. The relationship between the emotion of fear and impulsive actions is a very important concern within regular human interaction. Our brains can detect the danger even before we become afraid!

Fear and Anxiety

Ledoux says:

> Anxiety and fear are closely related. Both are reactions to harmful or potentially harmful situations. Anxiety is usually distinguished from fear by the lack of an external stimulus that elicits the reaction—anxiety comes from within us, fear of the outside world. The sight of a snake generates fear, but the remembrance of some unpleasant experience with a snake or the anticipation that you may encounter it are conditions of anxiety. Anxiety has also been considered as unresolved fear. Fear according to this view is related to the behavioural acts of escape and avoidance in threatening situations, and when these acts are thwarted fear becomes anxiety.
>
> Fear and anxiety are normal reactions to dangers (real or imaginary) and are not themselves pathological conditions. When fear and anxiety are more recurrent and persistent than what is reasonable under the circumstances, and when they impede normal life, then a fear/anxiety disorder exists. (1998)

Buddhist Perspectives on Fear

Fear as a 'moral emotion' is clearly presented in the discourses of the Buddha.

The Buddhist discussion on fear is somewhat different from the discourses about anger. Unlike anger, fear does not figure as an unhealthy root of behaviour, defilement or subliminal proclivity. Throughout the Buddhist discourses there is a visible ethical stance in the discussion of fear. Fear as dread of leading a bad life has strong ethical tones.

From an ethical point of view fear is neither good nor bad and the context is important. The fear of evil is to be cultivated. The Buddhist notion of a healthy conscience (*hiri-ottappa*) is important: *hiri* meaning shame of evil and *ottappa* meaning dread of evil. Also, fears consequent on excessive attachment to possessions and self-images, would obstruct contentment in this life and liberation from suffering. The roots delusion and greed provide a base for the emergence of fear. It has been mentioned that evil deeds may be done with four motives: partiality, enmity, stupidity and fears (A.IV.17).

Fear and Dread in Religious Life

There is an important discussion of 'fear and dread' in relation to the monk who has gone to the forest for a meditative life. As the monk lives alone in the forest he thinks about the possibility of encountering wild animals (A.III.99), especially snakes, as well as the possibility of having to confront tigers, leopards and bears. He may also have fears about old age and health, the availability of food and so on. According to the Discourse on Fear and Dread (*Bhayabherava Sutta*), the monk is gradually expected to master these areas of fear and dread (M.I.20–21). It is also said that if the monk has not got rid of defiling states of mind, even the rustling of fallen leaves, the breaking of a twig, and the movement of a peacock or deer may generate states of fear and dread. Also mentioned are those who are lustful, covetous, corrupt in heart, prone to anger and wickedness. If the monk harbours these defiled emotions, fear and dread will be generated. If a monk has these defiling emotions, he cannot secure concentration or delight in solitude. Those who master these conditions are described as end-makers of anguish.

The Buddha says: 'I frequent remote lodgings in forest and woodland wilderness, brahman, beholding two special reasons: beholding for the self an abiding ease here and now, and being compassionate for the folk who come after' (M.I.23–24).

Fear–Shame and Fear–Guilt Orientation

In the Gradual Sayings, the moral dimensions of fear are presented: fear of self-reproach (*attānuvāda bhaya*); fear of the reproach of others (*parānuvāda*); fear of punishment *(daṇḍa bhaya*); and fear of lower worlds (*duggati bhaya*). In fact, the first two are integrated as the Buddhist notion of conscience which is basically a fear–shame orientation rather than a fear–guilt orientation and this notion is found in *hiri-ottappa. Hiri is* shame of evil and *ottappa* is dread of evil. It is said that this positive sense of shame and dread is said to be an aid to self-control and personal autonomy as well as and aid to the development of social ethics.

There is an interesting rider about guilt and Buddhism, as some research indicates that early Buddhist tradition is more like a 'shame' culture like Japan rather than the guilt culture of the West that figures in the work of Sigmund Freud. In a study of emotion words in Sri Lanka that I did for a project of the East-West Center Culture Institute, I found that there was no Sinhalese word for guilt. But over the years the 'experience of guilt' is being seen in Sri Lanka, partly due to Western ways of thinking, so that Ruth Benedict's distinction into shame and guilt cultures may not always be applicable. Within the Buddhist doctrine, remorse and torment over past deeds interfere with the practice of concentration. In fact, it is said that evil done in the past may torment some people:

> Monks, as at eventide the shadows of the great mountain peaks rest, lie and settle on the earth, so monks, do these evil deeds that the fool has formerly done… lie and settle on him. (M.III.164)

Being tormented over past deeds interferes with the practice of concentration and the development of moral vigour for what is necessary is to put things right. In a study of the emotion lexicon and taxonomy that I made of Sri Lanka, it was difficult to find a Pāli/Sinhalese word for guilt. Compared with the society for which Freud wrote, guilt is not a central Buddhist concept, though the concept of confession (admission of wrongs done) is found in the community of monks. While at the level of Buddhist morality a healthy sense of shame and dread is advocated, at a more popular level, there is fear of ridicule and social disapproval (*lajjā-bhaya*) which is basically a shame orientation rather than a guilt orientation.

The Enigma of 'Objectless Anxiety' in Buddhism

While the notion that emotions are 'object-directed' is a paradigm in the philosophy of emotions, there has been significant interest in 'objectless anxiety' in the sermons of the Buddha. In Buddhist discourses, there innumerable instances, where emotions are directed towards specific emotions. For example: Videhika's anger at the slave Kali for getting up late on three successive occasions; the grief of Kisāgotami over the loss of her infant child. An emotion may be a loose kind of uncertainty, which the monk experiences in the forest and is described as dread.

The discourses describe an 'anxiety regarding the non-existent' (A.V.300). This is regarded as a subjective anxiety regarding the non-existent and an 'objective anxiety' regarding the existent. If he has lost some gold and grieves over it, that is objective anxiety. What is the anxiety which is subjective but does not exist? The eternalist who thinks that he will remain as an everlasting entity, hears the doctrine of the Buddha, the doctrine of the non-self and impermanence, and thinks 'I will surely be annihilated.' As a very insightful analysis, it may be said, the relationship between the self and anxiety breaks down, and it is this basic ambiguity between the self and the world, which makes objectless anxiety, this existential anxiety very revealing.

References

Buddha's Teachings.

Ledoux, Joseph. 1996. *The Emotional Brain.* London: Weidenfeld & Nicolson.

13
Destructive Emotions

In his conversation with Daniel Goleman the Dalai Lama said:

> Much human suffering stems from destructive emotion, as hatred breeds violence or craving fuels addiction. One of our most basic responsibilities as caring people is to alleviate the human cost of out-of-control emotions. In that mission, I feel that Buddhism and science both have much to contribute. (Goleman 2003)

In March 2000, a small group of internationally well-known philosophers and scientists sat down with the Dalai Lama to discuss issues which have a compelling urgency for the future of the world. Their focus was on destructive emotions. How do we replace these negative emotions with compassion, which is a positive emotion? Paul Ekman an expert on emotion studies, and Richard Davidson the neuroscientist, made a valuable contribution to this dialogue. Davidson focused on the pathology of anger saying that it can lead to rage and violence and that neuroscience could illuminate this search:

> Someone prone to pathological rage may be unable to anticipate those negative consequence of the extreme expression of anger. The inability

P. de Silva, *Mindfulness-based Emotion Focused Counselling*,
https://doi.org/10.1007/978-3-030-64388-1_13

> to anticipate these negative consequences appears to involve not just the frontal lobe but also the amygdala. There is a very recent study showing atrophy or severe shrinkage of the amygdala in people with a history of severe aggression. (Davidson and Begley 2013)

While the symposium on destructive emotions was a very valuable contribution and I have the book with me close for reference the psychological issues are always central. I am also exploring the ethical frontiers in this chapter.

I have presented a comprehensive study of the profile of anger but today we discern the emergence of destructive emotions in a world torn apart by crises and terror calls. In this chapter my focus is on Buddhist ethics—pathways for peace education. Richardson confirms that those who are brought up in a nurturing environment have a greater ability to regulate their emotions. In the contemporary world, the training in 'mindful emotions' has been a great success for generating a positive emotional climate and also developing mindfulness training, directed to countering anger, fear and depression: as I have shown in the earlier chapters.

Firstly, this chapter has a significant focus on *peace education* alongside the roots of war and conflict; secondly, exploring the moral dimensions of peace education; and thirdly 'exploring inner space' through meditation and mindfulness practice. As we are discussing peace education in the context of war, terrorism and conflict, we need to investigate the reasons for the collapse of moral values and explore solutions. I have emphasized the importance of mindful emotions as Davidson conveys, along with the moral dimensions and the blueprint for a nurturing society. The whole ethos of destructive emotions calls for a diagnosis. First, it is necessary to emphasize the vacuous nature of 'cold war peace'—the insidious role of the power of traumas of defeat and humiliation, and the memories of history. There is also a breakdown of ethics and responsibility within the technology of a war culture. Terrorism makes things more complex.

Restraints on Moral Identity

It is the 'wounds of war' that conditioned the minds of the defeated. And the kind of pseudo-peace that existed during the cold war in Europe was not based on mutual understanding and goodwill. Those who are wrecked by war and ruined and are struck deeply; and like the mythological phoenix that emerges from the ashes, they try to rise again from the embers. Here, we need to summon the near legendry words of the *Dhammapada*: 'Hatred can never be conquered by hatred, but it is love alone that can conquer hatred.'

Technological warfare has worsened the possibility of peace—*the memories of Hiroshima linger in our memories*:

> For scientists and others involved in the bomb, sympathy was inhibited by distance. They were only faintly aware of the people who were to be burned, blinded, blistered, shrivelled, irradiated and killed in Hiroshima. (Glover 2001)

In a remarkable study of the atrocities committed in Hiroshima, the Nazi genocide and Pol Pot's Cambodia, he says that in modern technological warfare, victims are distant and responsibility fragmented (Glover 2001). As Glover says, there is a sense of impersonality that separates the scientist who makes the invention of the deadly weapon from those who take decisions regarding its use. Also, the people who make the decisions are separated by a vast distance from the innocent victims. In this type of scenario, the *first casualty is ethics.* From here, when we move to global terrorism, we come to the border of moral anarchy.

While transmitted centuries ago, the message of the Buddha on the ethical and psychological dimension of war and peace is still relevant but needs a new vocabulary—*moral silence*: failure to verbalize and articulate one's moral beliefs; *moral deafness:* failure to listen to moral issues raised by others. *Moral blindness*: failure to recognize moral issues; *moral pessimism:* nothing worthwhile can be done. The fragmentation of responsibility of those who guide their nations, makes it easier for lapses in moral responsibility. When catastrophes take place at a distance, we need people with foresight, imagination and compassion.

> We need to make a distinction between peace as absence of war and peace as a state of tranquility founded on the deep sense of security that arises from mutual understanding, tolerance of other points of view, and respect for their rights. Peace in this sense is not what we saw in Europe during the four and half decade of cold war. The very premise on which it rested was fear and suspicion and the strange psychology of mutually assured destruction. (Dalai Lama 1992)

How does a nation deal with the shattering message of Hiroshima or the collapse of the World Trade Center in New York? How do we apply the ethic of non-violence? In a world torn by terror, crisis and chaos, to articulate a message of non-violence may look like holding up a red flag to a moving train. But Buddhism is not merely a message for times of calm and optimism. Its potentiality is also seen in moments of acute despair. Apart from the path needing to be at a collective level, there is no other path. Ideologies, identities and historical memories, and the wounds of grief and anger need a compassionate diagnosis. 'Memory without understanding may condemn people to repeat and suffer atrocities that so mark our humanity' (Glover 2001).

Terrorism of the kind that is found today was not present during the time of the Buddha. In a very elegant dialogue between Jurgen Habermas and Jacques Derrida, reflecting on the tragic events of 11 November 2002, Habermas considers certain forms of terrorism as a 'communicative pathology'. He says that certain forms of terrorism have no realistic goals, and if they tend to be nihilistic, they are not different from some of the criminal activity of today. Currently, the familiar political and social rhetoric is polarized between good and evil and no serious diagnosis is made for the restoration of the rule of law on a cosmopolitan order.

Jiddu Krishnamurti (1895–1986) says that the symptoms of far-reaching conflicts are seen in the clash of ideologies. The clash of ideologies may be cleared by rational dialogue, but use *of violence calls for a new model of peace education*. 'Fear, Pleasure, Sorrow, Thought, and Violence are all interrelated. Most of us take pleasure in violence, in disliking somebody, hating a particular race or group of people, having antagonistic feelings towards others. But in a state of mind in which all violence comes to an end, there is a joy which is very different from the pleasure of violence, with its conflicts, hatred and fears' (2014). Thus, if there is a different way of living, we shall be able to communicate with each other.

Krishnamurti writes a complete chapter on anger, the content of which is similar to the Buddhist analysis I have discussed in an earlier chapter. In fact, this book is on '*the education of the emotions*'. We need to explore new concepts and dialogues of peace education deeply within ourselves, within ourselves and our neighbours, and within the larger environment beyond us. In a classic sermon, presented several centuries ago, the *Kalahavivāda Sutta* of the *Suttanipāta* (vv. 862ff), the Buddha, in exploring new avenues of dialogue, emphasises that we need to replace an argument culture by a therapeutic culture of understanding each other. His criticism of racial, linguistic, religious and cultural identities generating continuous debate and argument as to who is right, presents a veritable perspective for peace education.

I shall conclude this chapter, with the poignant thinking of Thích Nh'ât Hạnh, the Vietnamese monk and philosopher. Reflecting on the futility, emptiness and devastation of war which he experienced, he has in his own way presented the ancient message of the Buddha, 'not through hatred, but love alone is the pathway for peace'.

Landscapes of War and Peace

> Life has left her footprints on my forehead,
> But I have become a child this morning
> The smile seen through leaves and flowers is back to smooth
> Away the wrinkles.
> As the rain wipes away footprints on the beach
> Again a cycle of death and birth begins.
> I walk firmly.
> I walk on thorns, but firmly, as among flowers
> I keep my head high.
> Rhymes bloom among the sounds of bombs and mortars.
> The tears I shed have become
> I feel calm hearing its sound on a thatch roof.
> Childhood, O my birthday is calling me, and the rain melts by despair.

I am still alive, able to smile quietly
The sweet fruit brought about by the tree of suffering.
Carrying the dead body of my brother, I go across the rice field
In the darkness.
Earth will keep you tight within her arms, dear one.
We have gone through a too deep a night.
This morning, yes, this morning, I kneel down on the green
Grass and I notice your presence
O, flowers that speak to me in silence,
The message of love and understanding has indeed come (1993–1996).

References

Dalai Lama (1992).

Davidson, Richard, and Sharon Begley. 2013. *The Emotional Life of Your Brain.* London: Hodder.

Glover, Jonathan. 2001. *Humanity: A Moral History of the Twentieth Century.* London: Pimlico.

Goleman, Daniel (ed.). 1997. *Healing Emotions: Conversations with the Dalai Lama, on Mindfulness, Emotions and Health.* Boston: Shambhala.

Goleman, Daniel, and the Dalai Lama. (2003). *Destructive Emotions: A Scientific Dialogue with the Dalai Lama.* Macmillan.

Krishnamurti, Jiddu. 2014. *Reflections on the Self*, new edn., ed. Raymond Martin. New York: KFI Publications.

14

Emotion Metaphors

I have already discussed the links between emotions and the body both with reference to Buddhism and Western thought. In this chapter, I am exploring a new and exciting field on emotion metaphors—not limited to the body. During the second part of this chapter, I will explore a few examples from the psychology of Buddhism. The thematic framework comes from a study done by Zoltan Kövecses (1986). This study focuses on *fear*, *anger* and *pride*. I am adding personal modifications to the examples, along with my classification and some of my examples. I will also look at the Buddhist discourses. As Buddhism uses both metaphors and similes, it should not be limited to embodied existence or to its vocabulary of liberation.

Metaphors for Fear and Anger

Physical agitation: he was trembling with fear.

Increase in heart rate: my heart pounded with fear; I began to feel my heartbeat clearly. As the student began his maiden speech, his heart

P. de Silva, *Mindfulness-based Emotion Focused Counselling*,
https://doi.org/10.1007/978-3-030-64388-1_14

was in the mouth. Lapses in heartbeat: my heart was having a lapse in heartbeat, when I realized that I did not find my purse in my pocket.

His face turned pale. His skin was prickling with fear. He was incapacitated by fear when he saw a large collection of white ants in the kitchen. A current went through my body as I listened to the ghastly murder story. The story of the murder made my hairs stand on end. Mobility: he was so terrified that he could not move his legs. She was frozen down to her boots. Inability to think: my mind went blank with fear.

He was wetting his pants with fear. Butterflies in the stomach. Dryness in the mouth. Body temperature: my blood ran cold.

Kövecses says that there are parallels regarding the body in fear and anger: increase in body heat; internal pressure; redness in the face and neck area, agitation and interference with accurate perception. Anger as fire is a central metaphor having its parallel in Buddhist discourses.

In general, the following metaphors summarize metaphors of anger: anger is a hot fluid in a container (boiling with anger); anger as smouldering; anger as insane with rage; anger at an opponent in a struggle; anger is something unleashed.

Buddhist Perspectives on Anger

> When anger does possess a man;
> He looks ugly; he lies in pain;
> What benefit he may come by
> He misconstrues as a mischance;
> He loses property (through fines)
> Because he has been working harm
> Through acts of body and speech
> By angry passion overwhelmed;
> The wrath and rage that madden him
> Gain him a name of ill-repute;
> His fellows, relatives and kin
> Will seek to shun him from afar;
> And anger fathers misery:
> This fury does so cloud the mind
> Of man that he cannot discern

This fearful inner danger.
An angry man no meaning knows,
No angry man sees the Dhamma,
So wrapped in darkness, as if blind,
Is he whom anger dogs.

Someone a man in anger hurts;
But, when his anger is later spent
With difficulty or with ease,
He suffers as if seared by fire.
His look betrays the sulkiness
Of some dim smoky smouldering glow.
Whence may flare up an anger-blaze
That sets the world of men aflame.
He has no shame or conscience curb,
No kindly words come forth from him,
There is no island refuge for
The man whom anger dogs.

The description of anger as fire is a common metaphor in the Buddha's sermons (A.IV.6–62). This is a short summary of a longer poem.

A Metaphor for Liberation, Beyond Suffering: Upstream and Downstream

'Right volitional attitude in coming to grips with the senses.'
Suppose a man is carried along in a
river by a current which looks delightful
and charming. Then a sharp-sighted man standing on the bank
seeing him calls out: 'Good man though you are carried along the river by a current
which looks delightful and charming, yet further down,
there is a pool, with monsters and demons.
When you get there, you will come to your death or painfulness',
Then that man, hearing the other's call,
struggles against the stream with hands and feet.

The Metaphors Are the Following

> 'A river current' is a name for craving.
> 'Looking delightful and charming' is a name of one's own sphere of perception.
> 'The pool further down' is the name for the five fetters belonging to the lower world.
> 'With waves' is a name or the five sensuous pleasures.
> 'With monsters and demons', a man's illicit for lure of women.
> 'Against the stream', is the name for freedom from craving.
> 'Struggle with hands and feet' represents the exercise of 'energy'.
> 'The sharp-sighted man' standing on the bank represents
> the arahant. (the perfected one. Itv.114)

Greed or craving is a concern common to both Buddhism and Christianity, where it is one of the seven deadly sins. Buddhism focuses on acquisitiveness, and covetousness. But in Buddhism, entanglement (*upādāna*) is a stage beyond craving and it is difficult to free one self. It is also an interesting metaphor as the entanglement may be either what is pleasurable or painful.

Metaphor for Defiling Emotions: Cleaning a Defiled and Stained Cloth

Vatthūpama Sutta (The Simile of Defiled Cloth)

If a piece of cloth were defiled and stained and a dyer dipped in some blue, yellow, pink or red dye, it would look poorly dyed and impure in colour. Because of the impurity of the cloth, so too when the mind is defiled a person will not have a happy destination. Whereas, if the cloth was clean, it would have been well-dyed and pure in colour and he would have a happy destination.

The following are the defiling emotions of the mind: ill will, anger, revenge, contempt, a domineering attitude, envy, avarice, deceit, fraud, obstinacy, presumption, conceit, arrogance, vanity, negligence (M.I.4).

The Bamboo Acrobat and Balancing Altruistic Emotions: How One Helps Another by Helping Oneself

A bamboo acrobat, having erected a bamboo pole said to his assistant: 'Climb up the bamboo pole and stand on my shoulder.' And Frying Pan climbed the bamboo pole and stood on his master's shoulders. The acrobat told Frying Pan: 'You look after me and I shall look after you.' Frying Pan replied that that would not work and that one needs to look after oneself: protecting oneself, one protects others and thus there is safety for both (SXL.VII.19).

A Turban on Fire

If on examination, a monk says: 'I usually remain covetous, with thoughts of ill-will, overcome by sloth and drowsiness, restless, uncertain, angry with soiled thoughts, with my body aroused, lazy or unconcentrated', then he should put in extra desire, effort diligence, endevour, undivided mindfulness and alertness, for the abandoning of the very same evil, unskilful qualities. Just as when a person whose *turban or head was on fire* would put forth extra desire, effort, diligence, endeavour, undivided mindfulness, and alertness to put out the fire on his turban or head… (A.x.51).

The Fool

Like spoons unable to taste
the flavour of the soup
are the fools who cannot see the truth
even though they live
all their lives among the wise. (Dh. v. 64)

Sadness as an Arrow

Seeking your own happiness, you should pull out your own arrow of lamentation, longing and sorrow (Sn 3.8).

Sadness is like a cotton fluff, blow it away (Sn.3.8).

Anger as Drops of Water

Anger is like drops of water on a hot plate (M.152).

Sadness as a Ball of String

> Just as a ball of string when thrown comes to an end by unwinding
> a wise man will make an end of pain. (D.2)

Craving as a Poisoned Arrow (M.I.105)

A man struck by a poisoned arrow wishes to know: who sent the arrow, what is the arrow made of, where does he live? By the time all these questions are answered, the injured man would have died. This is compared with the philosopher engrossed in metaphysical questions regarding who created the world and when did this happen, etc. without working out the path to liberation from suffering (as told by Thích Nh´ât Hạnh 1994).

> Passion is like scattered embers. (Thi.14)
> Like water on a white lotus do not adhere, passions do not stick in a liberated mind. (M.I.105)

Mindfulness

Watchfulness of a door keeper; instilling discipline like a horse trainer; persistence of an army defending a fortress; balance and vigilance of an acrobat (Buddhist sermons).

References

Buddhist Sermons.
de Silva, Padmasiri. 2005. *An Introduction to Buddhist Psychology and Counselling*, 4th ed. London: Palgrave Macmillan.
Kövecses, Zoltán. 1986. *Metaphors of Anger, Pride and Love*. Amsterdam and Philadelphia: John Benjamins.
Thích Nh'ât Hạnh. 1994. *Zen Keys*. New York: Harmony.

15

Compassion

Both the field of contemporary moral philosophy, and the drive towards positive mental health have brought compassion to the centre of current psychological issues. In philosophy, the excesses of the emotive theory of ethics, reducing statements of ethics to expressions of emotions have had a very critical response from philosophers like Bernard Williams (1972). Also, there is a revival of interest in moral psychology, and traditional studies like Philippa Foot's *Virtues and Vices* (1978) were coming to generate new dimensions for ethics. There is a real interest in traditional concerns like virtues and vices closer to Buddhism than some of the more epistemology-oriented trends in current moral psychology. Also, there is an important link to emotions. There has been a shift of interest to moral *sensitivity* and *character. Excessive concern with choice and volition may obscure the more rich and complex aspects of moral life, where the role of human emotions is more visible.*

Even in the preoccupation with choice, subjects like unconscious/subliminal motivation, involuntary sins, emotions and responsibility are issues frequently studied. Deciding is not merely a matter of choice of two alternative ways of responding to a situation but a decision about the kind of person one wishes to be. This is the holistic

P. de Silva, *Mindfulness-based Emotion Focused Counselling*,
https://doi.org/10.1007/978-3-030-64388-1_15

milieu within which questions are raised and answered. As there is a great convergence of moral psychology and ethics, this places the study of emotions in a new setting. Currently, Ledoux will say to discuss ethical choice and the role of volition in the complicated texture of human motivation without looking at the region of subliminal motives (Buddhist *anusaya*) would be like 'staging Hamlet without the Prince of Denmark. In fact, more important as Carl Jung (1875–1961) says, there can be 'subliminal goodness'. I have presented this idea in a new interpretation of the *Aṅgulimāla Sutta* (de Silva 2017, pp. 183–194) with parallels to the character of Raskoinikov, in Dostotevsky's *novel Crime and Punishment*.

Some insights from, Dialectical Behaviour Therapy (DBT), and the remarkable transformation of a drug addict, who after cure, through DBT, spent the rest of her life in a monastery. I am now doing more work on the SUBLIMINAL (both good and bad [*kilesa*] and I need to consult my *guru*).

A work that breaks new ground is Lawrence Blum's, *Friendship, Altruism and Morality* (1980). Current trends in Anglo-American philosophy have paid very little attention to emotions says Blum, and I shall present his views. In the latter part of this chapter I shall also present a very brief review of current trends. But Blum who initiated this early perspective on *emotions and morality* is particularly important. Blum's focus was on the caring relationship in the family. The neglect of the role of emotions in morality was due to the popular view of emotions as transitory, changeable and capricious: 'So, changeableness and capriciousness are not so much characteristic of all altruistic emotions as they are of weak, superficial or otherwise inadequate instances of them' (Blum 1980). He says that altruistic emotions are his central concern: compassion, benevolence, generosity, kindness, thoughtfulness, charity and love.

Moral philosophy needs to examine the logic of these emotions and I shall also present an integral perspective on altruistic emotions in Buddhism. This project needs to counteract the Kantian perspective on moral emotions. Though the popular opposition in ethics has been between the deontological ethics of Kant and the teleological consequentialism of the utilitarianists, there is room for a third alternative which emphasizes the altruistic view which is grounded in a direct concern for the wellbeing of others. An interesting perspective which has a focus on compassion as a moral emotion is found in the work of Schopenhauer (1965), *On the Basis of Morality.* This work opened up new horizons on compassion, especially as Buddhism had an impact on Schopenhauer.

My context for this inquiry is an interest in developing an alternative to Kantianism, in particular to his minimization of the role of emotions in morality and his exclusive emphasis on duty and rationality. I am influenced by Schopenhauer's critique of Kant's ethics and by his view of compassion as central to morality (Blum 1980). Buddhism does have a place for some of the utilitarian concepts of emotions as well as the notion of obligation and duties, but the vibrating directionality of the Buddha is in working for the welfare and happiness of others; *loving kindness*, *compassion*, *sympathetic joy* and *equanimity.* They provide the ideal ways of conduct for all living beings, including animals.

A point emphasized by Blum is the reaction to the high emphasis on will and choice in Kant. We need a new emphasis on character, emotion and human relationships. Also, this brings out an important link between ethics and moral psychology, which is a distinctive feature of Buddhism. Compassion is also an ego-transcending emotion. In fact, writing presently (2020, August), there is a remarkable resurgence of interest in compassion, care and human kindness. Even teachers who teach the nature of 'ethical dilemmas' in bioethics and environmental conflicts between ethics and ecology, have initiated the use of stories and parts of novels, where one can reach the base of human emotions and complicated springs of human motivation. Applied ethics need resurgent springs that add more colour to the logical battles that pervade their research and teaching. I have shown in the chapter on environmental counselling, how this new resurgence is emerging in environmental studies.

We need to get at the roots of the current crisis through what the several thousands of years, Buddha recorded in his sermons and I have done this with all humility in the chapter on Buddhism and environmental counselling.

Schopenhauer on Morality and Compassion

Schopenhauer looks at the anti-moral incentives of human behaviour and of these the most basic is egoism. Egoism is bound to the craving for existence and other ego-related activities, and the second is the incessant drive for sensuous pleasures. If these desires are opposed and blocked, wrath and anger emerge. The root of ill-will has many manifestations: envy and malice are intrinsically related to egoism. This analysis is very much reminiscent of the threefold craving in Buddhism, which I have presented in an earlier chapter. The craving for sensuous pleasures and craving for egoistic pursuits and the self-destructive urge emerges as a form of reactivity.

Compassion and Mental Health Care

Now that I have presented the value of compassion as an emotion, in keeping with the tenor of the present work on the therapeutic framework of Buddhist psychology, and the focus on 'Motivated Compassion' in the MA program on Buddhist counselling at the University of Hong Kong, I shall focus on compassion and mental health care.

In *The Compassionate Mind*, Paul Gilbert (2010), identifies two key qualities of compassion:

> The first the ability to be open to, moved by, and able to tolerate the suffering and distress of others in a nonjudgmental way. Second, is the desire, motivation and commitment to understand the source of suffering and to try to relieve it, by practicing appropriate ways of, a set of feelings, thoughts, and behaving.

Helen Spandler defines it as the following:

> While compassion might be thought of as an individual emotion, a set of feelings, thoughts, and motivation inside someone's head, it is actually a complex, multifaceted psycho-social process. Compassion develops, is

> enacted and supported (or inhibited) within relationships and contexts. (2018)

It is also necessary to have kindness and empathy for the practice of compassion:

> What is frequently left out of discussion of compassion, which appears to reduce it to empathy or kindness is the deep *awareness of one's own suffering* as well as the suffering of other living beings. (Spandler 2018)

In fact, one's understanding of personal vulnerability is important. It is not a weakness but a basic facet of one's experience of compassion for others. Another important point is that compassion has to be cultivated and Spandler recommends this horticultural metaphor. The collective notion of compassion is seen very often in Buddhist rituals, where a gift is offered to a monk in the context of grieving for someone lost. Compassion will grow in a healing and therapeutic environment, a point greatly emphasized by Spandler. The more vigorous it is as a part of moral life, the more its therapeutic potential will increase. Psychiatry is unfortunately often disease centred, a point which has been recognised by the positive psychology movement.

A Buddhist Perspective on Compassion

Mettā, Karuṇā, Muditā, Upekkhā are considered as the four sublime states. A Buddhist perspective on compassion has to be understood in the way that these concepts are interrelated. *Mettā* is rendered as loving kindness, *Karuṇā* as compassion, *muditā* as sympathetic joy, and *upekkhā* as detachment.

Buddhism is greatly focused on insight meditation and tranquility meditation, while compassion is doing practical things along with a dimension of compassion meditation. In an article entitled, 'Buddhism and Universal Compassion', there is a very good description of the four divine/sublime states:

> However early Buddhism did not rely on insight alone to develop universal compassion. It also developed meditative techniques of four divine or sublime states (*brahmavihāras*), loving kindness (*mettā*), compassion (*karuṇā*), sympathetic joy (*muditā*) and equanimity (*upekkhā*). Loving kindness is the desire for all beings to be well and happy, compassion is the desire for all beings to be free from suffering. To have sympathetic joy is to have joy when others experience good fortune and to wish that their good fortune continues. It is the opposite of feeling envy when others are fortunate. Equanimity is a state of calmness and mental balance with respect to the happiness and suffering of others. In early Buddhism, these four are interconnected, as well as the meditations to cultivate them. (Struhl 2018)

Contemporary Dialogue in the West

There have been a number of critical points attempting to point out that though compassion is a praiseworthy ingredient in our ethical life, it is not central to the ethical life. The objection is that it is unreliable as a guide, it is sentimental goodwill, and its presence depends on good fortune. In response, it is said mature and idealised good will is immune to such worries. People cannot just claim to have done a compassionate act, unless a person has an ethically good heart. It needs developing a certain kind of skill. In fact, it deepens a contextual focus, whether it is social service or working in a hospital. The focus here will be on compassion regarding human relations, offering differing forms of goodwill. Struhl calls it the Aristotelian approach: a role differentiated approach, an approach that sheds light on the way in which the virtues of compassion involve different forms of will depending on relations and context. Sometimes, we may call a person a compassionate person, looking at him over the years. Or, we may say that a particular act is compassionate. There may be a mother who is very compassionate to her children but may not act as a compassionate person in other contexts.

As I have illustrated earlier, the Buddhist approach is different as it is a more holistic skill, drawing multiple meanings from the doctrine of human suffering (*dukkha*); the four sublime states; developing compassion as a meditative state; as well as the practice of compassion in more secular activity like giving a beggar a meal or giving a donation to a project helping suffering children in Africa. Also, there is an integral link between the four sublime states and the doctrine of non-self. It is a complete way of life, and to make it a Buddhist practice all these ingredients need to work in an integral way.

Sociocultural Dimensions of Compassion

As presented by Helen Spandler, rather than seeing compassion as an individual emotion, exploring its sociocultural contexts, and the barriers to obtaining compassion in mental health services is emerging as a significant contemporary issue:

> Another limitation of the common understanding of compassion is that it is often seen as merely an individual quality, virtue or trait. Although it can be expressed by and through individuals, compassion is nurtured, cultivated (inhibited) within environments, cultures and contexts.
>
> The view that compassion can be facilitated, or inhibited within a different social and cultural system and thus extra efforts need to be made to create the conditions where compassion is more likely to flourish is important and thus within a Buddhist community regular sermon would focus and encourage listeners to cultivate compassion as a meditative state as well as inspiring social activities of helping those who are in need. That empathy, kindness and compassion have therapeutically healing powers is now recognised in neuroscience. Especially in aged care institutions, threat and force on patients would be counter-productive. (Spandler 2018, p. 129)

At REGIS where I live, I find the nurses whom I meet as remarkable models of compassion. I hardly know their religion, and any way Buddhists are very few. Culturally, they are very close to me, Nepal, India, Sri Lanka (my motherland), Thailand, South Korea, Japan, Philippines, China Cambodia, Vietnam. What a colourful expression of real compassion and human kindness. I keep to myself the message of Buddhism as the mindfulness path to move out of the cycle of human suffering, but it is this very Buddhist roots that open me like a flower to the bees around—to these wonderful people around. As I mentioned in my DEDICATION to the book-thy are the 'Unsung Heroes and Heroines of our Times', like their counter part, the fire Fighters of Australia whom, I have applauded with a poem that came from my heart: Animal Carnival (see, Appendix to the book).

References

Bagnoli, Carla. 2019. Compassion and Practical Reason: The Perspectives of the Vulnerable. In *The Moral Psychology of Compassion*, ed. Justin Caouette and Carolyn Price. London: Rowman & Littlefield.

Blum, Lawrence A. 1980. *Friendship. Altruism and Morality*. London: Routledge.

Cokelet, Bradford. 2019. The Virtues of Compassion. In *The Moral Psychology of Compassion*, ed. Justin Caouette and Carolyn Price. London: Rowman & Littlefield.

de Silva, Padmasiri. 2017. *Emotions and the Body in Buddhist Contemplative Practice and Mindfulness-Based Therapy*. London: Palgrave Macmillan.

Foot, Philippa. 1978. *Virtues and Vices*. Oxford: Oxford University Press.

Gilbert, Paul. 2010. *The Compassionate Mind*. London: Constable.

Schopenhauer, Arthur. 1965. *On the Basis of Morality*, trans. E. F. J. Payne. Indianapolis: Hackett.

Spandler, Helen. 2018. Challenges and Opportunities in Mental Health. In *The Moral Psychology of Compassion*, ed. Justin Caouette and Carolyn Price. London: Rowman & Littlefield.

Struhl, Karsten J. 2018. Buddhism and the Problem of Universal Compassion. In *The Moral Psychology of Compassion*, ed. Justin Caouette and Carolyn Price. London: Rowman & Littlefield.

Williams, Bernard. 1972. *Morality: An Introduction to Ethics*. Cambridge: Cambridge University Press.

16

Connectedness, Mental Health and Solitude

Those who value different types of social connections and enjoy the different types of relations do not fall into the predicament of being lonely. Levels of 'connectedness' vary but the pain of disconnectedness generates issues of mental health and personal harmony:

> The pain of feeling disconnected is expressed in many ways including physical illness, anxiety, depression, low productivity, substance abuse and domestic violence. We have all experienced the pain of disconnectedness whether it be feeling lonely at a party, being ostracized by a peer group or experiencing family breakdown. Thankfully such experiences are short lived and when we intelligently reflect upon them, we can learn and grow. However, when isolation is persistent and severe it brings lot of other problems with it. (Hassed 2008)

It is very necessary to distinguish *loneliness* from *solitude*:

> Social isolation is not the same as solitude. Solitude can be healthy, such as taking time to reflect, enjoying peace in meditation or enjoying being on the top of a mountain. *We can be connected and be in solitude at the*

P. de Silva, *Mindfulness-based Emotion Focused Counselling*,
https://doi.org/10.1007/978-3-030-64388-1_16

> *same time*. Conversely, we can be among many people and be socially isolated at the same time. (Hassed 2008)

The subject of solitude is important for Buddhists, as I discovered some of the regular, devoted practitioners at the Buddhist temple also lead very active social lives. Further, there is a great amount of material on loneliness and therapeutic resources, as I found in my own practice as a therapist. This is well brought out in the chapter on counselling for depression. But it is my thesis that a deep understanding of the *creative facets of solitude* offer a profound breakthrough and pathway for looking at loneliness:

Ours is an age where solitude tends to be discussed in the context of the problem of loneliness. However, in previous ages the capacity to seek fulfillment outside society has been admired and seen as a measure of discernment and inner security. In his lucid and highly readable book, Peter France shows how hermits, from the Taoists and ancient Greeks to the present day, have something vitally important to say to a society that fears solitude (1996).

> *Alone* has quite a different meaning, alone has beauty. To be alone means something entirely different. And you must be alone. When a man frees himself from the social structure of greed, envy, ambition, arrogance, achievement, status—when he frees himself from those then he is completely alone. That is quite a different thing. Then there is great beauty, the feeling of great energy.
>
> But loneliness is not that. Loneliness is the complete sense of being isolated from everything. I do not know if you have felt it. The more you are awake, the more you are questioning, looking, asking, demanding, the more you are aware of it: deep down in your consciousness, at all levels, you feel completely cut off. And that is one of the great sorrows—not being able to go beyond it, and being caught in that tremendous feeling with its great energy. (Krishnamurti 1997)

Hermits and the Blessings of Solitude

France gives a running commentary of different cultural versions of hermits and solitude. I shall give a kind of snapshot version of this stimulating work (1997). Due to the nature of the present work being focused on Buddhism, I have only selected references to Taoism/Confucianism (fascinating contrasting attitudes) as well as Henry David Thoreau, the environmentalist, the philosophy of melancholy, and solitude and emptiness in Thomas Merton. I shall contrast these profiles with an interesting *blend of the ethical foundations of a good society in Buddhism with the recluse on the track of ideal solitude.*

Confucius presents the traditional well-defined social relations between father and son, sovereign and subject, husband and wife, brother and brother and friend, and friend and friend. The Confucian virtue was described as *jen*, a basic sense of humanity: doing the right thing by one's fellow human beings. In fact, this is reminiscent of the Buddhist *Sigālovāda Sutta*, presenting ideal relations between parents and children, husband and wife, employer and employee, friend and friend, and recluse, and laymen.

Taoism offers an interesting contrast. Lao Tzu (Laozi) composed the celebrated *Tao Te Ching* (C. 道德经; Dàodé Jīng), a kind of manifesto for the solitary life:

> The essence of the teaching is that it is by withdrawing rather than asserting ourselves, through retreat rather than pursuit, by inaction rather than action that we acquire wisdom. We have to unlearn the superficial cleverness that we have developed to get on in society, to cease to compare with others, and to learn to live alone. (France 1996)

Solitude is healthy, according to the Taoist, because it removes us from the mutilating pressures of society and exposes us to the healing influence of nature (France 1996).

> There is no greater sin than desire,
> No greater calamity than envy,
> No greater adversity than pining for
> Something for oneself.

Therefore, he who knows enough is
Enough will always have enough. (France 1996)

Henry David Thoreau at Walden Pond

There has been much speculation as to why Thoreau went off to live as a hermit. This was his response to the question:

> I went to the woods because I wished to live deliberately, to front only the essential facts of life, and see if I could not learn what it had to teach, and not, when I came to die, discover that I had not lived. (France 1996)

His great idea was to lead a life where communion with nature would transform his life. Later he went to Walden Pond and built his own little cabin with the help of people and then planted his own vegetable garden. His life was greatly illuminated by living close to nature and his writings embody a kind of wisdom which just naturally dawned on him as a part of himself.

Thomas Merton and the Solitary Calling

Thomas Merton (1915–1968) was the hermit celebrity of the time; he sought solitude but had no commitment to obscurity and in this fascinating profile, we get a glimpse of a hermit's life—emotional, practical, psychological and spiritual. Merton described the solitary life in paradoxical terms:

> [O]ne who is called to solitude is not called merely to imagine himself as solitary, to cultivate the illusion that he is different, withdrawn and elevated. He is called to emptiness. And in this emptiness, he does not find points upon which to base a contrast between himself and others. On the contrary, he realises, although perhaps confusedly, that he has entered into *solitude that is really shared by everyone*. It is not that he is solitary, while everyone else is social: but that everyone is solitary, in a solitude

> masked by that symbolism which they use to cheat and counteract their solitariness....
>
> The solitary is one who is aware of solitude in himself as a basic and inevitable human reality, not just as something which affects him as an isolated individual. Hence his solitude is the foundation of a deep, pure and gentle sympathy with all other men whether or not they are capable of realising the tragedy of their plight. More—it is the doorway by which he enters into the mystery of God and brings others into that mystery by the power of his love and his humility. (France 1996)

'Withdrawal from other men can be a special form of love for them. It should never be a rejection of man or his society' (France 1996). Merton, author of an essay titled 'Anatomy of Melancholy', was appreciative of Zen Buddhism. In an essay entitled, 'Rain and the Rhinoceros', Merton reviews the play of rain in nature in a way that is close to Zen Buddhism, seeing modern man as having no time and no taste for solitude. Robert Burton's *Anatomy of Melancholy*, written in the seventeenth century, stimulated not just Merton but also Freud in his reflections on grief and depression (France 1996).

A Buddhist Perspective on Health, Wellbeing and Solitude

Buddhist philosophy combines a social ethic for the layman and a meditative life for the layman and monk. Solitude is not an end in itself. A layman also seeks solitude either in a retreat or few hours in daily life. A monk in his meditative life would often seek some sort of solitude. The ideal recluse is described in the celebrated *Bhaddekaratta Sutta* (The Discourse on the Ideal Lover of Solitude, M.III.187):

> One who dwells ardently
> By day, by night untiringly
> Him the tranquil sage has called
> The Ideal Lover of Solitude. (Nyānānanda 2012)

The forest and the root of a tree, and an empty hut, are standard descriptions for a monk's meditative life. An appropriate environment and suitable physical postures are recommended for meditation. Though, during contemporary times special meditation centres with modern facilities have emerged.

Mental Health Issues: A Buddhist Perspective

Attitude Towards the Self

Having now looked at connectedness and patterns of solitude, it would be most relevant to briefly describe the concept of ideal mental health and wellbeing from a Buddhist perspective. It is best described in the words of Erich Fromm:

> Well-being is possible to the degree to which one has overcome one's narcissism, to the degree to which one is open, responsive, sensitive, awake, empty.... Well-being means, finally to drop one's Ego, to give up greed, to give up chasing after the preservation and aggrandizement of the Ego, to be and experience one's self in the act of being; not in having, preserving, coveting, using. (Fromm 1964)

These words offer some stimulating parallels to the notion of emptiness in Thomas Merton's description of the ideal person. Fromm had a long correspondence with the German monk in Sri Lanka, Venerable Nyānaponika, and was inspired by Buddhism.

Reality Orientation

In the Western context, the normal individual is fairly realistic in his appraisal of his own reactions and abilities and knows what is going around him. It is the middle ground between running away from a situation and over-valuing one's skills. In Buddhism there is a deeper awareness and a critical encounter with the changing nature of things (*aniccā),* their basic unsatisfactoriness (*dukkhā*) and moving out of deep-seated egoism (*anattā).*

Self-Knowledge

After breaking the metaphysical and psychological frontiers of the ego with the practice of mindfulness, the mind will lose any form of rigidity, and clarity and luminosity emerges. In the moment-to-moment flow of life, mindfulness practice will help the individual to note, identify and label passing states of reactive anger, envy, conceit and yearning for things one does not possess.

Voluntary Control and Autonomy

As the mind becomes pliable and open, it becomes easy to break through automatic, conditioned and compulsive behaviour.

Ability to Form Sensitive and Satisfying Relations with Others

Instead of developing relations based on greed, power, domination, dependence and power, productive relations of care, friendship, trust and compassion emerge.

Body-Mind Integration

Such integration may be seen in ordinary life or is developed both in tranquility meditation and insight meditation

References

Burton, Robert. 1927. *The Anatomy of Melancholy*. New York: Farrar and Reinhart.

France, P. 1996. *Hermits: The Insights of Solitude*. New York: Chatto and Windus.

Freud, Sigmund. 1957. *Mourning and Melancholia*, Standard ed., vol. 14. London: Hogarth Press.

Fromm, Erich. 1964. *The Heart of Man*. New York: Harper & Row.

Hassed, Craig. 2008. *The Essence of Health*. Sydney: Random.

Krishnamurti, Jiddu. 2014. *Reflections on the Self*, ed. Raymond Martin, new ed. New York: KFI Publications.

Nyānānanda, Thero. 2012. *Concept and Reality in Early Buddhist Thought*. Kandy: Buddhist Publication Society.

17

Greed, Sensuality and the Acquisitive Drive

Buddhist psychology traces human suffering to unwholesome roots: greed (*lobha*), sensuality (*kāma taṇhā*) hatred (*dosa*), *ego* illusion (*moha*). Even in Christianity, greed is one of the seven deadly sins, and they have a wide-ranging vocabulary with the main vices being acquisitiveness, covetousness, cupidity, and the quiet and sombre virtues being humility, charity and veracity. Buddhism refers to three facets of craving for sensuous pleasures (*kāma-taṇhā*), craving for egoistic pursuits/acquisitiveness (*bhava-taṇhā*) and the craving for self-focused aggression/destructive urge:

> Ever true to its own acquisitive drive, greed has functioned under a multiplicity of aliases ranging from 'acquisitiveness' itself to 'covetousness', 'avidity', 'cupidity', 'avarice' and on to some of the more particularized metonyms like 'miserliness' or of course 'simony', the most recently coined of the lot. (Tickle 2004)

It is very interesting that in the same study, there is a reference to Buddhism:

P. de Silva, *Mindfulness-based Emotion Focused Counselling*,
https://doi.org/10.1007/978-3-030-64388-1_17

> Humility, charity and veracity is found within the Asian faiths, where they are taught as tools necessary to ward off or overcome sins, which are regarded as 'obstacles', so to speak, to the exercise of virtue. The Buddha, for instance, identified, greed, hatred and delusion as impediments to right living, naming them as 'three poisons' rather than created agencies. (Tickle 2004)

It is fascinating to discern these comments in a book series devoted to the study of the seven deadly sins, and also a book on greed written by Tickle describing grasping, avarice, covetousness and miserliness. In fact, the seven deadly sins, greed, pride, envy, sloth gluttony, lust, and anger figure as negative emotions in Buddhism, though the basic ethics, psychology, and metaphysics have certain differences. In the Buddhist practice of mindfulness, there is a specific focus on the conative and emotional side of our lives. Lust, anger and delusion, cover the motivational and emotional facets of our lives. These roots are related to a wide-ranging list of emotions. In fact, anger feeds on more than minor irritation and aversions, namely on envy, depression and boredom where the anger element is not very visible. Greed is more visible but often not seen as 'greed', as the tenor of daily life makes it difficult to unravel the margins of daily living, of earning and craving for 'this and that'. At this point a 'balanced life' is greatly recommended in Buddhist sermons.

Several sermons deal with the dimensions of a householder's life such as: working at a profession, earning, being thrifty and saving. In a later chapter dealing with 'environmental counselling' and Buddhist economics, the Buddhist analysis of a balanced and sustainable life will be provided. The Buddha did not limit his sermons to a critique of acquisitiveness and greed but also provided the details for leading a balanced life for householders as different from the more stringent ethics for the monks. In the context of meditation practice, the fever of lust is compared to a fire within; the physical tension of anger to being controlled by a forceful opponent; and delusion, to a person hopelessly entangled in a net (Analayo 2010). In the light of this metaphor, Analayo says the mindfulness practice is focused on both the conative and emotional side of the meditator. Chapter 6 is focused on the conative concepts of intention and volition.

One of the subtle points about human psychology emerged during the financial crisis, where excessive greed prevented the speculators from seeing the imminent collapse of their unending indebtedness to the banks. A delightful insight is presented through what is called, 'sand pile logic'. A child is making a beautiful sandcastle and gradually increases its height. The beauty increases with each layer… one more layer… one more layer… until it collapses. The financial crisis was built by the sandcastles of people nourished by unregulated bank loans. It was not merely an individual calamity but a social calamity.

Buddhism offers a kind of radical therapy:

> We are tempted to believe that certain achievements and possessions will give us enduring satisfaction. We are invited to imagine ourselves scaling a steep cliff face of happiness in order to reach a wide, high plateau on which we will live the rest of our lives; we are not reminded that as soon as we gain the summit, we will be called upon again into fresh lowlands of anxiety and desire. (de Botton 2004)

Sensuality and Boredom

The Buddha examined the nature of the threefold nature of craving in terms of the craving for sensuous pleasure (*kāma-taṇhā*), egoistic pursuits (*bhava-taṇhā)* and the craving for self-aggression (*vibhava-taṇhā*). In the manner that strong craving results in frustration incessant sensuous lust may end up in boredom. Man relishes the delights of sensuality with an incessant drive for variety and a vicious circle of unending pleasures. Søren Kierkegaard's depiction of the pleasure lover in his novel *Either/Or* written with strong sense of irony is a very mature perspective, which fits in well with the Buddha's presentation of the pleasure lover (Kierkegaard 1962). Man relishes the delights of sensuality and holds on to them with a strong tenacity. The pleasure drive renews itself with searching for variety and variegated forms of pleasure. When boredom emerge, he searches for more diversions. There is an endless process where he searches for more secretive and enigmatic pleasures. The ambiguity and inner contradictions in this lifestyle are very illuminating.

The concept of *kāma-taṇhā* has a very broad usage that goes beyond 'sexuality', as such it goes beyond mere 'sexuality' to sense-gratification. The Buddhist sermons refer to two important facets of (i) gratification of the five senses (ii) desires and passions of a sensual nature including sexuality. There is a natural predisposition in man to seek pleasure and be repelled by pain. As a pleasure principle, it is similar to the kind of pleasure principle presented by Freud (de Silva 2010). Unlike Western psychology, the Buddha's pleasure principle has a moral lining in addition to its therapeutic implications. A householder has a basis for legitimate sensual and sexual satisfaction. Complete abstinence and celibacy are for the monk. In the final analysis, it is not the sense organs or their impact that is crucial but the persistence and upsurge of the craving for sense gratification.

In an earlier chapter I referred to the subliminal level of activity for sensuality, anger and conceit. Further, when craving gets transformed into clinging there is also a hard layer for sensuality or egoistic pursuits. But the subliminal undercurrents (*anusaya*) may only be fully cleared in stages on the path to liberation. Western therapeutic systems including those of Freud do not have a spiritual goal of liberation, though up to a point Buddhism is able to share some of the therapeutic goals with Freud (de Silva 2010). As a liberation-oriented philosophy, it has a broader framework with a strong ethical focus, and based on that one has to understand the specific flavor of the concepts: though the basic psychology may be shared with most Western psychologies and therapeutic systems. In fact, the Buddhist analysis of mind, body and motivation may be profitably located alongside Western psychology, therapies and recent developments in neuroscience (de Silva 2017).

Ego-Oriented Behaviour

Ego-oriented behaviour has a number of cognitive roots in eternalism (*sassata-diṭṭhi*). It also has motivational roots in *bhava-rāga* and *bhava-taṇhā* and a subliminal base in *diṭṭhi-anusaya*. The craving for self-centered pursuits has its ideological roots in the dogma of personal immortality (*sassata-diṭṭhi*). There is a tendency to believe in a pure ego independently of the psycho-physical processes that constitute life. This bias towards egocentricity, rooted in the belief of an abiding ego manifests at various levels—linguistic, intellectual, emotional, ethical, and so on. The doctrine of egolessness (*anattā*) in the theory and practice of Buddhism, along with *aniccā* (constant change) and *dukkhā* (*suffering*), provides in a summary form the most central facets of Buddhism: as theory and noble practice. Practice involves different levels of depth and commitment, and it is a blend of moral conduct *sīla, samādhi* (practice of concentration) and *paññā* (insight through meditation).

This has to emerge as a way of life, day to day: refining ones understanding and practice. It is also a way of life that generates a tremendous refinement of human emotions. For those who fall a prey to the lure of possessions, acquisitions, fame, anger, and envy in the failure to obtain their longings, only a self-transforming change may bring about a radical change. The Buddha's compassion for transforming such people has been dramatized in the transformation of the thief Aṅgulimāla. There are little self-transcending acts that people are capable of performing that gradually nourish the intellectual and affective roots of liberation from the bondage of egocentric behaviour. This is the greatest journey in life—the path towards liberation.

Vibhava Taṇhā: The Drive for Self-Annihilation and Aggression

Though the craving for sense gratification and the craving for egoistic pursuits have been discussed in many studies, the craving for self-annihilation has not received the attention that it deserves. Building on a suggestion made by my teacher, the late Professor K. N. Jayatilleke (1920–1970), my post-graduate studies at the University of Hawaii, led me to the exploration of a fascinating study of Freud's death instinct and the Buddhist concept of self-annihilation and self-aggression (de Silva 2010). A very attractive scholarship offered by the East-West Center in Honolulu, Hawaii allowed me to pursue a PhD in East-West comparative philosophy, where I wrote a doctoral dissertation on Buddhism and Freud, with a focus on the philosophy of mind, which later inspired me to make the study of human emotions my hobby. Subsequently the East-West Center Culture Learning Institute offered me two-year professional training in emotion studies with a focus on the cross-cultural study of emotions: including Sri Lanka and many other cultures. This is the background to the present book on emotion studies. After I had completed an advanced diploma in counselling, my interest in emotion studies developed into the wider horizon of active counselling and mindfulness-based therapies.

While *bhava-taṇhā* arises with a conception of personality based on the dogma of personal immortality, *vibhava-taṇhā* emerges with the view that the physical and mental processes with the ego will be annihilated at death (*uccheda diṭṭhi*). Though on a superficial analysis, the two appeared to be diametrically opposed, against the larger background of the law of dependent origination, they are considered as merely contrasting attitudes of a man bound to craving. There are both similarities and differences between Buddhism and Freud on the craving for self-annihilation and the death instinct.

Buddhism accepts hatred (*dosa*) as one of the three roots of human behaviour along with greed and delusion as a base for aggressive behaviour and as a reactive response. The root hatred, moves people in frustration and despondency into self-destructive behaviour, including suicide. The alcoholic addict who knowingly courts disaster by continuously falling prey to alcohol and the man who in the final act of suicide exhibits moment to moment ambivalence—'to live' or 'court death', illustrates how people flirt with the death instinct. It is a vacillation between two aspects of craving. In fact, Freud was the first therapist to highlight the clinical significance of the concept of ambivalence. In addition to ambivalence, one of Freud's greatest insights was what he called the 'repetition-compulsion', the demonic path to self-destruction: a concept Freud presented in his work, *Beyond the Pleasure Principle* (1953). Freud was baffled by the concept of the death instinct and presented it as a riddle:

> So immense is the ego's self-love, which we have come to recognize as the primal state from which instinctual life proceeds, and so vast is the amount of narcissistic libido, which we see liberated in the fear that

emerges as a threat to life, that we cannot conceive how the ego can consent to its own destruction. (1953)

The most significant context in relation to the concept of *vibhava taṇhā* is found in the *Middle Length Sayings*:

> Those worthy recluses and Brahmins who lay down the cutting of (*ucchedaṃ*), the destruction (*vināsaṃ*), the disappearance (*vibhavaṃ*) of the essential being, these afraid of their own body, loathing their own body, simply keep running and circling round their own body. Just as the dog that is tied by a leash to a strong post or stake keeps running and circling round that post or stake, so do these worthy recluses and Brahmins, afraid of their own body, simply keep running and circling round their own body. (M.III, *Sutta* 102)

References

Anālayo, Ven. 2010. *Satipaṭṭhāna: The Direct Path to Realization*. Cambridge: Windhorse Publications.

de Botton, Alain. 2004. *Status Anxiety*. Camberwell, VIC: Hamish Hamilton.

de Silva, Padmasiri. 2010. *Buddhist and Freudian Psychology*, 4th ed. Melbourne: Shogam Publishers.

de Silva, Padmasiri. 2017. *Emotions and the Body in Buddhist Contemplative Practice and Mindfulness-Based Therapy*. London: Palgrave Macmillan.

Freud, Sigmund. 1953. *Beyond the Pleasure Principle*, Standard ed., vol. XVIII. London: Hogarth Press.

Kierkegaard, Søren. 1843, trans. 1962). *Either/Or*, vol. I & II, trans. Walter Lowrie. Princeton, NJ: Princeton University Press.

Tickle, Phyllis A. 2004. *Greed*. Oxford: Oxford University Press.

18

Pride, Conceit and Humility

I have presented a number of emotion profiles through anger, sadness, grief depression, fear, anxiety, envy and jealousy. But the emotions at the base of our concept of 'self' are very important from a Buddhist point of view. Invariably, now, we look at both psychological and philosophical/existential issues in the style of a dialogue with the West. We also need to clear up Western misconceptions of Buddhism, as I have done in the case of anger.

Robert Solomon says that the self is a pole of emotional judgment, that emotions are self-involved, and that in many emotions, the self is implicit or in the background. Anger for instance involves a judgment that the self has been offended and yet focuses on others. Resentment is also self-involved with a personal stance of defensiveness. But yet ultimately, it is a point of self-reference implying subjectivity (Solomon 1977). From a Buddhist point of view the questions that arise are about self-centred attitudes, being selfish, and whether emotions may be grouped as egoistic and non-egoistic. Even in recent literature, there is unwillingness to probe deeply into the issue of the *reality of the self*. The literature also avoids the moral criticism of emotions in the context of the activities of the self in emotions.

P. de Silva, *Mindfulness-based Emotion Focused Counselling*,
https://doi.org/10.1007/978-3-030-64388-1_18

I wish to cite two instances, where issues regarding the self in emotional activity are avoided. Leila Tov-Ruach makes the following observations: 'jealousy is one of those emotions that perceives a danger to the self at its center and all the varieties of jealousy depend on a "contextually determined state of the ego"' (1980, p. 477). But, having presented a very stimulating analysis of jealousy in relation to the self, there is a reluctance to take this analysis further and examine the status of the self-concept: 'Whether the sense of the unity of the self and protection that sense evokes is an illusion, is a question we must leave for another occasion' (Tov-Ruach 1980, p. 477).

Another work, this time by Gabriele Taylor, deals with the emotions of self-assessment, pride, *shame, guilt, and it makes the linkage to the emotions and the self very central.* But here again, the notion of the self does not receive sufficient critical analysis (1985). However, she makes a passing remark, that there is no unchanging object of consciousness, which may be referred to as a self, but that a concept of a moral agent requires a degree of connectedness between states of consciousness. While these classificatory remarks are important, they are not well integrated into the central texture of the work. A more focused discussion of the issues relating to the reality of the self would have been rewarding. The Buddhist position is that a false sense of the self feeds negative emotions of conceit, envy and jealousy. There can be a healthy sense of pride and here linguistic usage in different cultures is important.

Out of the modern philosophers, David Hume's position is interesting as he clearly stated that the *notion of the 'self' is a fiction.* Taylor's analysis is concerned with the reflexive nature of certain emotions like pride, shame, and guilt and with beliefs related to the emergence of these emotions, but the issue about the reality of the self, which is a Humean concern, is not pursued. Taylor does raise the issues about the Humean concern that excessive pride is vicious and examines the grounds for it: like a person's pride being disproportionate, badly grounded and excessive. She also says, that excessive pride being vicious may be due to 'an undue degree of self-preoccupation'. But the link between the Humean position about the unreality of the self and its relation to morally negative emotions is not discussed. This is of course a central concern of Buddhism—as the *cognitive distortions about the nature of the self and its relation to morally negative emotions is not discussed*. In Buddhism the cognitive distortions of the 'self' have implications for the psychology and ethics of Buddhism.

There appear to be objections against the use of strong generalities (like the self or ego) as a conceptual aid to tidy up the study of emotion taxonomies. But yet, it may be said that emotions may be understood at various levels of generalities. Also, there can be some integration between these various levels of generalities. While it may be futile to search for some absolute patterns of order for ordering levels of emotions, there are recurring residual patterns moving towards a unifying focus.

Terence Penulhum's paper on self-identity and self-regard raises certain significant issues about the idea of the self in our emotional lives (1969). He is raising the issue about self and emotions in Hume, but is also concerned with the broader issue of the 'idea of the self in our emotional lives' and then makes a reference to Buddhism. Penulhum says that the role the self plays in our thinking about some of the areas of the emotional life is important for Hume. 'There is an interesting historical contrast to Hume's procedure, one which would have surprised Hume if he had been aware of it… the Buddha is said to have argued that the Hindu view of the self as identical with the cosmic soul is false, somewhat as Hume rejects the substantial analyses of the self (Penulhum 1969). Thus, Penulhum presents a significant issue: What is the place of the self in our emotional lives? Also, if there are parallelisms between Buddhism and Hume, how does Buddhism deal with this problem? Penulhum also feels that Hume's attempt to link the emotion of pride to the sense of the self creates a problem, as there is a great deal of ambiguity in the use of words like *pride* and *humility*:

> Pride is often discussed in theological contexts as though it included all forms of inordinate self-concern or self-absorption, not only those that involve a high estimate of oneself. One very common form of self-absorption [de Silva's emphasis too] is obsession with one's own inadequacies, so that one can find oneself speaking of some apparent forms of humility as examples of pride in this sense. (Penulhum 1969)

Three important points that emerge in this discussion. Issues about pride and humility; the self and the passions; and the parallelism between

Hume and Buddhism. What is intriguing in this analysis is that if the self is a fiction, then are we to say that the passions are also a fiction? The answer to this query is that the idea of the self that plays a key role in the genesis of passions like pride is not the one he finds in the metaphysicians whom he attacks in his book, but perhaps has a kind of *personal continuity*, rather than any sense of strict *personal identity*: as Amélie Rorty points out, in discussing the relationship between passions and the self, Hume's project does not require that he shows the strict identity of a person's motivational structure. All that the common-sense idea of the self requires is that such changes form a continuous narrative (1990). Rorty's interpretation appears plausible and offers a satisfactory answer to Penulham's fears about Hume and Buddhism:

> It is not surprising that Derek Parfit saw Hume as a predecessor who defended a theory of personal continuity, rather than strict personal identity with the characterisation of that person's interests and motives. (1990)

Steven Collins's *Selfless Persons* (Collins 1982) provides an excellent study of the parallels between Hume, Buddhism and Parfit.

Hume describes how the idea of the self is derived from the passions of pride and humility: these are passions par excellence, bound to the idea of the self, though it is a fiction. 'It should therefore be surprising that the passions provide the distinctive elements that comprise the fictional idea of the self as distinguishable from a reorganization of impressions and ideas that compose external objects' (Rorty 1990).

Moral Criticism of the Emotions

What is conceived as a negative emotion in Buddhism is conveyed by the Pāli term *māna* and I shall consistently render this as 'conceit' rather than the looser translation as 'pride' which in cross-cultural usage has a more positive rendering. Hume slips from the use of pride as having a positive meaning to pride having a more negative meaning. Buddhism does not use the term pride as a blanket term to cover all kinds of concern and it has specific distinctive features. According to the Buddha, the basic egocentricity finds expression in three forms, craving, wrong conception of the personality and conceit. Thus, Penulhum's claim that in a theological context there is a loose usage of pride as a blanket term does not apply to Buddhism.

Māna (conceit) is metaphorically described as flying the flag implying a desire to advertise one self. Etymologically, the term implies to measure oneself against others; in formal usage it is considered a false notion. Finally, in Buddhism, humility is considered a virtue and is clearly distinguished from feelings of inferiority. What is described as the 'bias towards egocentricity' finds expression in craving, conceit and false views. Hume uses humility in a negative sense whereas in Buddhism, it is a positive virtue. In Buddhist ethics due humility is recognised.

> Humility is a rare virtue and an unfashionable one and one which is hard to discern. Only rarely does one meet somebody in whom it positively shines, in whom one apprehends with amazement the absence of the avaricious tentacles of the self… The humble man because he sees himself as nothing, can see other things as they are. (Murdoc 1970)

References

Collins, Stephen. 1982. *Selfless Persons*. Cambridge: Cambridge University Press.

Murdoch, Iris. 1970. *The Sovereignty of the Good*. London: Routledge and Kegan Paul.

Penelhum, Terence. 1969. Self-Identity and Self-Regard. In *Identities of Persons*, ed. Amélie Rorty. Berkeley, CA: University of California Press.

Rorty, Amélie Oksenberg. 1990. Pride Produces the Idea of Self. In *Identities of Persons*, ed. Amélie Rorty. Berkeley, CA: University of California Press.

Solomon, R.C. 1977. *The Passions*. New York: Anchor Press/Doubleday.

Tov-Ruach, Leila. 1980. Jealousy, Attention and Loss. In *Explaining Emotions*, ed. Amélie Rorty. Berkeley, CA: University of California Press.

Part IV

Practical Issues: Issues Linking Health, Temperament, Education, Work, Environment and a Resurgence in Moral Issues

19

Buddhist Perspectives on Addiction

Basic Buddhist ethics is based on five precepts. Refrain from: killing, stealing, violating the sexual codes, lying, and taking intoxicants (liquor and drugs). Self-control is the virtue of living according to basic ethical values as embodied in the five precepts. Though a monk's ethical code contains a variety of codes, the five precepts are also basic for monks. These five precepts are the focus of complex points of interpretation in modern society. Contextuality is important in their application but there is no doubt that the five precepts remain as the bedrock of Buddhist ethics.

Self-control is the virtue of living according to one's values, insofar as a person has the courage of his convictions and weaves the precepts into daily life, with wise understanding and mindfulness. Moral weakness may be occasioned by some. Amends may be made by recovering one's ethics. Those in whom the breakdown is habitual are bound to face various forms of suffering: punishment by the state, losing the approval of fellow Buddhists and most damaging—the remorse of having lived a bad life, and collecting what is described as 'bad *kamma*'. In the case of addiction to alcohol, these days counselling is offered and that is one of the themes of this chapter.

P. de Silva, *Mindfulness-based Emotion Focused Counselling*,
https://doi.org/10.1007/978-3-030-64388-1_19

From the point of view of counselling, the puzzle remains as to why many addicts take an extra drink knowing that they will suffer. The irresistibility of different types of addictions locates alcohol addictions in the vicious circle of gambling, smoking, drugs and irresponsible sexual behaviour. In fact, in a recent study, *Addictions: A Disorder of Choice* by Gene Heyman (2009), there is new insight: 'The varieties of voluntary human destructiveness are at the heart of many, if not most, literary accounts of the human condition.' This quote was highlighted by Liza Shean in an editorial review (2011). Heyman says, that contrary to the common view that addicts display compulsive and involuntary behaviour, they are making choices when they take to addiction, and they can also make a choice to move away from addiction.

I have talked about my experiences in counselling in *An Introduction to Mindfulness Based Counselling* (de Silva 2014). In the light of my reading and counselling work, I find an interesting observation by Michael Stocker very insightful. He observes that people in moods of apathy, tiredness and even despair see all the good to be won but lack interest, desire and strength (1979). I found that one has to handle a client's problem at the very early stages so that the client does not succumb to a vicious circle of addictions. The clients also need warmth, encouragement and perhaps exercises in mindfulness with a constant reminder of the dangers of habitual drinking.

In consuming drugs, alcohol and cigarettes and engaging in compulsive gambling, people knowingly chose to do things that they will regret. Socrates thought that to *know* what is morally right is to do it. But Aristotle deviated and said that the self-controlled person can master the passions to which weak people fall victim, thus emphasising the motivational factors. Both of them identified self-control with the 'rational' faculty. From my experience, I find that practising Buddhist mindfulness is more effective and it is even powerful when it is woven into daily practice.

Buddhist Resources for Managing Alcoholic Addiction

1. Clients with alcoholic addiction can recover when they decide to take charge of their lives. Taking responsibility for one's life is the starting point.
2. Clients need to accept that an addiction is hurting them and wish to overcome it. They need to realize that addictions cause suffering. In cognitive therapy, the therapist attempts to change the way that the addict perceives the situation of incessant temptation, by looking at his own thought patterns, which are described as being on 'auto-pilot'. The Buddha's celebrated sutta, *Vitakkasanthāna Sutta* (Pathways of Thought, M.I.118–122) is an ideal resource for Buddhist cognitive therapy.
3. Once the *cognitive framework of the addict changes, developing his motivational strength is crucial*. The client has to feel confident that they can change and manage their time during the period of withdrawal from alcohol while the therapist has to find the ways and means of ensuring the client's motivational strength. Family and close friends can certainly help. A crucial point at this level is taking small and detailed steps.
4. Mindfulness and the attentional stance are crucial. Clients are given simple exercises in mindfulness practice that helps to break through the *stimulus response in addictive behaviour*. It is helpful if they find alternative ways of spending their leisure time, away from the hustle and bustle of a hectic world, and enjoy the stillness of the evening at home, perhaps over a coffee. Regular visits to the temple are recommended. Some of my clients experienced an emptiness that comes in the evening and it is this sort of context that make them search for alcohol. Music, gardening, evening walks or immersion in some sport helps to generate new energy. Otherwise, the demon of boredom invades their leisure hours. If the person works regularly at an office, spending an enjoyable weekend with the family or going on a picnic are ways of relaxation. 'When you stop taking the drug of your choice, there is a hole in your life where the drug used to be. Suddenly you

are left with empty hours that you don't know what to do with' (Bien and Bien 2002).

Today, the work environment generates lot of stress, as there is an accelerated speed which is dominant in an office where there are computers, statistics, and new techniques of analysing data with a focus on speed and accuracy. In such a context, people get baffled when they encounter uncertainty and setbacks. In fact, Leslie Claxton describes this predicament in graphic imagery: 'the tempo of the hare's brain has to slow down and get used to the tortoise mind' (1977).

A solution to this kind of predicament has been offered by Csikszentmihalyi in a learning model of complete absorption and joy described as the 'flow'—a state in which people are so absorbed that nothing else matters (1978). Working with artists, mountain climbers, athletes, musicians and others in diverse occupations, it was found that people who got completely absorbed in what they did had no holes to fill with cheap entertainment or alcohol.

'The magic of the ordinary' is a concept I applied to a few of my clients with alcoholic addiction. The theme emerges from the inspiring essay by Thích Nh´ât Hạnh, 'Eating a Mandarin'. Having a great deal of self-compassion and caring for oneself helps in obtaining a wonderful recovery of wellbeing. The philosophy of contentment is one of the great Buddhist resources for working through the challenges of life. Self-compassion has to be supplemented by developing a sense of connectedness and healing relationship with others, as loneliness is also a kind of demon that invades addicts.

Case Study: The Magic of the Ordinary

Anthony is neither a gambler nor smoker. Further, he is not an alcoholic. He is very devoted to his family. However, he enjoys life at the higher levels, is attached to status, and is very generous with his wealth. Unfortunately, he has some conflicts with his boss and is transferred to another branch of the company, which is somewhat poor in providing him with both status and income. The work atmosphere is not very pleasant and he begins to drink more than he usually would. Without realising it, he starts having an additional drink and quietly slips into a kind of addiction. People at home are becoming worried. His wife's reaction to his behaviour makes things worse, and once, when driving, he nearly crashed his car.

Fortunately, friends and social workers recommend counselling. Counselling opens up a new dimension to being kind to oneself and others. Anthony does have a relapse but makes a comeback to normality. Further, counselling opens up a diversified agenda for the evening, of gardening, cooking, listening to music and evening walks with his wife. Counselling makes him realise that he can have an occasional drink and enjoy it rather than trying to drown his disappointments at work with constant drinks which lead to very angry moods. He gets a new job which provides an excellent change of atmosphere.

In the evenings, after work, his wife prepares something special, like a nice samosa, which he enjoys. He also has coffee and does not look for the bottle—it is the magic of ordinary pleasures. As Thích Nh´ât Hạnh said, the person who is happy and contented will enjoy even a simple thing such as eating a mandarin!

References

Bien, Beverly, and Thomas Bien. 2002. *Mindful Recovery: A Spiritual Path to Healing From Addiction*. New York: Wiley.

Claxton, Guy. 1977. *Hare Brain, Tortoise Mind*. New York: Eco Press.

Csikszentmihalyi, Mihaly. 1978. *The Psychology of Optimal Experience*. New York: Harper and Row.

de Silva, Padmasiri. 2014. *An Introduction to Buddhist Psychology and Counselling*, 5th ed. London: Palgrave Macmillan.

Heyman, Gene. 2009. *Addictions: A Disorder of Choice*. Cambridge, MA: Harvard University Press.

Sheean, Liz. 2011. Addictions: A Disorder of Choice: An Interview with Gene Heyman. *Psychotherapy in Australia* 17 (4): 26–31.

Stocker, Michael. 1979. Desiring the Bad: An Essay in Moral Psychology. *Journal of Philosophy* 76: 744.

20
Health and Emotional Experience

Two studies on health, emotions and mindfulness experience have emerged. The first study is *Conversations with the Dalai Lama on Mindfulness, Emotions and Health* (Goleman 1997).

Can the mind heal the body? How are the brain, immune system, and emotions interconnected? What emotions are associated with enhanced wellbeing? How does mindfulness function in a medical context?

It is only in the past twenty years that Western physicians, biologists, and psychologists have begun to comprehend the interrelationship between emotional states and mental and physical wellbeing. Buddhist thinkers, however, have been aware of the mind's healing capacity for more than two thousand years.

The second study, a more recent contribution, *Mindful Medical Practitioners* (Dobkin and Hassed 2012), is a more recent study on mindful medical practice. I shall refer to the first collection of articles for reference and then refer to the more recent studies, emerging out of teaching mindfulness to medical students. But a more useful study for the average reader is *The Essence of Health* (Hassed 2008). These studies are recommended as works for reference.

P. de Silva, *Mindfulness-based Emotion Focused Counselling*,
https://doi.org/10.1007/978-3-030-64388-1_20

Daniel Goleman, in opening up the emotions to health dialogue, says that states of mind foster either health or disease and he suggests that distressing emotions can undermine health. In fact, both the body and human emotions are important for health. Francisco Varela presents a focus on the field of immunology, as *the immune system is like a second brain*: a network of specialized cells that give the body a flexible identity. Also, somatic identity has very specific links with the neural network underlying cognitive life, and makes up the new field of psychoneuroimmunology. Chapters 3 and 4 present the concept of somatic intelligence and the role of the body in counselling.

Goleman makes a distinction between 'afflictive emotions' and 'nourishing emotions' in terms of their impact on health. Anxiety, anger and depression may increase vulnerability to disease, while equanimity and optimism have a positive impact on health:

> The new discovery in the last five or ten years is that states of mind can affect the strength of the immune system and the robustness of the cardiovascular system. The particular emotional states I am going to review are the only ones on which there has been scientific research to any degree. The afflictive states reviewed are anger or hostility; depression, which includes not just sadness, but also self-pity, guilt and hopelessness; stress which covers agitation, nervousness, and anxiety; and repression, or the denial of anxiety. The beneficial states reviewed are calmness, optimism, confidence, joy and loving kindness. (Goleman 1997)

Chronic anger affects the length of a person's life and makes them liable to heart disease and cancer. Anger generates cynicism and hostility and affects one's relations with other people. Depression can often interfere with recovery from some initial sickness and also poses the threat of heart disease. For stress and anxiety, there is valuable material in Hassed (2008) which I shall explore later. Denial and repression have to be handled with Buddhist techniques of mindfulness. I have discussed the role of the subliminal level of anger, sensuality, greed and conceit in Buddhism with great detail in Chapter 4. Regular practice of mindfulness will certainly help to deal with denial and repression.

Wholesome Emotions and Healing

In ordinary discourse we speak of detachment, optimism and a relaxed state of mind. In traditional Buddhism, emotional balance is presented through what is described as 'equanimity' (*upekkhā*) which has many dimensions. In recent psychological studies in the West (Wallace and Shapiro 2006), 'affective balance' involves, freedom from emotional vacillation. Apathy and inappropriate emotions are well presented. 'Affective apathy' involves emotional deadness, and 'hyperactivity' involves excessive elation and depression, hope and fear, infatuation and aversion.

Five dimensions of equanimity are described in Buddhist texts. (i) It is used as a neutral feeling between pleasurable and painful feelings. (ii) It is used to refer to even-mindedness in the face of success and loss. Praise and blame occur within the definition of the eight vicissitudes of life: loss and gain, disrepute and fame, praise and blame, pain and pleasure. (iii) There is the equanimity that emerges within the spectrum of meditative states with different states of absorption. (iv) There is the equanimity used in the context of the celebrated four sublime states: loving kindness (*mettā*), compassion (*karuṇā*), appreciative joy (*muditā*) and equanimity (*upekkhā*). Though these are meditative states, they also function at the level of social discourse: for instance, treating friend and foe alike. In today's world one is now living at a time when because of the constant bushfires, floods, earthquakes and tornadoes, one can become infected with what is called 'compassion panic'. Equanimity may also at times degenerate into bland indifference. (v) Equanimity is also one of the seven factors of enlightenment.

Having social connections and developing a chain of friends is the best positive trait to deal with loneliness. The extent to which people have friends provides emotional support. What Goleman calls the 'human connection buffer' is sure to make you feel that you are not alone in the world of stress and conflict. Goleman adds that a good sense of humour and being open is good therapy, though not necessarily medically effective.

According to Francisco Varela et al., 'the interaction between the mind, the nervous system and the immune system provides a physiological basis for the influence of emotion on health' (1999). The study of responses between the nervous system and the immune system is called psychoneuroimmunology (psyche for the mind and neuro for the immune system): immunology being a new field.

The Brain and Emotions

Richard Davidson is a pioneer in the neuroscience of emotions. An associate, Clifford Saron has presented a summary of his work, which is central to understanding the link between emotions and health and how the brain organises our emotional life in Davidson and Begley, *The Emotional Life of Your Brain* (2013). When we look at the structure of what we describe as an emotion, it is necessary to break down its components. The first focus is: (i) cognitive dimension, judgments and thoughts related a state of feeling; (ii) observed behaviour like a gesture of anger or gentleness; (iii) facial expression, a spontaneous expression; (iv) a body sensation, involving lower brain centres that control the autonomic nervous system and the release of hormones where the effects are long lasting. A second focus is the cerebral cortex, where we focus on the emotional response.

Emotions can also be described in terms of 'approach behaviour' and 'withdrawal behaviour'. The left side of the brain is associated with approach behaviour and the right side of the brain is associated with withdrawal behaviour. It has been found that damage to each side has different consequences.

One very important contribution to an understanding of basic emotions is the revival by Paul Ekman of a Darwinian thesis. This thesis is that basic emotions are manifested in the face: anger, fear, sadness, joy and surprise. I have discussed the recent work of Paul Ekman and the Darwinian heritage in Chapter 5.

There have been many recent studies; one is the role of the amygdala in emotional experience and the other is the ground-breaking concept of 'neuroplasticity', a thesis by Richard Davidson, which I have discussed in earlier chapters.

Joseph Ledoux in his recent work, *Emotional Brain* (1996), says the amygdala is very quick—it makes a direct connection but is not very precise, because most of the sensory information goes via the other path, the path to the neocortex, where it is analyzed through several circuits while a response is formulated. The amygdala quickly assesses the nature of the sensory data.

The Clinical Uses of Mindfulness

In this section, I will summarize the role of mindfulness in health and healing, using a few central points provided by Jon Kabat-Zinn. He introduced a range of meditative techniques to the mainstream Western medical setting. In the hurly burly of the world, running after this and that, it is necessary to *slow down and explore the value of stillness* and to not lose contact with our own experience. This is true of both the mind and the body and the concept of healing is important:

> Have you considered the inner resources, perhaps even the wisdom that already exists in your body and mind? If you can uncover it and develop a way to use this energy, then perhaps, together with your doctors, you can move towards greater levels of health and healing. This is not curing but healing. (Kabat-Zinn 1990)

This is not a replacement for medical treatment but a supplement to it. Aspects of mindfulness training include: non-judgment, patience, acceptance and trust. Also important are non-striving, letting go and having a beginner's mind. He says that the therapists themselves do not teach the Buddhist *sutta*s but introduce them according to context and relevance. The most important thing is to trust in one's inner-being. Non-judgment includes seeing clearly without judging and non-striving is not to push to gain certain ends. The notion of a beginner's mind adds certain freshness to each project you do. Letting go is important as we tend to cling stubbornly to certain projects.

References

Davidson, Richard, and Sharon Begley. 2013. *The Emotional Life of Your Brain*. London: Hodder.
Dobkin, Patricia Lynn, and Craig Stephen Hassed. 2012. *Mindful Medical Practitioners*. Switzerland: Springer International.
Goleman, Daniel (ed.). 1997. *Healing Emotions: Conversations with the Dalai Lama, on Mindfulness, Emotions and Health*. Boston: Shambhala.
Hassed, Craig. 2008. *The Essence of Health*. Sydney: Random.
Kabat-Zinn, Jon. 1990. *Full Catastrophe Living*. New York: Delacorte.
Ledoux, Joseph. 1996. *The Emotional Brain*. London: Weidenfeld & Nicolson.
Varela, Francisco, Evan Thompson, and Eleanor Rosch. 1999. *The Embodied Mind: Cognitive Science and Human Experience*. London: MIT Press.
Wallace, Alan B., and Shauna Shapiro. 2006. Mental Balance and Well-Being. *American Psychologist*, October.

21

Exploring a Buddhist Theory of Humour: Humour as Pedagogy

Renowned meditation teacher Joseph Goldstein says:

> A sense of humour is indispensable in the practice of the dhamma, both in retreat and on the roller coaster of our life in the world. When we reflect for a moment on the quality of mind a sense of humour implies that we see that it creates some inner space. Being able to see the humour, the lightness, and the emptiness of the phenomena is really a great blessing during those times when we become caught in the various dramas of our lives. (1993)

One of the questions I have encountered in Australia is that Buddhism is essentially a serious concern with the challenges and conflicts in life, which involves exploring a way out of what the Buddha described as *dukkha* which though rendered as 'suffering' is almost untranslatable. It is a basic human predicament along with features of impermanence and the emptiness of what we consider as the ego and egoistic pursuits. Zen Buddhism explored ways of using humour to get the message of the Buddha across. When used for educating people who have an overburdened ego it is an instrument of skillful pedagogy. The Zen Masters were looking at the polarities and conflicts that people faced and with finding

P. de Silva, *Mindfulness-based Emotion Focused Counselling*,
https://doi.org/10.1007/978-3-030-64388-1_21

a way through dialectical conflicts for meaningful intervention through a sensible middle ground.

The question whether the Buddha smiled and whether Buddhism has a sense of humour are two different types of questions. I shall only briefly present the answers given by scholars to the question whether or not the Buddha smiled and will then present my own interpretation of a Buddhist theory of humour:

> There were those among Buddhist scholars who clearly would have preferred to believe that the Buddha never laughed at all, especially after his enlightenment experience at Bodhgaya. The Buddha's wisdom and the Buddha's mission seemed to require the ultimate in seriousness, gravity and solemnity. There was no objection to the suggestion that the youthful Siddhartha Gautama laughed during his self-indulgent period in his father's palace. In fact, laughter might well be seen as a characteristic expression of the frivolity and sensuality of his early life, prior to the discovery of the Middle Way and the Four Noble Truths. Laughter seems inextricably bound up with the young Gautama's self-indulgence. (Hyers 1989)

The scholastic attempt to deal with the apparent contradiction between laughter and enlightenment resulted in Bharata's theatrical treatise of six forms of laughter: *sita,* a faint smile, serene, refined and subtle; *hasita* which reveals the tips of the teeth; *ihasita*, a broader smile accompanied by modest laughter; *apahasita*, a more pronounced laughter associated with the movements of the head, shoulder and arms; *apahasita*, loud laughter that brings tears to the eyes, and *atihasita*, uproarious laughter. It has been observed that the Buddha displayed in certain contexts, *sita*, a reserved and tranquil, smile (Hyers 1989, pp. 266–277).

According to Hyers, the Buddha sees the contradiction/juxtaposition between his enlightened state and the unenlightened world of greed and sensuality. But I wish to add personally, the natural expression of the Buddha at the contradictions in layman's life would be compassion, though it is inevitable that the Buddha sees the contradictions. The only other useful study I have seen is Thānissaro Bhikkhu's *The Buddha Smiles* (2015). Though a useful study, it does not contain anything like the incongruity theory of humour, I am presenting.

Ñāṇavīra Thero on the Incongruity Theory of Humour

Venerable Ñāṇavīra (1920–1965) was a British philosopher who became a Buddhist monk later. He came to Sri Lanka with another scholar who was named as Ñāṇamoli after his ordination as a Buddhist monk. He and Ñāṇavīra Thero were ordained at Island Hermitage. Ñāṇavīra moved into a forest hermitage in Bundala, south of Sri Lanka. He belonged to the existentialist philosophical tradition of Søren Kierkegaard (1813–1855) and Martin Heidegger (1889–1976). His theory of the incongruity theory of humour was close to Kierkegaard's philosophy of humour.

Existentialist philosophy sees a kind of contradiction between everyday existence and the 'deeper cracks, fissures and holes in it which we ignore'. Sometimes, we honestly see them and laugh at them to keep them at a distance and through literary devices like a play we laugh and exorcise them to neutralize them. We need to be honest that through a comedy we are laughing at our own foibles. And if we conceal the true nature of things from ourselves, we do not follow the existentialist path of awareness through which we realize our own faults.

Venerable Ñāṇavīra Thera's work, *The Tragic, the Comic and the Personal* (1987) was a trailblazer for the present study. This work focuses on the contradictions within the temporal and shaky foundations of our sense of self—this is the father of all contradictions in our lives. Thus, he says that when we laugh at a comedy or weep at a tragedy what we are really doing is busying ourselves repairing all the little crevices that have appeared in our familiar world during the course of the day or week that if neglected go deeper into ourselves:

> The tragi-comedy of the human (*puthujjana*'s) situation as apprehended by the authentic man in his lucid anxiety is the source of all tragedy and comedy on the purely ordinary level. Whereas the inauthentic man laughs or weeps, without knowing why he does so—in other words irresponsibly. The authentic man, when he laughs at something is serious minded... he laughs and weeps with understanding and this gives his humour a depth and an ambiguity that escapes the inauthentic man. (Ñāṇavīra 1987)

Ñāṇavīra Thera sees interesting similarities in the incongruity theory of humour developed by the Danish existentialist thinker, Soren Kierkegaard and in fact, before ordination, he was a British existentialist philosopher by the name of Harold Musson.

Humour and Irony in Kierkegaard's Novel, *Either/Or* and the Buddha's Depiction of Sensuality

I shall present three versions of the incongruity theory of humour: Søren Kierkegaard (1813–1855) and Buddhism on the contradictions in the life dominated by sensuality; the book which led to a television documentary/satire of Alain de Botton on status anxiety; facets of Zen humour; along with parables from the sermons of the Buddha.

Kierkegaard presents three life styles in his philosophical novel, *Either/Or*: Firstly, the aesthetic life of pure sensuality; secondly, of seduction followed by boredom and melancholy and the ethical-mature life of marriage; and thirdly, religious life and their opposition. These conflicts are presented in a dialectical mode. Unbridled sensuality without commitment necessarily ends in boredom. His portrayal of sensuality, egotism and the flight from boredom describes in a graphic way the incongruities of the way of sensuality—similar to the Buddha's critique of sensuality. Kierkegaard wrote an academic thesis on 'irony' and thus his theory of humour had much depth (1843).

Kierkegaard writes through pseudonyms, keeping an impersonal distance, which helps him to develop a refined theory of irony. The seducer's diary presented in a theatrical medium captures the essence and the dilemmas of a life pervaded by a deep incongruity—which the seducer does not see but the audience sees. Pure erotic life is colored by enigmatic obstacles, both secretive and surprising, whereas conjugal life, in its ethical strands, stands for candor, open-heartedness, revelation and understanding. This is what the Buddha rejected and described as the *kāmasukhallikānuyoga*.

We are not always humiliated by failing to get what we wish, though it is only if we have not invested too much in our pride. In the way that Kierkegaard focuses on the contradictions in the pure life of sensuality, this study has a focus on pride and humiliation. Both the life of sensuality and human pride have figured in Chapters 17 and 18 of the present work. This chapter presents the same theme in a literary medium with the addition of a rare theme in Buddhist studies, Buddhism and humour. It is a most effective instrument of pedagogy. The important point, is that our level of expectation colors our sense of humiliation. This predicament presents the fissures and broken pieces of our lives through stories, drama and plays—with good humour, humility, veracity and mindful understanding of the application of Buddhist insights. It is only by opening our minds to a sensibility of mindfulness that, for instance, we see the early buds of envy and conceit within us. Today, in society at large, people are going through what the psychologists calls 'an identity crisis' and people are not aware that a hidden sense of pride, conceit and envy are besetting their daily lives.

In the television documentary, created from de Botton's *Status Anxiety* there is dramatization of status anxiety, and how it is fueled by jealousy and envy, the human emotions. Buddhist mindfulness of negative emotions clears us from disguised anger that feeds insidious envy.

The Buddha has emphasized the role of subliminal anger (*paṭigha anusaya*) which is at the root of human frustration. What is important is that television comedy has a therapeutic role in bringing to the surface our little anxieties, envy and false pride. With a laugh we come back as normal human beings. An English poet, Geoffrey Chaucer said, 'Envy is full of sorrow at another man's goodness and prosperity but joyous in another person's misfortune.'

Humour as Pedagogy in Zen Buddhism

Both Søren Kierkegaard and Ñāṇavīra Thera were focusing on the inner contradictions in the lives of people. They were looking at the polarities and conflicts that people faced and finding a way through a skillful pedagogy. Zen Buddhism presents humour as an aspect of its skillful pedagogy. Here is an example of conceptual blockages. The Zen Master was once asked to utter a profound truth, and he said: 'There is a river', but a younger follower, disappointed, repeated the question and the Master said: 'All right, there is no river'. This is an example of collapsing categories and the limits of dualistic thinking:

> The more people succumb to dualistic thinking in response to these polarities, the more they become trapped in conflict. And the more we as interveners buy into these dualities, the less effective we are in helping others to find a constructive way to move forward. However, if we are able to see these polarities as guideposts for finding a way through conflicts—and that each movement of them is an essential part of a larger truth that conflict presents we can achieve profound and meaningful intervention. (Mayer 2015)

The value of what are described as koans in Zen Buddhism is that we can often find deeper middle ground beyond conflict. Often the presentations are beautifully nuanced with a touch of humour which is a strong point in their pedagogy. Zen Buddhism was also integrated into Dialectical Behavior Therapy (DBT). DBT practice holds the concepts of acceptance and change together and Zen offers a rich harvest of their teachings and humour.

The Buddha's Use of Parables

In 'The Parable of the Raft', a man after crossing the river, carries the raft on his head. The Buddha says that the *dhamma* is to be practiced and this parable is a critique of the person who is intellectually engrossed in the *dhamma* without practicing it, merely displaying knowledge in debating and talks. Having embarked for the beyond, one has to exert oneself and gradually cross over with the aid of the raft.

The second parable is that of the 'Poisoned Arrow'. The Buddha cites the tragic predicament of a man shot with a poisoned arrow who refuses to allow the doctors to treat him until a number of questions are answered. Who shot the arrow? What is the arrow made of ? Where does the man who shot the arrow live? By that time these questions are answered, the man will be dead. This is compared to Māluṅkyaputta who gets it into his head, to find answers to speculative questions regarding the beginning and the end of the world without practising the *dhamma*. The Buddha also uses numerous analogies with a touch of humour.

> Though all through life the fool
> Might wait upon the wise
> No more dhamma can be seen
> Than the spoon the taste of soup.

References

Goldstein, Joseph. 1993. *Insight Meditation.* Boston: Shambhala.

Hyers, C. 1989. Humour in Zen: Comic Midwifery. *Philosophy East and West* 39 (3): 267–277.

Kierkegaard, Søren. 1843 [trans. 1962]. *Either/Or*, Vol I & II, trans. Walter Lowrie. Princeton, NJ: Princeton University Press.

Kinkāns, Vladimirs. 2015. Humor and Laughter in the Pedagogical Communications. *Society Integration Education. Proceedings of the International Scientific Conference* II: 375–385.

Mayer, B. 2015. *The Conflict Paradox*. San Francisco: Wiley.

Ñāṇavīra, Thera. 1987. *The Tragic, The Comic and the Personal*. Kandy: Buddhist Publication Society.

Thānissaro, Bhikkhu. 2015. *The Buddha Smiles*. San Diego, CA: Forest Monastery.

22

A New Agenda for Environmental Counselling

Mediating Through the Broken Circle of Ecology, Economics, Ethics and Human Wellbeing

In recent times, environmental issues have come into the centre of debates in politics and society with a welter of conflicting concerns of a dialectical pattern within ecology, economics, ethics and human wellbeing. This chapter uses the term 'environmental counselling' in a new way: different from what is traditionally described as environmental counselling. Global warming is one of a number of ecological crises that threaten the very existence of the plant and animal species that share the earth with us. Due to conflicting debates and misinformation, there is lack of clarity regarding the integration of our ecology with ethics, economics and human wellbeing. In my recent book on conflict studies, using a parable from the Buddhist sermons, the 'Palāsa Jātaka', I use a dialectical model of understanding current social, economic and ecological challenges (de Silva 2018).

The inability to see these conflicting zones in their relative importance denotes a lack of vision—a theme which is beautifully captured

P. de Silva, *Mindfulness-based Emotion Focused Counselling*,
https://doi.org/10.1007/978-3-030-64388-1_22

in a parable on Mulla Nasrudin's attempt to find his lost keys. Mulla was searching for his lost keys under the street lamp, and a man passing by inquired where he had lost the keys. The Mulla replied, 'In my living room'. The stranger baffled, asked, 'Then why are you searching for them here?', And the Mulla replied, 'The light is better here.' Many who speak on the environmental crisis fail to realize, as the Buddha said, that happiness is found within ourselves. That is where human greed rides roughshod over our lives, as when *greed dominates, we lose sight of significant environmental values*. This is the lesson we draw from the Mulla story.

We are now coming to recognize that the project of gaining mastery of nature springs from a number of assumptions specific to Western industrial society: that happiness and well-being lie in the satisfaction of our material needs and sensual desires; that the basic orientation of human kind is one of conflict and struggle at subjugation; and that nature must be conquered and made subservient to the satisfaction of our desires. We can also see that these assumptions are fallacious ones which if not challenged and replaced soon, may well have grave consequences (Bodhi 1987).

Here is the story from the 'Palasa Jātaka', which is a beautiful parody on the use of non-replenishable fossil fuels. A bird that had eaten the fruit of a Banyan tree voided its excrement on the trunk of a Judas tree. A golden goose says to the tree deity: 'Do not allow the Banyan tree to grow, as every tree on which a Banyan tree springs is destroyed by its growth.' The Banyan tree wrapped around the Judas tree consumed soil, water and nutrition. As time went by, all happened as the golden goose had predicted. The Banyan tree sent down roots which wrapped round the trunk of its host and consumed its own share of soil, water and nutriment. The Banyan tree grew bigger and stronger until it split the Judas tree. Then, the Judas tree toppled to its death. This is a graphic parable for the present day, typifying the kind of dialectic in the *conflicting zones of economics, ecology and human wellbeing*. The Banyan tree thus represents the use of carbon-based fuels. The emission of carbon dioxide in invisible small quantities, apparently harmless, menaces the civilization that depends on it. There is a dilemma here: placing restrictions on emission means limiting productivity and limiting productivity will usher in lay-offs of personnel and possible recession.

Now for the moral of the parable: unmitigated greed contributes to the resistance corporate leaders show to curbing carbon emissions. Greed is backed by the strong impulse to dominate and control. When delusion sets in—the screen that cannot go beyond darkness—we are unable to find the key. The reality of this dilemma is well seen today in the current critique of the mining industry and the ensuing debates about the use of coal. But like Mulla, we are seeking for answers elsewhere!

The mining industry is one that has detrimental social and environmental consequences, particularly when not conducted with proper planning and regulation. The extraction of fossil fuels is an industry that provides great economic profit, which allows the owners and shareholders to overlook its human impact. Also, there is strong political pressure for people seeking employment. Both the vegetation and animal populations are at risk. Some mining activities need to be blocked to preserve biodiversity. There are also clear links between extraction activities, water contamination and loss of biodiversity. The chance of contracting lung diseases creates important health issues. Developing countries experience many issues like loss of access to water. While formal regulation by the government and delegated institutions for water management and for the Great Barrier Reef etc., are important, there are many voluntary societies that engage in issues pertaining to climate and environment.

The movement for renewable energy sources has gained considerable momentum during recent times. This is an alternative which needs to make headway, while the use of coal needs to be limited. Above all, in farming communities, often beset with drought, water management is the centre of discussion and controversy. There are conflicting dualities between coal and employment on the one side, and the destruction of the environment, pollution of water, harming animals and biodiversity on the other. Yet, it is darkened by misinformation regarding environmental damage and private corporate self-interest. Where there is darkness, we need some light from genuine specialists on the subject, beyond dialectical conflicts. What is the path for a workable synthesis?

It needs honesty, a great deal of soul-searching, and some realism as to what is possible.

Mending the Broken Circle of Economics, Ecology, Ethics and Human Wellbeing

Fritjof Capra (b. 1939) commenting on the ecological crisis, says: 'It is a crisis of intellectual, moral and spiritual dimensions' (Capra 1983). According to Capra, apart from the ecological and economic consideration, it is a crisis of intellectual, moral and spiritual values. In fact, in the context of the Buddhist perspectives on the environment, it is a crisis that has moral and spiritual dimensions. This point refers to the importance of *dhamma niyāma* (the lawful nature of things), *citta niyāma* (lawful nature of the mind) and *kamma niyāma*, (the moral dimensions of the mind). Let us first take the moral dimension. The first precept in Buddhist ethics is that of non-killing.

The celebrated Buddhist monk from Vietnam Thích Nh´ât Hạnh says that ethics involves development of moral character which is beyond formal precepts. For him, callous destruction of the environment would run counter to an extended Buddhist sense of the first precept. The second ethical point relates to the rights of future generations to whom we are responsible in our attitude to the environment. A third point is the position of animals, and issues pertaining to biodiversity as, for instance, the controversy around coalmines in Australia. The Buddha captures the essence of the moral law (*kamma niyāma*) in the *Aggañña Sutta* which presents as a fanciful myth, the world cycle; how moral dimensions have an impact on nature; and an environmental ethic coming down the centuries to a world where exploitation of nature has been prominent: 'Since folk are ablaze with unlawful lust, overwhelmed by depraved longings, obsessed by wrong doctrines, on such as these the sky rains not steadily. It is hard to get a meal. The crops are affected with mildew and grown to mere stubs' (*Gradual Sayings*, I, 159). This passage also indicates the Buddhist *dhamma niyāma* (the lawful nature of things). In fact, in the Middle Length Sayings, the Buddha says, that if people lead bad lives fed by human greed, the four elements, fire, water, earth and air will revolt.

Today, there are bushfires, floods, earthquakes and tornadoes in a relentless repetition. The role of human greed indicates the importance of having the *citta niyāma* (the lawful nature of the mind). A mind defiled by human greed feeds environmental destruction. These three laws provide a philosophical, psychological and moral basis for genuine environmentalism. It is of profound interest that the Buddha, in the *Mahāhatthipadopama Sutta* (M.I.186–191), says that the four elements would revolt if we do not safeguard our future. That is the reason why the destruction of the environment, at its deepest levels, is a spiritual crisis.

Ecology

The global economy is a subsystem of global ecology, and as Herman Daly in his book, *Beyond Growth* (1996), says:

> The environment is a large circle such that the economy is a box inside the circle, and the pathological frontiers of exploiting nature have eaten into our economy. The ecosystem performs three important functions: first, it provides natural resources as food, fibre, fuel, bio-diversity and drugs. Second, it performs essential services as photosynthesis, regulation of atmospheric gas, water and climate, formation of soils and pest control; third, the ecosystem absorbs water—including sewage and garbage, and in fact all fuels, solid gases and heat.

Following the spirit of the '*Palāsa Jātaka*', Venerable Bodhi says that ecology and economics are, 'locked in an intense wrestling match'. Ecosystem ethics considers that the most important moral imperative is the maintenance of a healthy ecosystem. This is crucial as we regard considerations of future generations as important as our consideration of other humans, plants and animals.

Economics

Recent studies in neurology indicate that though our 'want system' (craving level) dominates the 'like system'. The cultivation of mindfulness, compassion and empathy may bring internal attunement with other people. Greed and envy destroy a sound mind. The good resonance circuits of the brain make us attuned to others. But conventional economics has lost its way and no longer maximizes human happiness. The primary error is model blindness since when the only tool you have is a hammer, every problem looks like a nail (Gittins 2010).

It is narrow in the sense that it is concerned with only one aspect of our lives: the material, having nothing to say about the social or spiritual. Even more narrowly, they focus on those aspects of our lives that can be traded in the marketplace.

Today, new advances in psychology, evolutionary biology, neuroscience and ecology have thrown up new frontiers of knowledge and the new science of positive psychology.

Psychology, Ethics and the 'Work Environment'

Many psychologists believe that: 'People in advanced industrial societies are psychically numbed as a result of being *cut off from nature* and unable to feel the beauty of the world… The pervasive influence of advertising promises to fill the void, and we spend the time pursuing commodified substitutes, that never really satisfy' (Loy and Goodhew 2005). Michael Sanders's recent work on the erosion of moral values in an era of market triumphalism, sums up the ailments of the time. He says that apart from the factor of greed which played a role in the financial crisis, the expansion of market values to spheres of life where they do not belong such as health and education was very destructive. In addition to human greed, the dominant market values were a stumbling blow to human values. His work (Sanders 2012) is a landmark for our time.

Getting back to economics, alternative economic models geared towards sustainability and contentment are important. The collapse of the stock market and the financial crisis illuminate a new context for economic activity, where markets collapse beyond human expectations within a constant gambling mania. Two little metaphors will illuminate the collapse of economic activity.

1. Using the sand pile logic example again: take a child completely immersed in making a castle of sand. Every new addition of a pile of sand adds a tremendous sense of delight till at some point, the whole structure collapses. Ramo (2009) says that changes in complex economic systems, whether they are ecosystems or stock markets, often takes place, not in smooth transition, but as a consequence of fast catastrophic events. Those who gamble their way up the corporate ladder, with lack of transparency are oblivious that contained within these gigantic structures are embedded the very seeds of collapse.
2. The 'Monkey Trap' story contains a very Buddhistic insight on human greed. The trap is constructed in such a way that there is a banana inside an empty coconut shell with a very small opening—just enough for the monkey to put his hand in but not enough room to take the banana out. The monkey suffers and eventually discovers that if he 'let's go' and takes his hand out, the suffering is gone!
3. In the world's biggest economies, by some repetitive compulsion, people are tied to the 'hedonic treadmill'. The law of diminishing returns is applicable to both economics and hedonics. The third ice cream is not as pleasant as the first. The law of diminishing returns works the same way. In a study called, *The Joyless Economy,* Tibor Scitovsky illustrates how many people do not get the balance right between work and leisure. He recommends a positive psychology of work, life and leisure.
4. Contentment and a balanced life is the Buddhist way. The monk, Venerable Ānanda, recommends frugality for monks. When a monk receives new robes, the old robes are used as coverlets; when coverlets are old, they are to be used as mattress covers; and when they are older, they are to be used as rugs; and then the rugs are to be used as dusters; and then the tattered dusters can be kneaded with clay and used to

> repair cracked floors and walls. Frugality rather than extravagance—humility rather than conceit. The ability to appreciate the success of the other person rather than being envious are Buddhist values.

In traditional Ladakh culture, they have a very insightful meaning of frugality: not collecting things in old cupboards, but making much out of little, such as we find in Venerable Ānanda's advice to the monks regarding use of old robes. In the sermons of the Buddha, there is a beautiful description of wastage by people who are callous regarding the social values of sharing food without wastage. In the story of the wood apple eater those who waste food are compared to the wood apple eater. He shakes the branches with both ripe and unripe fruit, collects what he wants and then lets the other fallen fruit rot. There is also advice regarding accumulation of wealth. It should be like the way that a bee collects nectar from a flower without injuring the plant.

Pathways of Buddhist Environmental Ethics

I have looked at ecology and economics. The third field is ethics, or more aptly, 'environmental ethics'. Due to the unprecedented challenges to the planet, there have been different types of issues: the first ones were concerned with specific issues like the use of biocides; deforestation and loss of wilderness; extinction of animal species; cruelty to animals. Some have been specially focused on gold mining in Thailand, or mining in the Kakadu National Park in Australia's Northern Territory, or more recently the Adani Coal Mine in Queensland. It is difficult to look at these issues impartially and aim at a balance, where the new factors of politics, employment for people without jobs and corporate greed play a role. Another group of problems, relevant for a Buddhist perspective are the moral perspectives for the non-human world—animals, plants, ecosystems and nature. Here, there have been among environmentalists, a rejection of any anthropocentric ethics in preference to biocentric ethics.

If humans have destroyed the environment in a rapacious way, if neglect of the environment caused the bush fires destroying thousands of innocent animals, a philosophical attempt to reinforce, 'Anthropocentric environmental Ethics', at this time, when the world is collapsing, looks a little like 'Nero playing the flute when Rome was burning'!

WE need a sensible balance of anthropocentric and biocentric ethics. The great Vietnamese thinker, Thích Nh'ât Hạnh says, in contemporary times, we need to extend the violation of the first of the Buddhist five precepts to the 'destruction of the environment and insensitivity to the loss of animal lives', in this process, the rights of future generation is also a new ethical code. A biocentric component to environmentalism, supplementing anthropocentric perspectives is a very sane recommendation, making ethics *contextual.*

References

Bodhi, Bhikkhu. 1987. Preface to *Buddhist Perspectives on the Environmental Crisis*, ed. K. Lassendel. Kandy: Buddhist Publication Society.

Capra, Fritjof. 1983. *The Turning Point: Science, Society and the Rising Culture*. New York: Bantam.

Daly, Herman E. 1966. *Beyond Growth: The Economics of Sustainable Growth*. Boston: Beacon Press.

de Silva, Padmsiri. 1998. *Environmental Philosophy and Ethics in Buddhism*. London: Macmillan.

de Silva, Padmasiri. 2018. *The Psychology of Buddhism in Conflict Studies*. London: Palgrave Macmillan.

Gittins, Ross. 2010. *The Happy Economist*. Crows Nest, Sydney, NSW: Allen and Unwin.

Loy, David, and Linda Goodhew. 2005. Consuming Time. In *Hooked*, ed. Stephanie Kaza. Boston: Shambhala.

The *Palasa Jātaka* (No. 307), *Jātaka*, vol. 3.

Ramo, J.C. 2009. *The Age of the Unthinkable*. London: Little Brown.

Sandel, Michael. 2017. *What Money Can't Buy: The Moral Limits of Markets*. London: Penguin.

Scitovsky, Tibor. 1992. *The Joyless Economy: The Psychology of Human Satisfaction*. Oxford: Oxford University Press.

23

Beyond Greed: Emotions of Generosity and Altruism

The negative emotions of greed, anger, fear, depression, envy and jealousy have already been covered in this book. The chapters on compassion and healing emotions make amends for the negative. Now we need to look at the positive emotions. A great deal of therapy involves compassion, empathy and the efforts to help people in distress. Though I did not discuss this point earlier, environmentalism as a way life and the love of nature has a lively emotional dimension. The present chapter on the emotions of generosity and altruism makes a significant Buddhist contribution to the debate. The tender emotion of altruism is in striking contrast to the egoism and the selfishness of individuals. In fact, at the ethical level, the practice of higher levels of sacrifice strikes a note of genuine selflessness. There have been descriptions of self-sacrifice by universally acclaimed individuals. There have also been exemplary people living quiet lives of humility, patience and kindness to others. In fact, Erich Fromm used the distinction between the 'having mode' dominated by power, greed, acquisitiveness, and the 'being mode' of love, sharing and generosity. Buddhism makes a similar distinction between the greed type of personality (*rāga carita*) and generous type (*cāga carita*):

P. de Silva, *Mindfulness-based Emotion Focused Counselling*,
https://doi.org/10.1007/978-3-030-64388-1_23

> The practice of giving is universally recognized as one of the most basic human virtues, a quality that testifies to the depth of one's humanity and one's capacity for self-transcendence. In the teaching of the Buddha, too, the practice of giving claims a special place of eminence, one which singles it out as being in a sense the foundation and seed of spiritual development. In the Pāli *suttas*, we read time and again that 'talk of giving' (*dānakathā*) was invariably the first topic to be discussed by the Buddha in his graduated exposition of the dhamma. (Bodhi 1995)

Venerable Bodhi also says that whenever the Buddha delivered a sermon to an audience comprising people who did not yet regard him as a teacher, he would start by emphasizing the value of giving. Topics like teaching on moral excellence, the law of *kamma* and the quest for renunciation would be offered later. In fact, the act of giving is an early expression of a more demanding sacrifice, the perfection of giving (*dāna pāramitā*).

One important dimension of moral behaviour is altruistic behaviour. In fact, moral behaviour is at a very general level, altruistic behaviour. It is the desire to promote one's own welfare and those of others. In the West, especially due to the writings of Max Weber (1864–1920), there is a tendency to see in Buddhism, a dichotomy between working for one's own good and that of others: 'Salvation is an absolutely personal performance of the self-reliant individual. No one and no social community can help him' (Weber 1958). But the Buddhist *suttas* take the position that by protecting oneself, one protects others and by protecting others, one protects oneself.

Dana referred to as 'giving' and *cāga* is used in the following way: (a) abandoning, giving up, renunciation; (b) liberality, generosity. While *dana* is used more for almsgiving to monks, the monks in return give back the noble gift of the *dhamma* to the people. Eradication of greed is an important quality that reverberates of Buddhist altruism. This disposition also helps to weaken the attachment to excessive wealth and the possessive structures of self-centred behaviour. At the level of moral excellence, defilements of covetousness and avarice lose their power, and we build positive emotions of liberality and compassion. The evils of miserliness, wastefulness and envy of the wealth of others thin out. Following those precepts ensures a balanced and righteous life (*dhamma cariyā*, *sama cariyā*).

The Buddha also praises the person who earns in a righteous way and gives to the needy. Developing such positive character strengths is an aid for spiritual development.

The Humanistic Culture

Today contexts for self-sacrifice and giving have widened due to the complexities of a changing world. People can give in terms of their time, energy. The numbers of people who need help and assistance have increased. The issues include lack of proper housing, poor nutrition, disease and disability. Also, people can travel to countries where assistance is needed. The bushfires, tsunamis, floods and earthquakes are frequent and volunteers help in addition to what governments may do. In Melbourne, in a fundraising event, kids who had collected money in a saving box handed over all their pocket money for a children's hospital Easter, fund-raising event. The suffering in the world is so intense, that some of the social workers have developed 'compassion fatigue'.

The Buddha's advice in such contexts is to exercise a sense of realism through equanimity. This a balancing factor through which people understand the doctrine of *dukkha* (human suffering), cushioning its effects. Equanimity is the balancing factor underpinning kindness, compassion and altruistic joy. This concern is important in grief counselling. Peter Singer, in a study on saving lives focused on Africa, says that collective efforts to pool money, time, the UN, and very compassionate and wealthy people, can handle the whole predicament of people in dire distress (Singer 2009). These are modern dimensions to the practice of altruism.

References

Bodhi, Bhikkhu (ed.). 1995. *Dana: The Practice of Giving*. Kandy: Buddhist Publication Society.
Fromm, Erich. 2013. *To Have or to Be?* London: Bloomsbury.
Singer, Peter. 2009. *The Life You Can Save*. Melbourne: Text Publishing.
Weber, Max. 1958. *The Religion of India*. Glencoe, IL: The Free Press.

24

Contemplative Education

It is time to review broadly the concept of 'contemplative education' as a discipline which illuminates a broader setting for the practice of meditation:

> The faculty of voluntarily bringing back a wandering attention, over and over again is the very root of judgment, character and will. An education which should improve this faculty would be an education par excellence. But it is easier to define this idea than to give practical instructions for bringing it about. (James 1950)

Jon Kabat-Zinn says that William James was not aware of the practice of mindfulness when he penned this passage but would have been delighted to discover that, in the practice of mindfulness, there was certainly an education for discovering that faculty of bringing back a wandering attention over and over again (2005, p. 17).

There is a great contemplative tradition across a wide spectrum. There are those who have interiorized their outlook, such as the Christian desert fathers, the Himalayan yogis, Sufi saints, Thomas Merton and the Buddhist forest monks. At the other end, are those who have displayed active interconnection with the world, such as the present Dalai Lama,

P. de Silva, *Mindfulness-based Emotion Focused Counselling*,
https://doi.org/10.1007/978-3-030-64388-1_24

the twelfth century mystic, Hildegard of Bingen, Thích Nh'ât Hạnh, Mahatma Gandhi and Martin Luther King.

The teaching of contemplative education in the classroom is basically a training for life rather than a trade. Being calm is the first asset. Your mind may take a creative turn and move towards new horizons. It will also gain a basic sense of balance in challenging circumstances.

The Epistemological Outlook of Contemplative Education

Education programmes, in general, develop a students' skills for 'critical thinking': focusing on the validity and the assumptions of an argument, especially the validity of the data presented to support a certain position/hypothesis. Clarity of thinking is very important and it builds learning skills, especially analytical skills, in breaking an issue into components. In fact, the Buddha was described as an analyst rather than a dogmatist as he would present the arguments supporting a certain thesis. The Buddha divides questions into four types: those which ought to be explained categorically; those which ought to be replied with a counter question; those which ought to be set aside (for example, if a flame of a candle dwindles, it is meaningless to ask, where it went); and those which ought to be explained analytically. He also said, one should not accept anything based purely on faith, on authority; on likes and dislikes; or because the majority accept it. These qualities show that he combined the best of the analytical approach to philosophical issues with a basic contemplative approach to liberation, a quality that stands out in the Buddhist contemplative approach.

Today, those who encourage the development of contemplative education say that in addition to logical and analytical skills, we need to develop the experiential, self-reflexive and contemplative dimensions of learning. It includes knowing through silence: beholding and witnessing the contents of our consciousness. The practice of meditation can be integrated into a broad-based contemplative, inward-looking, educational curriculum that is blended with compassion and empathy for others: qualities that cut across different groups (social, religious or ethnic). Also, it has to be emphasized, that contemplative education may be added to the school curriculum, not as a substitute for the current rational–empirical perspective, but as a supplement. Contemplative techniques ranging from poetry to meditation may be designed to quiet and shift the habitual chatter of the mind, so that the mind develops skills of deepened awareness, concentration, and self-knowledge and helps one to develop *confidence and trust within oneself.* This is important in daily life. When problems emerge, often it may be a temporary bodily ailment, the mind is capable of searching for alternative ways of handling it in a calm way. Deeper questions call for in-depth absorption.

In the context of understanding specific issues like the 'nature of the self' and such basic issues, there are different layers of understanding. There is also an 'existential dimension', where we confront issues which are described as the 'hard knocks of life', which have been the focus of both existentialism as a philosophy and existential therapy. There are different contexts for existential perspectives in the teachings of the Buddha. Understanding one's own vulnerability, having self-compassion and working through issues in general, is an existential approach:

> Have patience with everything unresolved in your heart and try to love the questions themselves as if they were locked rooms or books written in a foreign language. Don't search for the answers, which could not be given to you now, because you would not be able to live them. And the point is to live everything… Live the questions now. Perhaps then, someday far in the future, you will gradually, even without noticing it, live your way into the answer. (Rilke 2001)

One of the most important facets of contemplative knowledge is its 'self-reflexive' quality, as Krishnamurti observes: listening to the operation of your own minds. He considers self-knowledge as the beginning of freedom. One who listens to one's mind would open up to others. He considers self-knowledge as the beginning of freedom; one that is not weighed down by accumulated layers of learning by facts and theories.

The Psychological Frontiers of the Contemplative Perspective

In contemporary times, mindfulness-based therapies have been greatly integrated into therapy. This is entirely consistent with the aim of overcoming suffering and improving the welfare of all sentient beings. This work has gained a new momentum with the recent discoveries in neuroscience by Richard Davidson and Daniel Siegel. Cognitive behaviour therapy has extended its frontiers to the management of depression and mindfulness-based pain management.

Mark Epstein is the best commentator on the Buddhist contemplative approach in therapy. Epstein says that the Freudian technique of 'evenly suspended attention' and the bracketing of the critical faculty while listening to clients offers a marked resemblance to that of the Buddha: though there is no evidence that Freud was influenced by Buddhism. Naropa University in Colorado was a pioneer in developing a contemplative tradition within the psychology department. Now, in many universities, formal academic programmes have integrated mindfulness and related contemplative psychology.

Contemplative Ethics and Moral Psychology

Compared with the emerging interest in contemplative education, philosophy and therapy and even recent trends in moral psychology, a contemplative ethics needs to be developed. The discipline of ethics is generally divided into two facets according to the history of Western traditions of ethics: meta-ethics and normative ethics. Meta-ethics does not directly participate in the practical activity of reflecting and discussing ethical issues but is like a spectator reflecting on the very practice of ethics: like a spectator looking at a game of soccer who understands the rules of the game but is not playing soccer. An interesting recent development has emerged among teachers of ethics to broaden and diversify engagement in dialogue, especially where there is a polarization of views. Also, this tradition has changed the rules of the game by going beyond mere consistency, validity and inferences drawn from standard ethical theories.

The focus on proof and disproof has to be replaced by communication and especially by paying heed to the role of human emotions in ethics. Most classroom tutorials emphasize the skill to critically evaluate the presentation, rather than to understand it. As an example, the great fascination for moral dilemmas, such as whether Peter should steal a drug to save his wife's life, has highlighted the importance of a new kind of pedagogy for the classroom. It ought to be one where the students get immersed in the issues and do not just pass 'logical judgments' as an answer. Many questions, like some of the moral dilemmas, call for a full immersion of the class in the discussion, imaginatively identifying with different facets of the dilemma. In fact, some of the modern techniques of teaching use narratives, stories, fiction, drama and biographies. One such experience I had was during a class on 'existential ethics' using Søren Kierkegaard's novel *Either/Or* at the University of Hawaii.

In a similar vein, Wittgenstein talks about the rough road:

> The more narrowly we examine actual language, the sharper becomes the conflict between it and our requirements. (For the crystal purity of logic was, of course not a result of investigation: it was a requirement). The conflict becomes intolerable, the requirement is now in danger of becoming empty—we have now got onto slippery ice where there is no friction and so in a certain sense the conditions are ideal, but just because of that, we are unable to walk. We want to walk, but also just because of that, we are unable to walk. We want to walk; so we need friction. Back to the rough road. (1953)

The meaning of friction in the above statement may be interpreted as a reference to the uncertainties and chaos of our lives. But the philosophical worldviews that pervaded the times of Wittgenstein, dominated by the rational–empirical method, which attempted to find neat answers to well formulated questions, had no place for ethical dilemmas, polarized and conflicting views on moral issues, chaos and uncertainty—the rough road of life. Ethics which are self-reflexive, experiential and contemplative are more suitable for the rough road. To deal with the apparent contradictions, paradoxes and the dialectical movement of things, a contemplative approach is helpful. In contexts of adversity, we need mindfulness and a reflective turn of mind, rather than a logical formulation for making choices. It is such a perspective, as James remarked, that is the root of judgment, character and will. This is not to deny the importance of rules and precepts, which are crucial for Buddhist ethics, but we also need a mind immersed in reflective concerns of morality and, most important, the moment to moment flow of morality.

Of the prominent philosophers in the West, Iris Murdoch remains the best exponent of a contemplative perspective on ethics, as she compares the moral journey to a person going on a pilgrimage. It is a metaphor which we may admirably use in the context of Buddhism. Murdoch says that apart from the ethics that emerge when making a choice, what is important is the moral perspective that pervades continually, in the moment to moment flow of life: 'I would regard the daily, hourly, minutely attempted purification of consciousness as the central and fundamental arena of morality' (1956). This is not to deny the value of moral principles, precepts and theoretical perspectives and criteria for evaluating good and bad actions in Buddhism but we also need to look at their wellsprings in the deeper reflective/meditative base in Buddhist ethics. Bernard Williams, a moral philosopher, reflects what other philosophers say:

> We do not always arm with theories, in the hurly burly of our moral lives, and deep reflection brings a relevant wellspring of the moral emotions within ourselves. In Buddhism, morality is a practice blended with mindful awareness. Moral action that does not work has been compared to people in a rowboat putting tremendous effort and exertion into rowing across a river, while failing to untie the rope attaching the boat to the dock.

The building of character was also important for an early ethicist, Aristotle. For Buddhism, the moral and what may be described as 'spiritual transformation' has a strong base in the transformation of character.

Ethics of Compassion

The chapter on compassion ties in neatly with discussion of ethics in this chapter. Compassion as an emotion has a role in the motivation of people. Lawrence Blum (1980) says that altruistic action can sometimes be motivated by consideration of duty alone. He argues rather that actions motivated by compassion have a particular *value* arising from the expressive qualities of compassionate action. In fact, Caouette and Price, the editors of a new book, *The Moral Psychology of Compassion* (2018) say that compassion can have a distinctive value in creating trust and a sense of collaboration between physician and patient. Another important point mentioned by them, is that in crossing frontiers to ethical theories, compassion might be considered as a source of *evaluative knowledge*. It can thus disclose the evaluative properties of a situation, like perception disclosing the perceptible properties of things. Compassion, certainly is a valuable source of moral knowledge. As our main concern in this chapter is the role of contemplative knowledge, it is necessary to emphasize that *mettā* in Buddhism is a meditative state: universal and boundless, without barriers, extended to all sentient beings. It is blended with empathy for the suffering, as well as kindness, sympathetic joy and equanimity.

References

Blum, Lawrence A. 1980. *Friendship. Altruism and Morality*: London: Routledge.
Caouette, Justin, and Carolyn Price (eds.). 2018. *The Moral Psychology of Compassion*. London: Rowman & Littlefield.
James, William. 1950. *The Principles of Psychology*. New York: Dover Publishing.
Kabat-Zinn, Jon. 2005. *Coming to Our Senses*. New York: Dover Publishing.
Kierkegaard, Søren. 1843 [trans. 1962]. *Either/Or*, Vol I & II, trans. Walter Lowrie. Princeton, NJ: Princeton University Press.
Murdoch, Iris. 1970. *The Sovereignty of the Good*. London: Routledge and Kegan Paul.

Rilke, Rainer Maria. 2001. *Letters to a Young Poet*, ed. Amélie Rorty and trans. Stephen Mitchell. New York: Modern Library.
Wittgenstein, Ludwig. 1953. *Philosophical Investigations*. Oxford: Basil Blackwell.

25

Work Ethics, Emotional Intelligence and Mindfulness

A work on human emotions is incomplete, unless we explore the role of emotional intelligence in the workplace. Further, it has been observed by leaders in the workplace, that when we deal with people, we are not dealing with the challenges of logic but with people who are creatures of emotions. In fact, when Daniel Goleman published his groundbreaking book, *Emotional Intelligence* (1996), he opened up a whole dimension of new interests. Furthermore, the chapter on healing emotions concerned a work that Goleman edited with a number of illustrious scholars, including The Dalai Lama.

This chapter opens up the question of emotional intelligence as a work ethic and also what Buddhist contemplative practice contributes to it. Of course, Golcman did explore this facet of IQ or emotional intelligence in his work but I shall refer to his contributions to this field, of emotions in the work ethic, later in the chapter.

P. de Silva, *Mindfulness-based Emotion Focused Counselling*,
https://doi.org/10.1007/978-3-030-64388-1_25

The Shifting Sands of Work Ethic and Ethical Theories

The growth of applied ethics in philosophy generated a great deal of interest in the relevance of ethics and values to environmental issues (see Chapter 22), biomedical concerns, as well as business, management, and the work ethic. In the late 1990s, there was a call to replace a fragmented curriculum with a more holistic one, integrating the emerging disciplines. Environmentalists dominated this scenario and Alastair Gun, at that time responded thus:

> To achieve a sustainable society, we need the specialized skills of many people, environmental scientists, planners, economists and educators. But skills on their own is not enough. We need a shared vision—an environmental ethic. (1993)

In the early 1990s, the Harvard Business School responded to these emerging tides in the educational and professional world: *there was a re-discovery of purpose in the management field.* The need to emphasize corporate responsibility and accountability rose to the surface and the MBA curriculum provided a formal model. Thus, business education had to be more than a transfer of skills but an activity that engages one's character and values, spurs one's imagination and sense of meaning and one's sense of responsibility and accountability (Piper 1995). But competing ethical theories and arguments, made scholars realize that a new management ethic is necessary.

A New Management Ethic

Shift of perspective emerged from the work of a neurologist on the nature of intelligence. Antonio Damasio, a neurologist who studied the impairment of patients who had damaged the prefrontal amygdala circuit, made an important discovery. He found that the patients' decision making was flawed, *not because of any deterioration of their reasoning powers, but because they could not experience certain feelings and emotions.* While they had the requisite knowledge, attention, memory, ability to use language, make calculations and do any 'logical reasoning', there was a marked alteration in their ability, as such, to experience feelings, and one would say, emotions. The patient, Phineas, who had experienced a brain injury showed that there was a discrepancy between rationality and the ability to experience emotions and thus displayed irresponsible behavior in coming late to the office at his workplace.

The damage to the brain implied an inability to experience the emotional and ethical facets in working life, thus leading to a degenerated character. This was the groundbreaking discovery of Antonio Damasio (1994). More recently, the writing of Joseph Ledoux (1996) and David Goleman has been followed by a stream of literature on the role of emotions in personal and public life, and especially on the workplace. It was a shift from an argument culture to a kind of therapeutic culture, with new resources for a management ethic.

Exploring New Pastures for a Work Ethic

Having described both the malady and remedy, Cairnes says, that to comprehend things in this way, one needs a special kind of intelligence. This is a fresh pathway for attaining the kind of targets needed to *blend intellect, spirit and emotions.* This approach engages one's character, stirring the moral imagination and raising the sense of responsibility. *Instead of summoning ethical principles, protocols and directives, we befriend our private demons of fear, depression, despair and anger;* we accept and work with our limitations and we consider the obstacles we face as our teachers. This is to work at a radically *deeper level* and this, brings a sense of connectedness to all the realities around us. It is a blend of emotional resurgence and a kind of therapeutic approach to work. In the current contemporary world, we need a philosophical framework of this kind to deal with the complexities and tensions in the workplace, home and society.

To embrace all parts of ourselves, pain, uncertainty and a seeming crisis (not a real one) is a *mark of real self-compassion.* The point that one can work on pain and apparent disappointment and make them a basis for transformation is what Carl Jung termed as converting brass into gold—emotional alchemy. This is what today, a neuroscientist like Richard Davidson describes as resilience. Once you blend it with the approach of contemplative meditation, we re-teach a thing's loveliness which we earlier did not see. Adversity may be transformed into insight, compassion and renewal. There is also a concept referred to as AQ: Adversity Quotient.

Goleman published the groundbreaking work on emotional intelligence in 1996. He was partly voicing the new revolution in work ethics that was emerging at the time, though his own work was based on the scientific discoveries pertaining to the brain and new psychology.

The Search for an Emotionally Intelligent Organisation

The important thrust of this section is to emphasize the point that reinventing a new management ethic means that those who work, as well as those who lead, have to find a deep sense of purpose and a passion for what they do. Such a sense of purpose and passion for what they do may heal the fragmentation that there is between work, home and life, and society. The integration of emotional intelligence or emotional literacy into corporate life has been a thesis that is unfolding in the work of Howard Gardner, Peter Salovey and J. M. Meyer. Its popular exposition is expressed by the focused research of David Goleman (1996).

Goleman presents the concept under five components:

1. Knowing one's emotions and self-understanding. The ability to monitor feelings from moment to moment is crucial to psychological insight. It is said that those who have a clear knowledge of their feelings are better pilots of their lives. My usage of *self-awareness* refers to a self-reflexive, introspective attention to one's own experience, sometimes called *mindfulness* (1996, p. 315).
2. The ability to manage one's own emotions. This type of skill helps people to manage their own emotions. This type of skill helps people

to manage the stress and anxieties of daily life and also the adversities and ups and downs of life.
3. The ability to use emotions to reach desirable goals, thus increasing one's productivity and effectiveness.
4. Being sensitive to the emotions of others. People who are empathetic begin to understand the social signals of others.
5. The art of handling relationships with others and the management of the emotions of others. The art of handling relationships with others and the management of the emotions of others is a skill that takes time to attain, develop and apply.

The Concept of Emotional Intelligence: Some Philosophical Issues

Philosophers have discussed the issues pertaining to the dichotomy between rationality and emotions, and the idea that emotions do not have any epistemic status or claims to knowledge. As far as I am aware, hardly any philosopher has yet attempted to look at the specific concept of IQ. But there has been one attempt, a misunderstanding that calls for a detailed response. E. M. Adams says that we do not have a conceptual framework to critically assess our feelings, emotions and impulses. He also says that instead of critically assessing our feelings, emotions and impulses, we follow a therapeutic and treatment approach, to control or transform emotions (Adams 1998). Of course, Goleman does not clarify this process of awareness in detail, except for saying that this refers to the practice of mindfulness.

Adam's criticism calls for an answer in the light of the discussion we had in Chapter 24 on contemplative education. *The practice of mindfulness and rational criticism do not exclude each other.* Often, they may be complementary, and in other contexts like in the problem of addictions, bodily arousal in *akrasia* (temptation), respond better to mindfulness practice. There are also specific therapies like that of Albert Ellis's, Emotive Cognitive Therapy, which combines the analysis of false beliefs pertaining to emotions with therapy. We have to move away from Adams's dualistic thinking and find more holistic ways of finding resources to heal the fragmentation in our lives.

Adams's criticism may be summarized thus:

1. The mere awareness of one's own feelings and impulses (and those of others) does not make one's resulting feelings rational. It is not a rational procedure.
2. Intelligence is a cognitive matter involving comprehension and critical judgment.
3. Issues pertaining to the emotions need to be examined within an epistemological or educational framework, not a therapeutic one.

Epistemological Issues

The term emotional intelligence may be replaced by a phrase like 'emotional sensibility' and 'emotional maturity'. Also, there are many contexts, where we look at reason and emotion in ritualized opposition, but we can also see contexts where they supplement each other. Here recent discoveries in neurology are helpful. One such instance is Antonio Damasio's groundbreaking discovery that morality and rationality were dependent on the proper functioning of emotional circuits in the prefrontal cortex (Damasio 1994) giving direction to and for controlling our perception and belief formation. Ronald de Soysa says: 'Like a scientific paradigm, our emotions are better at stimulating research in certain directions than at finding compelling and fair reasons for their own adoption.' According to Damasio, the thesis is that emotions rather than being sand in the machinery of action, can actually promote rational behaviour in situations of indeterminacy. *Positive emotions play a role in rational decision making*. Finally, Adams does not understand that mindfulness practice can enhance emotional sensibility. I wrote a long article as a response to Adams's criticism and sent a copy to Goleman who was thrilled. He liked it and immediately sent me a book which he had written with the co-authorship of another scholar, on business ethics and emotions.

The Emotionally Intelligent Workplace

Carry Cherniss and Daniel Goleman edited a recent work on emotional intelligence in the workplace (2001). In the years following Goleman's book on emotional intelligence and competency in the workplace have been under review. Some are purely cognitive, but most of them are emotional competencies such as self-confidence, initiative and team work. The important question is how does emotional intelligence develop in an entire organisation? Goleman works out three clusters of EQ. The first is very important for the contemplative dimension.

The first is the *self-awareness cluster*, where the focus is on emotional self-awareness, indicates the importance of recognizing and being aware of one's own feelings and how they affect one's performance. Self-awareness is the path to recognizing one's own strengths and weaknesses. Where the self-assessment is accurate, it may be considered as a superior performance, and indicates a great deal of self-confidence. Thus, emotional self-awareness, accurate self-assessment and self-confidence are the hallmarks of this culture.

The second is the *self-management cluster*. This cluster refers to managing internal states, impulses and resources. It manifests as the absence of distress and disruptive feelings. This combines a sense of trustworthiness when others are aware of one's skills and conscientiousness: being careful, self-disciplined and scrupulous in attending to one's responsibilities. The need to achieve and taking initiative is important, as initiative is a key to understanding outstanding performance. Thus, emotional self-control, trustworthiness, conscientiousness, adaptability, the achievement drive and initiative, stand out for this second cluster.

The third, is the s*ocial awareness cluster* which manifests in three kinds of competencies. Empathy gives people a good awareness of the emotions of other people, their concerns also their needs. They can pick up non-verbal cues like emotions on the face and to some extent the voice. In a larger group, skills prevent stereotyping and seek variety, as with a doctor who sees patients or someone who manages jobs in the workplace. Social awareness also needs to help grasp the unstated needs and concerns of another which is a mark of a successful salesman, thus taking into consideration, the customer's view. The third is organisational skills to read the currents of emotions and political realities of a group.

In reality, these competencies do not work in a watertight compartment but blend in different ways. Across clusters, they help one another to mix and blend and integrate.

The leadership styles presented by Goleman are fascinating and they expand current dialogues about leadership.

Visionary type: has self-confidence, is very positive, mobilizes others and has the ability to expand to new visions when there is a need.
Affiliative type: has empathy, build bonds and has the skill of conflict management.
Democratic type: promotes teamwork, collaboration and communication. Creates harmony in a group, especially when there is need.
Coaching type: has empathy and helps others develop. Has emotional awareness and develops long-term strengths.
Coercive type: is very negative.
Pacesetting type: tries to get quick results and is very negative.

References

Adams, E. M. 1998. Emotional Intelligence and Wisdom. *Southern Journal of Philosophy* 36 (1): 1–14.

Cairnes, Margot. 1998. *Approaching the Corporate Heart*. Sydney: Simon & Schuster.

Cherniss, Cary, and Daniel Goleman. 2001. *Emotional Intelligence in the Workplace*. New York: Jossey-Bass.

Damasio, Antonio R. 1994. *Descartes' Error: Emotion, Reason, and the Human Brain*. New York: Avon Books.

Goleman, Daniel. 1996. *Emotional Intelligence*. New York: Bloomsbury.

Gun, Alastair S. 1993. 'Culture as a Resource for Sustainability'. Paper presented at the IRC *Conference on the Transmission of Environmental Values*

Through Culture, Ethics and Education. Information and Resource Center, Singapore.
Ledoux, Joseph. 1996. *The Emotional Brain*. London: Weidenfeld & Nicolson.
Piper, Thomas. 1995. In *Management Ethics: Theory, Cases and Practice*, ed. Gordon L. Clark and Elizabeth Prior Jonson. *Sydney*: Harper Educational.
Weinhardt, Justin, and Aden Dumaisnil. 2018. Compassion in the Workplace. In *The Moral Psychology of Compassion*, ed. Justin Caouette and Carolyn Price. London: Rowman & Littlefield.

26

Mindfulness-Based Cognitive Therapy

I have already discussed depression from different perspectives and brought it within the province of understanding for a kind of layman's ethic—for grief counselling, and beyond excessive medicalizing depression, and issues of daily life. If neglected these can generate depression. The important relationship of the central links of sadness to depression, need early attention. I have also, following Erich Fromm, looked at the social dimensions of depression as alienation and taken some contexts beyond the clinic to the home and the workplace. This is precisely the path for exploring depression and is not merely for the person subject to a cycle of depressive episodes. I wanted to explore depression in a human setting. There is an authentic rationale for what I have written in Chapter 8.

I have myself gone through depression: authentic, existential and experiential. This was a deeply shattering phase in 1994, which ultimately culminated in the tangible insights of life. I was in a clinic for one week—and saw a very sad gap between the inmates of the ward and myself. After one week, I discovered the possibility of a sane, very rich life outside. I only needed the will and confidence that I could go out to have a wonderful life outside. That was the best way of paying homage

P. de Silva, *Mindfulness-based Emotion Focused Counselling*,
https://doi.org/10.1007/978-3-030-64388-1_26

with love and compassion to my wife, whom I lost a few years ago in Singapore (de Silva 2014, Chapters 16, 17). When one is in and out of depression, one sees two worlds but can have a glimmer of beautiful optimism that one can come out of a shattering phase in life.

I wish to recall the words of Wolpert on depression that I quoted in Chapter 8:

> The human spirit has the ability to come to grips with the most challenging times and during such times, one should turn towards the experience of pain, sadness, fear, worry, anger rather than a moving away from such a context to a spirit of abandonment. We need to face life as if each moment of life is precious, look at the movement of apparent suffering, with openness and a sense of vitality and then things become different. (1999)

This background helps me to look at MBCT for depression. I have looked at MBCT briefly for pain management—in the context of work done by Vidyamala Burch and Risa Kaparo—and I have drawn on some of its insights. But I wish to devote this chapter to the MBCT way of managing depression. But whatever the issues we focus on, Wolpert's call has inspired me and those who take to MBCT. Further, there is a common link that inspires most of the mindfulness-based therapies, of both pain management and depression management:

Mindfulness lies at the core of Buddhist meditative practices, yet its essence is universal. It has to do with refining our capacities for paying attention, for sustained and penetrative awareness, and for emergent insight that is beyond thought but can be articulated through thought. Thus, the practice of mindfulness lends itself beautifully to the kind of synthesis with cognitive therapy reflected in the following volume:

> Strictly speaking, mindfulness is not a technique or a method, although there are many different methods and techniques for its cultivation. Rather, it is more aptly described as a way of being, or a way of seeing, one that involves coming to our senses in every meaning of the phrase. (Segal et al. 2002)

The basic premises of MBCT may be summarized. It is basically the cultivation of awareness through mindfulness practice, an attitudinal framework characterized by non-striving, acceptance and a genuine interest in experience. It draws on the central Buddhist theme of vulnerability, which needs to be balanced by contextual pragmatism, and equanimity regarding the ups and downs in life. The diagnosis is forced on the *habitual autopilot*. It is rumination as a particular style of self-critical, self-imposed, repetitive, negative thinking. Experiential avoidance makes one try to avoid one's real predicament and conscious self-knowledge is recommended which paradoxically helps and which is different from rumination.

What is important from a Buddhist perspective is that there is a focus on body sensations and emotions. The MBCT program is done in an eight-week class format. In this book, I am interested in the focus on feelings/emotions. Interpretation of events plays a large role in determining moods. Understanding the extent of this can be very helpful. First, in rumination, there is experiential avoidance of certain emotions: getting away from difficult emotions. Avoidance creates more suffering. In Buddhist thought, pain is inevitable but not suffering. Work done on the emotions and the body is important, as keeping unwanted emotions at bay without understanding and experiencing creates additional layers of suffering.

In Buddhism, the transition from feeling to emotions and bodily feelings is a kind of entry point to emotions. The body can be seen as a window to the mind. It is through the body that the unfinished processes of emotional re-awakening emerge. Earlier, I have emphasized the important links between the body and emotions. The links between thoughts and emotions are greatly emphasized also in MBCT. But, the role of the body in depression is central. Directly experiencing bodily sensations is a part of the therapy:

> [T]he body is part of the feedback loop that maintains depression. The sensations of heaviness, fatigue, sagging posture and muscle tightness associated with the experience of depression can be one of the factors perpetuating the experience. Seeing this offers some important clues in

> learning to use the body as an ally in reversing the feedback loop. (Crane 2009, pp. 3, 52)

Getting caught up in the thought processes relating to emotions is also a problem. This problem is dealt with by a process called de-centering thoughts: identifying what are just mere thoughts and not emotions! Feelings, the body and emotions are all a focus in MBCT therapy which is dependent on context, and the different phases of the eight-week program. Learning to turn towards, befriend and engage with difficult experiences and to extend them to normal experiences is a key component of the MBCT program. Avoidance of difficult emotions is a reason for relapse into depression. It is said that the participant should turn inwards and learn to infuse warmth, kindness and compassion towards the inward process. Habitual patterns of avoiding difficult emotions should be replaced with an attitude of acceptance, kindliness and a kind of curiosity. Thus, the radical reformation in MBCT is to convert a habitually self-critical and judgmental person into an open, interested, warm and accepting person. What interests me most, is the central role difficult emotions play in depression, as well as the role played by a positive emotional outlook in coming back to normality.

References

Crane, Rebecca. 2009. *Mindfulness-Based Cognitive Therapy*. London: Routledge.

de Silva, Padmasiri. 2014. *An Introduction to Buddhist Psychology and Counselling*, 5th ed. London: Palgrave Macmillan.

Segal, Zindel V., Mark Williams, and John Teasdale (eds.). 2002. With a foreword by Jon Kabat-Zinn. *Mindfulness-Based Cognitive Therapy for Depression*. New York: Guilford Press.

Wolpert, Lewis. 1999. *Malignant Sadness*. London: Faber and Faber.

27

Compassionate Mental Health Care

This chapter has three important facets: challenges for today's medical practitioners and the role of compassion in the physician, the logic of compassion as an emotion, and issues pertaining to ageing and mental health.

Challenges to today's medical practitioners are many as they have to deal with many issues: new surgical procedures, diagnostic skills, referrals, and a growing body of consultative procedures. But another important ingredient for treatment is the background of compassion in the physician focused on the patient's suffering and the emotional resonance from the patient directed towards human suffering. Recently, with the emerging face of 'moral psychology', a new socio-cultural model that focuses both on new perspectives and barriers to compassionate care is visible.

There are many causes or triggers for depression and anxiety. One rarely finds the one in the absence of the other. Thus the clinical picture is often mixed. We can inherit a genetic disposition to depression or anxiety but whether or not that disposition will be triggered depends on a variety of things, many of which are in our control. Major life stress can make a genetic disposition more likely to express itself. Mental health services are

P. de Silva, *Mindfulness-based Emotion Focused Counselling*,
https://doi.org/10.1007/978-3-030-64388-1_27

often engaged in health crises such as self-harm, suicidal tendencies and depression. But it must be emphasized that changing lifelong negative attitudes is central for healthy living. Here, we need positive concepts of ageing well. Having negative attitudes to ageing is poor coping. Having lived in a retirement village for over fifteen years, the following words of Carl Jung ring in my ears:

> A human being would certainly not grow to be 70 or 80 years old if this longevity had no meaning to the species to which he belonged. The afternoon of human life must also have a significance of its own and cannot be merely a pitiful appendage to life's morning. (Vaillant 2002, p. 143)

In the context that Jung refers to, what we get is not mere compassion, but 'elevated compassion', a tremendous respect for the client. These insights on ageing well, emerged from a landmark Harvard study. While I shall take issue pertaining to elevated compassion and ageing well in a subsequent section of this chapter, the message for the compassionate physician is more than that of moderating depression and anxiety:

> What is less clear from current evidence is to what extent one can change life-long negative attitudes and to what extent doing so can reverse the negative effects on health. But there is enough research on the beneficial effects of improving mental health for heart diseases, cancer, immunity and other conditions to suggest that it can.
>
> So, attitude is crucial for healthy ageing. Research has found that people who have more positive perceptions of ageing, lived seven and a half years longer than the ones with less positive perceptions. (Hassed 2008, p. 207)

The need for compassionate mental health care is our main concern. According to Paul Gilbert, the first key ingredient of compassion is the ability to be open to, to be moved by and to be able to tolerate the suffering and the distress of others in a non-judgmental way. The second is the attempt to relieve it by appropriate ways of thinking, feeling and behaving. Though compassion at the first sight appears an individual emotion, it is a multifaceted emotion with social dimensions. What we need is a culture of *real* compassion.

Another limitation is to see compassion as an individual quality as it is cultivated through a social setting, in inter-dependent relationships, so that there is appreciation in those who give and receive compassion. Compassion is both deeply personal but yet social and cultural. In a hospital culture the doctor, nurse and the patient generate interpersonal bonds. As the Vietnamese philosopher monk Thích Nh′ât Hạnh described with a horticultural metaphor, the seeds of compassion need to be cultivated and nurtured in different communities and cultures, and thus socio-cultural systems are central to the practice of compassion (Ekstrom 2012).

But one has to be aware of different cross-currents of individualism in society. Compassion has to be located in each individual's deep awareness of suffering. Furthermore, efforts have to be made to locate where true compassion would flourish, especially in therapeutic communities. Current neuroscientific evidence indicates that there is a variety in the healing process, through kindness, compassion and recovery. We could say that compassion should be a part of the moral life of a society, strengthening its therapeutic and healing value.

Today, as Ekstrom says, service provision is extremely de-contextualized and individualized. That is one reason to emphasize the need for socio-cultural roots for compassion, strong roots that feed a whole system.

References

Ekstrom, Laura. 2012. Liars, Medicine, and Compassion. *Journal of Medicine and Philosophy*, April.

Hassed, Craig. 2008. *The Essence of Health*. Sydney: Random.

Vaillant, George E. 2002. *Ageing Well: Surprising Guideposts to a Happier Life*. London: Scribe.

28

Developing a Moral Psychology of Emotions: A Prologemena

I have been interested in developing a moral psychology of emotions in Buddhist perspective, as my next effort to write on ethics and emotions. As a preliminary background to this interest, I am restricting this chapter to the moral psychology of anger.

Anger as a Moral Emotion: Biology and Physiology and Neuroscience

Out of the standard list of emotions, anger has a pre-eminent place. (i) It is found among animals, and associated with distinctive elicitors, physiological responses, action tendencies and expressive behaviour. (ii) As I have already discussed earlier in this book, Paul Ekman has demonstrated the universality of emotions on the face. (iii) It is physiologically distinct from other emotions. (iv) Affective neuroscience indicates that anger is associated with the activation of the amygdala, hypothalamus and grey areas of the mid-brain. Darwin's work discussed in an earlier chapter gives more information on anger and the evolutionary heritage

P. de Silva, *Mindfulness-based Emotion Focused Counselling*,
https://doi.org/10.1007/978-3-030-64388-1_28

of animals. But it is only in recent times that anger as a moral emotion has been recognized.

Profile of Anger Beyond Physiology

Anger is often considered as a judgment that transgress accepted norms and codes of behaviour and often generates the need for punishment and even a kind of retribution. Unfair and illegitimate judgments then prevail. Another way of describing the context for anger is as a response to injustice. Anger is sometimes directed to positive pro-social behaviour about fairness and poverty, when relieving the suffering of a group of people is ignored.

Guilt and Shame

In the discussion on guilt in Buddhism, I mentioned the difficulties of finding a word for guilt in a Sinhalese, as early Buddhist culture was more shame-focused. My own research indicated the importance of shame in the emotion vocabulary for Sinhala, though in the contemporary world Sinhalese do experience guilt due to the impact of the West. Guilt dominated in Freudian culture and writings. In the West guilt is a prominent moral emotion.

Guilt has been seen as contributing to moral motivation. As people feel guilty, they confess, make reparation, engage in self-criticism and sometimes seek punishment. Paul Ekman who worked on a list of basic emotions and has a place for both guilt and shame:

> Both guilt and shame are sometimes regarded as basic emotions. It is not implausible that they both evolved to play roles in social behaviour. But another possibility is that these emotions are learned by-products of other emotions that are more fundamental… On the face of it, guilt has striking similarities to other emotions. (Ekman and Davison 1994)

I shall conclude this chapter with the following words:

> We began with the observation that emotions typically arise when people make moral judgments, and went on to observe that the emotions in question are ones that involve self- or other- directed behaviour. The actual moral emotion that arises on any occasion will depend on what kind of transgression has taken place. We have looked at two of these emotions in detail: anger and guilt. We suggested that these emotions are particularly important in Western morality, because they arise in response to autonomy, norm violations, and autonomy norms are central in Western morality. (Prinz and Nichols 2010, p. 111)

This is an interesting theory emerging from recent studies in moral psychology. It contrasts with the physiological, somatic and neurological foundations of anger, presenting us with a challenging conclusion that in spite of these dimensions, anger has contextual links with moral dimensions in settings like breaking promises and righteous indignation. In the Buddhist psychology of emotions, the moral dimensions play a role in the causal setting, but physiology plays a role in embodied emotions while neurological insights are also significant.

Buddhism and Moral Anger

The moral psychology of emotions is a very recent and emerging field. In my next phase of writing I shall explore this field, especially, anger, sadness, compassion and pride. But I wish to clear up some points of misunderstanding regarding the issues of anger and Buddhism as expressed in a recent exploration of the subject by Cherry and Flanagan (2017).

Owen Flanagan presents a valuable introduction to the subject including different theoretical approaches from ancient to contemporary times. The basic battlegrounds are *philosophical* through Aristotle, the Stoics, Buddhism and current concerns of social justice. My presentation emerges from the psychology and the counselling perspectives of Buddhism, also the current work in mindfulness and neuroscience:

> In any case, it is not as if the *Buddhist thinks we can just will our way out of anger.* Most of the therapy required to overcome anger is social work

> of a philosophical sort. Some of the work is straightforwardly epistemic, overcoming false beliefs, and metaphysical, replacing these false beliefs with true beliefs about the ultimate nature of things. (Flanagan 2000, p. xxii)

I agree with him that following Śāntidēva (685–763 CE) we focus on anger as a process of conditioning factors but beyond this Flanagan misses the whole message in the early Buddhist *Satipaṭṭhāna* and the recent dialogues on mindfulness practice. The chapter on anger in my book proves that the *Buddhist approach is therapeutic.*

Buddhist Meta-Awareness: The Ekman–Dalai Lama Dialogue

Ekman says:

> I completely agree that each emotion can be enacted constructively or destructively. To have a choice about how you are going to enact an emotion you must be aware of the emotion as it is arising, of the 'spark before the flame', or in Western terms, the impulse before the action. Then if you are aware in your consciousness that an emotion is arising, you should be able to adjust the level and the way in which you respond. (Dalai Lama and Ekman 2008, p. 23)

The Dalai Lama says:

> This is very true, because in the meditation text, there is the role of the two main faculties that are being constantly used—one is mindfulness and the other one, Alan Wallace calls, 'meta attention', a form of self-awareness.

Meta-awareness indicates the role of self-awareness in training the practitioner to a point where the person is able to detect, even before the actual emotion or the propensity to the actual emotion has arisen. Emotion triggers refer to a person's appraisal of the event, though the person is not conscious of making it. A further point about triggers is our typical lack of awareness of the emotion, and that a part of us can monitor the emergence of an emotion and watch what is being experienced. When a person is well trained in meta-awareness, he is able to predict that he may fall prey to the emotion of anger. According to my meditation teacher, this is evidence of a very developed state of mindfulness. Body sensations play a crucial role and they are among the entry points of anger but one can accept body sensations without needing to react (de Silva 2017).

In deep meditation practice *one goes beyond morality,* where it is neither good nor bad, neither yours nor mine, and it is a process which emerges, stays for a while and passes away. In another context, Flanagan says, Buddhists try to 'destroy anger' (2000, pp. 259–281). A Buddhist makes anger an object of meditation (*dhammānupassanā*), and also derives insight from the emergence and passing away of a process. The chapter on anger presents a viable perspective of understanding the early Buddhist perspective on anger, along with a brief review of the Tibetan Buddhist perspective. Buddhists do not 'destroy' anger but convert it into a process of developing awareness of the rise and fall of psychological/bodily states. As Venerable Nyānaponika says, Buddhists do not throw away anger but with a little magic convert it into a great source of insight or use antidotes, as discussed in one of the chapters earlier.

Future Studies

I am at leisure working on a Moral Psychology of Emotions, using poetry, using new insights on women and emotions, children and emotions, central concerns like forgiveness, roots of neglected areas of guilt, how ambition generates a temporary cloud over, otherwise a contented mind, re-visiting contentment and many such fascinating poems, often presented to the poetry club at REGIS, where I live.

A Poem to Conclude My Journey

Compassion, kindness and resilience are close to my heart,

With self-compassion, and refined SOFTNESS set apart-
With this recipe -a stone can melt, it can crack, transform,
And reach the hearts of others, give them strength, warmth, and turn a cold day, to one of beaming sun,
Then seconds will change to minutes and then to years.
And make your journey and mine—just the same.
Remember, when friends disagree and sometimes angry;
And turn to devious paths that kindles their intellect!
We are creatures of SOFT hearts and mind, though single,
And the rhythms of our hearts in musical rhymes mingle!

References

Cherry, Myisha, and Owen Flanagan (eds.). 2017. *The Moral Psychology of Anger*. New Kingston, PA: Rowman and Littlefield.

Dalai Lama, and Daniel Goleman (eds.). 2004. *Destructive Emotions: A Dialogue with the Dalai Lama*. New York: Macmillan.

de Silva, Padmasiri. 2017. *Emotions and the Body in Buddhist Contemplative Practice and Mindfulness-Based Therapy*. London: Palgrave Macmillan.

Ekman, Paul, and Richard Davison (eds.). 1994. *The Nature of Emotions*. New York: Oxford University Press.

Flanagan, Owen. 2000. Destructive Emotions. *Consciousness and Emotion* 1 (2): 67–88.

Prinz, Jesse, and Shaun Nichols. 2010. Moral Emotions. In *The Moral Psychology Handbook*, ed. John Dorris. Oxford: Oxford University Press.

29

Integrating the Thematic Structure of Counselling Emotions

Part I

Mindfulness of the daily run of different emotions, through self-empathy, and converting negative emotions into positive ones, through what Carl Jung described as emotional alchemy, converting 'brass into gold'—sums up the basic thematic structure of the book, with the aid of some of the elegant recent works in 'Contemplative Neuroscience',—sums up what is new in this work on counselling emotions. And there is an ingenious way of presenting this approach through a poem with brevity, clear focus, and a rhythm that appeals to those who are looking for optimism in a disturbed world today.

Opening Your Heart and Mind to the Beauty That Is Within You

There is gold within you, to see on your part,
In the deepest layer of your heart,
To understand yourself better,
Be grateful to others, resilient to and confident, together
Then steadily you will be able to hear,

P. de Silva, *Mindfulness-based Emotion Focused Counselling*,
https://doi.org/10.1007/978-3-030-64388-1_29

A golden voice within, very near.
Is it a paradox that through SILENCE you can HEAR?
Calmness is central to hear your emotions in self-empathy.

The ocean may be rough and windy at times,
But you see the calm and steady waves at other times,
A long rebounding silence with endless ripples emerging.
Yes, the deeper layers within you, is calm and reassuring.
In a world outside, with great chaos, strife and confusion,
One calm person, will see the way to building a mine of resilience,
Which is the positive way—great empathy, not mere endurance.
The seeds of empathy you have, but you have yourself grow,
A deep awakening, while loosening the hold of your own ego,
Then all the noise subsides, and see the colors, and their nuances,
As in a mirror, you see your own past-the anger of a child,
it passes away, as she runs across to catch a butter fly far away,
Then her great joy when she sees a whole parade of butterflies
Yellow, white, red, brown and orange, all the way.
The anger that your spouse has shown, aside,
Is resting on a thin wide, those you love, also hurt you alone,
And those whom you hurt, love you along.

Converting Brass into Gold, Emotional Alchemy

Now you know, there is gold in your anger, sadness and fear,
How anger is very slippery, sadness need not end in melancholy.
Carl Jung said, on, emotional alchemy, converting depression,
Into deeply felt love and grief is a way of keeping love alive, Develop, a new passionate momentum of meaning in life
Convert, anger into calm but fearless, passionate stand for you,
And have your say, use its momentum in your own way.
People with quiet humility shine in their charming way,
And as he sees himself as 'nothing' can see others with empathy.
With a little magic, 'boredom' can be replaced by the ever presence of mind with something fully absorbing, with great joy!

All this is like an artist doing wonderful things, by mixing colors,
Depicting land and sky and the delicate nuances of emotions alike,
Has a finer thread of nuances, mirrored in the body and *psyche.*
See the finest blends of the nuances of emotions in self empathy.

Presenting the Thematic Structure of Emotions in Anger

Part II

Cooling the Flames of Anger

Anger is natural to pain and frustration,
When it is injustice, we call it, 'Righteous indignation'.
When justifiable anger is brushed aside
You need some room to move about,
Touch it, fondle and caressing around.
'Then you discover, that it is a wonderful gift with a wrapper,
Hidden beneath is lots of tension and stress,
It is fatiguing and eats away your calm and health,
You can be determined, passionate, assertive,
But neutralized with patience, as you may
Being both calm and yet passionate to win your way (see, Rick Hansen, *Resilient*, On Anger).

FIREWORKS! A Study of Anger in Children
Anger has three qualities: Ambiguity/Ambivalence, Invisibility, Volatility

I get angry when I want to,
I get angry when I don't
I'll get angry when I'll try to
I'll get angry when I won't.
I get angry when I am threatened,
I don't get angry when I am threatened,
I get angry when I am sad
Anger is a good thing
And then again it is bad
Now we're got started
I am feeling glad.

(This poem has contradictions, which we call *ambivalence*—anger is both good and bad).

In the Bosom of Family Life There Is Ambivalence

The anger that your spouse has shown, aside,
Is resting on a thin divide,
As those whom you love, also hurt you alone,
And those whom you hurt, love you along.
Perhaps, as someone said, 'occasional anger adds a bit of spice',
To add color and nuance to deeply embracing love.
I do not mean 'theatrical anger', used as an artifice,
Used by a spouse to get things done,
As that has no real flame for the ignition we need!
Affectionate love does not really need such a prior lead,
As it is just spontaneous and natural, you read,
In their face and body, no matter who takes the lead!

The Volatility of Anger

Anger creeps in and adds its own flavour
To jealousy, which involves love/hatred of the beloved,
Contempt for the rival, thus it's a possessive fix, threatened
It is also a threat to self-esteem and self-love cracking,
Thus, it is anger revolving around a person—egocentric.
Anger feeds envy, resentment, malice, spite, hatred,
Revenge, hostility, ill-will, and the worst, ingratitude.
The saddest insight is that anger may convert grief to depression.
Finally, it is a roller-coaster for competitive greed, failing
As their 'sand castles' are toppling down,
All this is a very long picnic, with anger, up and down.
Anger is a thread that ties many emotional knots, and tangles.
Loosening them with mindfulness, clears you of these 'entanglements'.

The Invisibility of Anger: The Subliminal

There are hidden tendencies below conscious level,
If someone passes a comment, a low-level comment at you,
Your body is excited, face turns red, and you are not aware
That a little revolution has caught you inside, unawares.
But if you have practiced, 'mindfulness' over time,

you know to 'slow down'. These are dormant tendencies,
lying below the conscious level, creating all discrepancies,
To your normal self, cool and steady, like sunshine lit,
Called '*anusaya*' in Buddhist study, for anger, greed and conceit.
If you have a hardened center of accumulated scars, you need
To clear the mind with mindfulness practiced all along,
The mind becomes calm, the body becomes steady,
And that is what we call, 'resilience'—a mind re-born.
Constant anger is reactive, and weaves knots and tangles,
And your brain absorbs all these webs—all that may be cleared.
Resilience as different from reactivity creates more peace, calm,
Awaken your natural intelligence to deal with life's, any alarm.

(This profile of anger may be taken as a model for fear and sadness, with the insights into the logic of each emotion).

30

Preserving the 'Green Carpet' and the Animals, in Times of Turmoil

Part I

There Was a Garden in My Heart

A Message from the Humming Birds.
Two Poems: Preserving and Destroying the Green Carpet.

There was a garden in my heart,
Now, it's an ecosystem torn-apart,
Humming birds are crying, sighing.
It was a wonderful green carpet,
We guarded a real, green carpet.
But we are crying, while singing, as now it's not clean.
The earth is dying, as it is not green.
It needs lots of water and again to be green.
The recurring drought has killed all the shoots,
As if a man has been walking on it in iron boots.

Remember! We control pests,
We pollinate plants,

P. de Silva, *Mindfulness-based Emotion Focused Counselling*,
https://doi.org/10.1007/978-3-030-64388-1_30

As we fly, we are also seed carriers,
Do not forget we have honey combs,
In our limbs! And in early morning,
When we have a delicacy,
Porridge and honey,
I always remember you.
We transform muddy marshes and green-lands,
Weaving a mosaic of green and red patches,
Which like an art piece that matches.
We are not scavengers,
But we do clean up the mess of smelling rubbish,
And keep the forest clean with a touch of 'real finish'.

A Carnival of Animals

Dedicated to the Fire Fighters of Australia.

If you love animals, whether they are cats and dogs,
Cobras and crocodiles, spiders and mosquitoes, or a singing bee,
Kolas, monkeys, tree climbers, water divers—whatever they be
Will see nature's rich tapestry through mountains and forestry.

Through winter and spring, summer and autumn,
In the lives of multi-colored birds, in ways loving and solemn,
Nature's own rhythms of tooth and claw,
Affection for their mates and sympathy for their kind.
To save their delicate lives in a bush fire crisis, for you and me.
Spider is a great artist, a cycle wheel in silken thread on a ceiling!
The center is firm, around the axis, spokes in directions no railing.
A dainty little insect is to be caught in this tricky gossamer trap.
I have blocked your way to the trap, hurry, get out of the way!

Cobra

Between the yellow landscape and the amber evening light,
It breaks in on, an elastic trail, moving, moving within my sight,
In soundless mystery, long winding lateral oily gloss,
Slipping along greasy ribs, on the grass and patches of moss,

Dragging, slipping, dragging, the stealthy prowler, is the cobra,
Voice of my education says,' the royal cobras are to be honored,
Not the demonic ones;
But the voice of my culture says, 'What is royal and demonic,
Are just in your mind, Treat them all alike, like kings and queens!'

Crocadile

Jagged crested dawdler, studded with craggy blotches, large, ponderous, powerful jaws, with canonical teeth, lizard like, skin plated, carnivorous, what carnal delicacy you moan for?
But no worries, as we shall have you all—around
In a well- protected pond and garden with a beautiful fence, around, we can be friends for life: children like to play with you,
And domesticate a fiery tribe with care and compassion to be.

BOREDOM is a dominating emotion of our times today.
But there is a wonderful way of turning it around, and making this a most stimulating journey.

BOREDOM IS INTERESTING: A PARADOX OF OUR TIMES

If you begin exploring the nature of BOREDOM,
I can bet, you will never get bored, as you have the freedom,
To move inside, outside and across, within its own kingdom.
The colorful nature of something, dubbed as a colorless lump,
But it's an adventure to a colorful land: tedium, apathy, humdrum,
Listlessness, lethargy and a dramatic turn to Hamlet,
'sicklied over with the pale cast of thought':
Going round and round in thinking—'to be or not to be'.

The culture of mindfulness living, opens new lights.
The mind is fickle and flighty, pursuing fanciful flights,
It flies across to a revolving stage, entrance to exit,
And back again to the entrance—a merry go round!
It is time, we learned the art of restraining the mind,

Through mindfulness practice, you gain tremendous, new ground!
'The faculty of bringing back a 'wandering attention',
Over and over again is the root of judgment, character and will'.
A self-controlled mind, brings great joy and harmony
Above all, the 'little man' boredom now flies away.
These shackles of bonds to passing alluring things,
with wandering thoughts; is called—**calibrating boredom**.

There is reacting against those who have, what you do not have,
Thus feeling, angry and empty, restless—drive this demon away,
This damage to developing a sound mind is—**reactive boredom**.
Restless man, ceaseless running mind, is the slave of a system
Unknown, running through him is an autonomic nervous system.
It is damaging—it is **searching boredom,** a paradox, he is searching for boredom—perhaps it lulls him down to sleeping apathy.

Next calls for sympathy to give him some relish and zest for life—it is **apathetic boredom.**

When things go wrong, as some times they will,
When the road you are trudging seems uphill, And when
funds are low and debts are high,
Yet you need to smile without a sigh,
Do rest a bit till you gain your strength,
But never quit!
In the midst of winter, come an invisible summer. Albert Camus
When you are honest and make your way, even before summer,
Beautiful Spring blossoms, magic purple bunches,
Greet you on the way.

Part II Coming Home

You are missing the unshakable roots of inner calm,
By running away to foreign lands,
Which is stress, clearly to your body and mind,

My expert says, you need to 'rest and digest' (parasympathetic);
Not revolve like an engine, 'flight or fight' (sympathetic side);
Enjoy a great morning with the rising sun,
See, the brilliant, scarlet setting sun,
At night, hear the soothing music of a distant flute...
This is the road to inner peace.
In your daily life, you may collect little bits of 'hurt',
That is natural to have lovely goals with you,
But share your ups and downs with others,
With a majestic heart,
Anna, below shows the way: (Talk to graduating class).
'We need a window to living in the present',
See the lilies in the field; exhaust the little movements-
soon it dies-do not miss the majestic movements of life—
Remember, you are the sole guardian of your life,
Your particular life, as I call,
Not the life at the desk, the bus or the bank account, your particular life, as I call not the life at the desk, the bus or the bank account but your heart and soul.
Make your own choice!
'If we must not do, what we really want to do,
Or must do, what we really do not want to do-without a choice.
This in short is BOREDOM. Anna Quindlen, Pulitzer Prize Winner

31

Interoception: Where Many Roads Meet

'Interoception' is basically the sense of our body's 'internal state'. It is how we feel and understand what is happening inside ourselves and it also controls autonomic motor movements.

I. It is a skill a meditator develops to sense the interior of the body.
II. It is a path discovered in some mindfulness-based therapies (Bruno Cayoun); Research, Lauri Nummenma, Finland.

Body sensations as crucial elements in emotions.

III. It is a path presented by recent work in neuroscience (Daniel Siegel).
IV. It is integrated in the interpretation of Buddhist texts and regular mindfulness practice (Ven. Dhammajīva).
V. The focus of the present study is the body and emotions.

P. de Silva, *Mindfulness-based Emotion Focused Counselling*,
https://doi.org/10.1007/978-3-030-64388-1_31

A Poet's Description

The focus is on ATTENTION
On the sensitive internal world of BODILY STATES.
While the five senses bring all the sensory excitements,
In mindfulness practice, such disturbance is minimized,
No entrance to the sensory excitations, all windows closed.
We have access to the *Sixth Sense*—includes sensations
in limbs, body's motion, tension and relaxation of the muscles,
And the state of our internal organs, lungs, heart and intestines.
Such bodily facets of awareness also is a base for our intuitions, *And gives shape to our emotions.*
There is a neural net around the internal organs.
It is a gateway to other people around,
And finally links to reflection and the mind-
A Seventh sense as a link with 'mind-sight'.
Practice of mindfulness, body scans, breathing exercises,
Would fine tune, the rhythms of the body-mind linkages,
in our emotional lives.

Body Sensations Are Basic Elements of Emotions

Body sensations are a basic links between body and mind,
Research indicates that different emotions were found,
Linked to different patterns of bodily sensations called 'maps',
And they were culturally universal without any lapse,
Consistent with East Asian and Western European participants,
It is claimed that this is consistent with mindfulness meditation (Bruno).
Body sensations are basic elements in emotions (Lauri Nummenma).

Body sensations in reality are neither physical nor mental.
A real link between body and mind- it is relational.
Different patterns of bodily sensations present to us,
Distinct emotions, made of thoughts, body sensations,
And the need to react; emotions emerge at the pre-conscious,

Level, and at times remain at the subliminal level,
With the potential of being aroused, by stimuli, like rudeness,
Arousing anger, a threat arousing fear, a tragic loss, for sadness.
The first reaction is from the body, which if mindfully trained,
Will remain calm and undisturbed.

Four basic features of body sensations are very integral,
To understand their texture and force is central,
Mass, from the lightest to the heaviest experience,
Motion, from the stillest to the most agitated,
Temperature, from the coldest too the hottest,
Fluidity, from the loosest to the densest.
These are four characteristics of 'interoception'.
Anger, tends to manifest, dominant increased temperature,
Which is heat and motion, and increased heart rate and agitation,
Sadness is related predominance of mass, with heaviness,
In head, neck and shoulder, and decreased fluidity,
Affecting the throat; Fear predominance of decreased fluidity,
With constriction of affecting chest and abdomen,
And increased temperature.

Deeper Facets: The Buddhist Contemplative Path (Blending Some Prose with the Poetry)

Buddhist practice for developing mindfulness has a deeper source in contemplative practice, with a focus on the 'sixth sense', going beyond the five senses.

1. Five senses bring information with the transmitting of neural impulses to smell, taste, sound, touch and visual image.
2. While the five senses bring information from the outside world, a consciousness independent of the five senses emerge in deep meditation states. This is described as the *sixth sense: anindriya paṭibaddha viññāṇa*: a consciousness unrelated to the senses.

Stage 1

In insight meditation, the breath is seen as an 'air draft' than a breath, as a *vibratory pattern.* The air is the 'Striker' element that pushes; the point of touch is the tip of the nose or the lips—'Solidity'. Rubbing on the lips is 'Ignition'. Moist element is 'liquidity' (also described as 'cohesiveness'—as ice to water).

Stage 2

In deep meditation, the movement of these four elements is considered as a flow of vibratory patterns. As the meditation proceeds, the breath will calm down, and relaxed peace appears. The gap between the in and out breath disappears, and the meditator experiences the 'Breath Body'. According to my meditation teacher, the experience of the BREATH BODY (*passambayaṃ kāyasaṅkhāraṃ*) is a strategic turning point in the contemplative efforts. The body is seen as an 'other' *(parato)*, losing the misplaced focus on the notion of the self.

At this point, I am at the feet of my teacher, learning.

(Beyond this point, one has to consult your meditation Guru. Attending a retreat is the best way to get trained on this path).

Appendix I

Poetic Metaphors: Four Stages of vipassanā ñāna—Insight

Sāmañña-phala Sutta, Volume 2, *Sutta* 2, *Dīgha Nikāya*

Poetry in this book can be supplemented with four poetic metaphors.

1. Mastering the five hindrances: sensual desires, aversion, boredom, restlessness and worry, sceptical doubt.

   Thus, estranged from lusts, aloof from evil dispositions, he enters and remains in the First Rapture. His body is suffused with joy and ease born of detachment: 'As if a skilful nurse had scattered perfumed soap powder in a metal basin, and then sprinkling it with water drop by drop, will knead it together that the ball of lather with the moisture is drenched and permeated with and without'.
2. He suppresses discursive reasoning, mind becomes lucid and sharp and there is ease born of joy and rapture, and they experience a deep happiness of their lives. This is non-thinking *vipassanā ñāna* (insight).

P. de Silva, *Mindfulness-based Emotion Focused Counselling*,
https://doi.org/10.1007/978-3-030-64388-1

Also, see the arising and passing of phenomena. It is as if a current of cool water arising from a spring enters a pool and the spring would pervade, fill, permeate and suffuse the pool with cold waters.

3. Equanimity (*upekkha*) is predominant, going beyond the joy of rapture, serene and peaceful. 'Suffused with ease but no extra joy in it'. Like lotus flowers in a tank grown up in water but, *not rising above water*, but so pervaded, drenched and permeated with the cool water.
4. Goes beyond both elation and dejection, and it is strengthening stage 3. A state of pure self-possession.

Like a man rapt in in a clean white robe, suffusing the whole body, and no spot not suffused therewith. A state of complete self-purification.

There is also a fifth stage focused on impermanence, which is hard to capture in poetic metaphors.

There are many variations of this structure in other presentations and it depends on the practitioner's guide. But what is outlined above is quite authentic as it is from the sutta literature.

References

Adams, E.M. 1998. Emotional Intelligence and Wisdom. *Southern Journal of Philosophy*.

Alston, W.P. 1967. Emotion and Feeling. In *The Encyclopedia of Philosophy*, vol. 2. New York: Macmillan.

Anālayo, Ven. 2010. *Satipaṭṭhāna: The Direct Path to Realization*. Cambridge: Windhorse Publications.

Aronson, H.B. 2004. *Buddhist Practice on Western Ground*. Boulder, CO: Shambhala Publications.

Averill, James. 1980. Emotion and Anxiety: Sociocultural, Biological and Psychological Determinants. In *Explaining Emotions*, ed. Amélie Rorty. Berkeley, CA: California University Press.

Bagnoli, Carla. 2019. Compassion and Practical Reason: The Perspectives of the Vulnerable. In *The Moral Psychology of Compassion*, ed. Justin Caouette and Carolyn Price. London: Rowman & Littlefield.

Begley, Richard J., and Sharon Davidson. 2012. *The Emotional Life of Your Brain*. New York: Penguin.

Bennett, M.R., and P.M.S. Hacker. 2003. *Philosophical Foundations of Neuroscience*. Oxford: Blackwell.

P. de Silva, *Mindfulness-based Emotion Focused Counselling*,
https://doi.org/10.1007/978-3-030-64388-1

Biegler, Paul. 2011. *The Ethical Treatment of Depression*. Cambridge, MA: MIT Press.

Bien, Thomas. 2006. *Mindful Therapy*. Boston: Wisdom Publications.

Bien, Beverly, and Thomas Bien. 2002. *Mindful Recovery: A Spiritual Path to Healing From Addiction*. New York: Wiley.

Blum, Lawrence A. 1980. *Friendship. Altruism and Morality*. London: Routledge.

Bodhi, Bhikkhu. 1987. Preface to *Buddhist Perspectives on the Environmental Crisis*, ed. K. Lassendel. Kandy: Buddhist Publication Society.

Bodhi, Bhikkhu (ed.). 1995. *Dana: The Practice of Giving*. Kandy: Buddhist Publication Society.

Burch, Vidyamala. 2008. *Living With Pain and Illness*. London: Piatkus.

Burton, Robert. 1927. *The Anatomy of Melancholyd*. New York: Farrar and Reinhart.

Cairnes, Margot. 1998. *Approaching the Corporate Heart*. Sydney: Simon & Schuster.

Calhoun, Cheshire, and Robert Solomon (eds.). 1984. *What Is an Emotion? Classic Readings in Philosophical Psychology*. Oxford: Oxford University Press.

Caouette, Justin, and Carolyn Price (eds.). 2018. *The Moral Psychology of Compassion*. London: Rowman & Littlefield.

Capra, Fritjof. 1983. *The Turning Point: Science, Society and the Rising Culture*. New York: Bantam.

Cayoun, Bruno. 2015. *Mindfulness-integrated CBT for Well-being and Personal Growth*. Oxford: Wiley.

Cherniss, Cary, and Daniel Goleman. 2001. *The Emotionally Intelligent Workplace*. New York: Jossey-Bass.

Cherry, Myisha, and Owen Flanagan (eds.). 2017. *The Moral Psychology of Anger*. New Kingston, PA: Rowman & Littlefield.

Claxton, Guy. 1977. *Hare Brain, Tortoise Mind*. New York: Eco Press.

Cokelet, Bradford. 2019. The Virtues of Compassion. In *The Moral Psychology of Compassion*, ed. Justin Caouette and Carolyn Price. London: Rowman and Littlefield.

Collins, Stephen. 1982. *Selfless Persons*. Cambridge: Cambridge University Press.

Crane, Rebecca. 2009. *Mindfulness-Based Cognitive Therapy*. London: Routledge.

Csikszentmihalyi, Mihaly. 1978. *The Psychology of Optimal Experience*. New York: Harper and Row.

Dalai Lama, and Daniel Goleman (eds.). 2004. *Destructive Emotions: A Dialogue with the Dalai Lama*. New York: Macmillan.
Daly, Herman E. 1966. *Beyond Growth: The Economics of Sustainable Growth*. Boston: Beacon Press.
Damasio, Antonio R. 1994. *Descartes' Error: Emotion, Reason, and the Human Brain*. New York: Avon Books.
Damasio, Antonio. 2000. *The Feeling of What Happens: Body and Emotion in the Making of Consciousness*. London: Vintage.
Darwin, Charles. 2015. *Expression of Emotions in Man and Animals*. London: HarperCollins.
Davids, Rhys. 1914. *Buddhist Psychology*. London: Bell and Sons.
Davidson, Richard, and Sharon Begley. 2013. *The Emotional Life of Your Brain*. London: Hodder.
de Botton, Alain. 2004. *Status Anxiety*. Camberwell, VIC: Hamish Hamilton.
Deigh, J. 2004. Primitive Emotions. In *Thinking About Feeling*, ed. R.C. Solomon. Oxford: Oxford University Press.
de Silva, Padmasiri. 1992a. *Buddhist and Freudian Psychology*, 3rd ed. Melbourne: Shogam Publishers.
de Silva, Padmasiri. 1992b. *Twin Peaks: Compassion and Insight*. Singapore: Buddhist Research Society.
de Silva, Padmasiri. 2005. *An Introduction to Buddhist Psychology and Counselling*, 4th ed. London: Palgrave Macmillan.
de Silva, Padmasiri. 2008. *Introduction to Mindfulness-based Counselling: The Magic of the Ordinary and the Elegance of Small Things*. Ratmalana, Sri Lanka: Sarvodaya Printers.
de Silva, Padmasiri. 2010. *Buddhist and Freudian Psychology*, 4th ed. Melbourne: Shogam Publishers.
de Silva, Padmasiri. 2014. *An Introduction to Buddhist Psychology and Counselling*, 5th ed. London: Palgrave Macmillan.
de Silva, Padmasiri. 2017. *Emotions and the Body in Buddhist Contemplative Practice and Mindfulness-Based Therapy*. London: Palgrave Macmillan.
de Silva, Padmasiri. 2018a. *The Psychology of Buddhism in Conflict Studies*. London: Palgrave Macmillan.
de Silva, Padmasiri. 2018b. *Ma Ma Foundation Lectures*. University of Hong Kong. (Available on the Internet).
de Silva, Padmasiri. 2018c. *The Buddhist Psychology of Emotions and Humour*. London: Palgrave Macmillan.
Dhammajīva, Uḍa Ēriyagama Mahāthero. 2008a. *In This Life Itself: Practical Teachings on Insight Meditation*. Meethirigala: Nissarana Vanaya.

Dhammajīva, Uḍa Ēriyagama Mahāthero. 2008b. *Towards Inner Peace*. Meethirigala: Lithira Publishers.

Dobkin, Patricia Lynn, and Craig Stephen Hassed. 2012. *Mindful Medical Practitioners*. Cham, Switzerland: Springer International.

Drury, Maurice O'Connor. 1973. *The Danger of Words*. London: Routledge and Kegan Paul.

Ekman, Paul. 2003. *Emotions Revealed*. New York: Weidenfeld and Nicolson.

Ekman, Paul, and Richard Davison (eds.). 1994. *The Nature of Emotions*. New York: Oxford University Press.

Ekstrom, Laura. 2012. Liars, Medicine, and Compassion. *Journal of Medicine and Philosophy*, April.

Engler, Jack. 2006. Promises and Perils of the Spiritual Path. In *Buddhism and Psychotherapy across Cultures*, ed. M. Unno. Boston: Wisdom.

Epstein, Mark. 2007. *Psychotherapy without the Self*. New Haven: Yale University Press.

Evans, Dylan. 2001. *Emotion*. Oxford: Oxford University Press.

Flanagan, Owen. 2000. Destructive Emotions. *Consciousness and Emotion* 1 (2): 67–88.

Foot, Philippa. 1978. *Virtues and Vices*. Oxford: Oxford University Press.

France, P. 1996. *Hermits: The Insights of Solitude*. New York: Chatto and Windus.

Freud, Sigmund. 1953. *Beyond the Pleasure Principle*, Standard ed., vol. XVIII. London: Hogarth Press.

Freud, Sigmund. 1957. *Mourning and Melancholia*, Standard ed., vol. 14. London: Hogarth Press.

Freud, Sigmund. 1958. *Remembering, Repeating and Working-Through*, Standard ed., vol. 12. London: Hogarth Press.

Freud, Sigmund. 1966. *Analysis, Terminable and Interminable*, Standard ed., vol. XXIII. London: Virago.

Fromm, Erich. 1994. *The Art of Listening*. London: Constable.

Fromm, Erich. 2013. *To Have or to Be?*. London: Bloomsbury.

Gardner, Howard. 1983. *Frames of Mind: The Theory of Multiple Intelligences*. New York: Basic Books.

Germer, Christopher K. 2009. *The Mindful Path to Self-Compassion*. London: Guilford Press.

Gilbert, Paul. 2010. *The Compassionate Mind*. London: Constable.

Gittins, Ross. 2010. *The Happy Economist*. Crows Nest, NSW: Allen and Unwin.

Gladwell, Malcolm. 2005. *Blink: The Power of Thinking Without Thinking*. London: Penguin.

Glover, Jonathan. 2001. *Humanity: A Moral History of the Twentieth Century*. London: Pimlico.

Goldie, Peter. 2002. *Emotions: A Philosophical Exploration*. Oxford: Clarendon Press.

Goldstein, Joseph. 1993. *Insight Meditation*. Boston: Shambhala.

Goleman, Daniel (ed.). 1997. *Healing Emotions: Conversations with the Dalai Lama, on Mindfulness, Emotions and Health*. Boston: Shambhala.

Goleman, Daniel, and the Dalai Lama. 2003. *Destructive Emotions: A Scientific Dialogue with the Dalai Lama*. Macmillan.

Goleman, Daniel. 1996. *Emotional Intelligence*. New York: Bloomsbury.

Greenberg, Leslie. 2008. *Emotion Focused Therapy*. Washington, DC: American Philosophical Association.

Gun, Alastair S. 1993. Culture as a Resource for Sustainability. Paper presented at the IRC Conference on the Transmission of Environmental Values through Culture, Ethics and Education. Information and Resource Center, Singapore.

Haggard, P. 2008. Human Volition: Towards a Neuroscience of Will. *Nature Reviews Neuroscience* 9: 934–966.

Hanson, Rick. 2018. *Resilient: How to Grow an Unshaken Core of Calm, Strength and Happiness*. New York: Harmony.

Hart, Tobin. 2004. Opening the Contemplative Mind in the Classroom. *Journal of Transformative Education* 2 (1): 28–46.

Harris, Richard. 2006. Embracing Your Demons: An Overview of Acceptance and Commitment Therapy. *Psychotherapy in Australia* 12: 2–8.

Hassed, Craig. 2008. *The Essence of Health*. Sydney: Random.

Hassed, Craig, and Stephen McKenzie. 2012. *Mindfulness for Life*. Wollombi, NSW: Exisle Publishing.

Hassed, Craig, and Richard Chambers. 2014. *Mindful Learning*. Wollombi, NSW: Exisle Publishing.

Heyman, Gene. 2009. *Addictions: A Disorder of Choice*. Cambridge, MA: Harvard University Press.

Higgins, Kathleen, and David Sherman Sherman (eds.). 2012. *Passion, Death and Spirituality: The Philosophy of Robert C. Solomon*. Heidelberg, New York, and London: Springer.

Hokanson, J. E., and M. Burgess. 1962. The Effects of Three Types of Aggression on Vascular Processes. *The Journal of Abnormal and Social Psychology* 64 (6).

Horwitz, Allan A. V., and Jerome Wakefield. 2007. *Loss of Sadness*. Oxford: Oxford University Press.

Hyers, C. 1989. Humour in Zen: Comic Midwifery. *Philosophy East and West* 39 (3): 267–277.

Jacobson, Nolan Pliny. 1966. *Buddhism: The Religion of Analysis*. New York: Humanities Press.

James, William. 1884. What Is an Emotion? In *Readings in Philosophical Psychology*, ed. Cheshire Calhoun and Robert Solomon. Oxford: Oxford University Press.

James, William. 1950. *The Principles of Psychology*. New York: Dover Publishing.

Jayatunga, Ruchira. 2012a. *Let Us Be Mindful*. Ganemulla, Sri Lanka: Printwell Printers.

Jayatunga, Ruchira. 2012b. Mindfully Managing Anger. In *Let Us Be Mindful*. Ganemulla, Sri Lanka: Printwell Printers.

Kabat-Zinn, Jon. 1990. *Full Catastrophe Living*. New York: Delacorte.

Kabat-Zinn, Jon. 2005. *Coming to Our Senses*. New York: Dover Publishing.

Kaparo, Risa. 2012. *Awakening Somatic Intelligence: The Art and Practice of Embodied Mindfulness*. Berkeley: North Atlantic Books.

Kenny, Anthony. 1963. *Action, Emotion and Will*. London: Routledge & Kegan Paul.

Kierkegaard, Søren. 1843: trans. 1962. *Either/Or*, vol. I & II, trans. Walter Lowrie. Princeton, NJ: Princeton University Press.

Kinkāns, Vladimirs. 2015. Humor and Laughter in the Pedagogical Communications. *Society. Integration. Education. Proceedings of the International Scientific Conference*, vol. II, 375–385.

Kövecses, Zoltán. 1986. *Metaphors of Anger, Pride and Love*. Amsterdam and Philadelphia: John Benjamins.

Krishnamurti, Jiddu. 2014, new edn. *Reflections on the Self*, ed. Raymond Martin. New York: KFI Publications.

Kumar, Samit. 2005. *Grieving Mindfully*. Oakland, CA: New Harbinger Publications.

Ladner, Lorne. 2004. *The Lost Art of Compassion*. New York: HarperCollins.

Ledoux, Joseph. 1996. *The Emotional Brain*. London: Weidenfeld & Nicolson.

Loy, David, and Linda Goodhew. 2005. Consuming Time. In *Hooked*, ed. Stephanie Kaza. Boston: Shambhala.

Lutz, Catherine. 1995. Need, Nurturance and the Emotions on a Pacific Atoll. In *Emotions in Asian Thought*, ed. Joel Marks and Roger Ames. New York: State University of New York Press.

Lyons, William. 1963. *Philosophy Papers*. New York: Humanities Press.
Lyons, W. 1980. *Emotion*. Cambridge: Cambridge University Press.
Marks, Joel (ed.). 1986. *The Ways of Desire*. Chicago: Precedent.
Matthews, Bruce. 1983. *Craving and Salvation: A Study in Buddhist Soteriology*. Waterloo, ON: Wilfrid Laurier University Press.
Mayer, B. 2015. *The Conflict Paradox*. San Francisco: Wiley.
Murdoch, Iris. 1970. *The Sovereignty of the Good*. London: Routledge and Kegan Paul.
Ñāṇānanda, Thero. 2012. *Concept and Reality in Early Buddhist Thought*. Kandy: Buddhist Publication Society.
Ñāṇavīra, Thera. 1987. *The Tragic, The Comic and the Personal*. Kandy: Buddhist Publication Society.
Neu, Jerome. 1990. Jealous Thoughts. In *Explaining Emotions*, ed. Amélie Rorty. Berkeley, CA: University of California Press.
Nussbaum, Martha. 1991. Compassion and Terror. *Daedalus* 132: 20–26.
Nussbaum, Martha. 2001. *Upheavals of Thought: The Intelligence of Emotions*. New York: Cambridge University Press.
Nyānaponika, Mahāthera. 1983. *Contemplation of Feelings*. Kandy, Sri Lanka: Buddhist Publication Society.
Nyānaponika, Thero. 2014. Managing Anger. In *An Introduction to Buddhist Psychology*, Padmasiri de Silva, 182–183. London: Palgrave Macmillan.
Oatley, Keith. 2004. *Emotions: A Brief History*. Oxford: Blackwell.
Parkes, Graham. 1990. The Transmutation of Emotions in Rinzai Zen and Nietzsche. *The Eastern Buddhist* XXIII: 1.
Penelhum, Terence. 1969. Self-Identity and Self-Regard. In *Identities of Persons*, ed. Amélie Rorty. Berkeley, CA: University of California Press.
Piper, Thomas. 1995. *Management Ethics: Theory, Cases and Practice*, ed. Gordon L. Clark and Elizabeth Prior Jonson. Sydney: Harper Educational.
Prinz, Jesse. 2004. *Gut Reactions: A Perceptual Theory of Emotions*. Oxford: Oxford University Press.
Prinz, Jesse, and Shaun Nichols. 2010. In *The Moral Psychology Handbook*, ed. John Dorris. Oxford: Oxford University Press.
Radden, Jennifer. 2000. Love and Loss in Freud. In *The Analytic Freud, Philosophy and Psychoanalysis*, ed. Michael P. Levine. New York: Routledge.
Ramo, J.C. 2009. *The Age of the Unthinkable*. London: Little Brown.
Ricard, Matthieu. 2006. *Happiness: A Guide to Developing Life's Most Important Skill*. New York: Little Brown.
Rilke, Rainer Maria. 2001. *Letters to a Young Poet*, ed. Amélie Rorty and trans. Stephen Mitchell. New York: Modern Library.

Rinpoche, Lama Glendun. 1992. *Working with Emotions: Carlton North*. Vic: Zambala.

Rorty, Amélie Oksenberg. 1990. Pride Produces the Idea of Self. In *Identities of Persons*, ed. Amélie Rorty. Berkeley, CA: University of California Press.

Rumi, Jalaluddin. 1995. *The Essential Rumi. Trans. by Coleman Barks*. San Francisco, CA: Harper.

Sandel, Michael. 2017. *What Money Can't Buy: The Moral Limits of Markets*. London: Penguin.

Schopenhauer, Arthur. 1965. *On the Basis of Morality*, trans. E.F.J. Payne. Indianapolis: Hackett.

Scitovsky, Tibor. 1992. *The Joyless Economy: The Psychology of Human Satisfaction*. Oxford: Oxford University Press.

Segal, Zindel V., Mark Williams, & John Teasdale (eds.). With a Foreword by Jon Kabat-Zinn. In *Mindfulness-Based Cognitive Therapy for Depression*. New York: Guilford Press.

Sheean, Liz. 2011. Addictions: A Disorder of Choice: An Interview with Gene Heyman. *Psychotherapy in Australia* 17 (4): 26–31.

Siegel, Daniel. 2007. *The Mindful Brain*. New York: Norton.

Singer, Peter. 2009. *The Life You Can Save*. Melbourne: Text Publishing.

Solomon, Robert, C. (Ed.). 2004. *Thinking About Feeling*. Oxford: Oxford University Press.

Solomon, Robert C. 2007. *True to Our Feelings: What Our Emotions are Really Telling Us*. New York: Oxford University Press.

Solomon, R.C. 1977. *The Passions*. New York: Anchor Press/Doubleday.

Spandler, Helen. 2019. Challenges and Opportunities in Mental Health. In *The Moral Psychology of Compassion*, ed. Justin Caouette and Carolyn Price. London: Rowman & Littlefield.

Spinoza, B. 1963. *Ethics*. New York: Hafner.

Stocker, Michael. 1979. Desiring the Bad: An Essay in Moral Psychology. *Journal of Philosophy* 76: 744.

Storr, Anthony. 1966. The Concept of Cure. In *Psychoanalysis*, ed. C. Rycroft. London: Constable.

Struhl, Karsten J. 2018. Buddhism and the Problem of Universal Compassion. In *The Moral Psychology of Compassion*, ed. Justin Caouette and Carolyn Price. London: Rowman & Littlefield.

Sumedho, Ajahn. 1998. *Four Noble Truths*. Taiwan: Amaravati Publications.

Taylor, Gabriele. 1985. *Pride, Shame and Guilt: Emotions of Self-Assessment*. Oxford: Clarendon Press.

Thanissaro, Bhikkhu. 2015. *The Buddha Smiles*. San Diego, CA: Forest Monastery.
Thích Nh'ât Hạnh. 1994. *Zen Keys*. New York: Harmony.
Tickle, Phyllis A. 2004. *Greed*. Oxford: Oxford University Press.
Toby, Hart. 2004. Opening the Contemplative Mind in the Classroom. *Journal of Transformative Education* 2 (1): 28–46.
Tov-Ruach, Leila. 1980. Jealousy, Attention and Loss. In *Explaining Emotions*, ed. Amélie Rorty. Berkeley, CA: University of California Press.
Vaillant, George E. 2002. *Ageing Well: Surprising Guideposts to a Happier Life*. London: Scribe.
Varela, Francisco, Evan Thompson, and Eleanor Rosch. 1999. *The Embodied Mind: Cognitive Science and Human Experience*. London: MIT Press.
Wallace, Alan B., and Shauna Shapiro. 2006. Mental Balance and Well-Being. *American Psychologist*, October.
Weber, Max. 1958. *The Religion of India*. Glencoe, ILL: The Free Press.
Weinhardt, Justin, and Aden Dumaisnil. Compassion in the Workplace. In *The Moral Psychology of Compassion*, ed. Justin Caouette and Carolyn Price. London: Rowman & Littlefield.
Wolpert, Lewis. 1999. *Malignant Sadness*. London: Faber and Faber.
Williams, Bernard. 1972. *Morality: An Introduction to Ethics*. Cambridge: Cambridge University Press.
Wittgenstein, Ludwig. 1953. *Philosophical Investigations*. Oxford: Basil Blackwell.
Yalom, Irvin. 2003. *The Gift of Therapy*. London: Piatkus.
Zoltán, Kövecses. 1989. *Metaphor and Emotion*. Cambridge: Cambridge University Press.

Author Index

P. de Silva, *Mindfulness-based Emotion Focused Counselling*, https://doi.org/10.1007/978-3-030-64388-1

Subject Index

P. de Silva, *Mindfulness-based Emotion Focused Counselling*,
https://doi.org/10.1007/978-3-030-64388-1

The manufacturer's authorised representative in the EU is Springer Nature Customer Service Centre GmbH, Europaplatz 3, 69115 Heidelberg, Germany. If you have any concerns regarding our products, please contact ProductSafety@springernature.com

Printed and bound by CPI Group (UK) Ltd, Croydon, CR0 4YY

30/09/2026

02225457-0012